Advance Praise for *The Art and Science of Stick Fighting*

"'Everything should be made as simple as possible, but no simpler.'—**Albert Einstein**. In the twenty-three years that I have been practicing stick fighting, I have read many elaborate texts on this topic. Master Joe Varady has taken the beautiful but complex art of stick fighting and distilled it down to its fundamental core. Master Varady provides expert guidance and a solid road map of well-organized competencies, drills, and clear illustrations to help beginners and experts alike on the road to individual mastery. Whether you are looking to incorporate this amazing martial art form into your school's curriculum or are looking for a combat-tested, weapons-based martial art, *The Art and Science of Stick Fighting* is a must-have book for martial artists."
—**Juan (Little John) Cruz,** third-degree black belt,
Doce Pares Multi-style System

"Upon reading Master Joe Varady's *The Art and Science of Stick Fighting*, it is clear that he has not only a technical mastery of stick fighting but a deep and knowledgeable appreciation of the historical and cultural background that helps form the art. The thorough and detailed descriptions of the moves are accentuated by appropriate cultural references that help put them into a better context, allowing for a deeper understanding of answering not just how and what but also when and why. Master Varady's writing makes it easy for the layperson to quickly understand, and the technical acumen and skill presented gives the experienced martial artist plenty to expand upon. The many different arts compiled into one single book is impressive and thorough in its scope and detail. This book is a well-thought-out encyclopedia of moves and history that will serve as a handy reference for stick fighting enthusiasts at any experience level, including the veteran teacher that needs more to add to their teaching knowledge and repertoire. There were many drills and methods in this book that were new to me and were explained with great detail, and with beautiful pictures to help illustrate the essence of the drills.

"I highly recommend this book to anyone serious about learning more on the art of stick fighting, not just from one single style but from a multitude of styles, countries, and backgrounds."
—**Brian Scott**, eight-time World Eskrima Kali Arnis Federation World Full-Contact Stick Fighting Champion, professor of martial arts at the University of Colorado Boulder, fourth-degree black belt Doce Pares eskrima, fourth-degree black belt freestyle karate (state and national champion), first-degree black belt Hawaiian kenpo/kajukenbo, brown belt Brazilian jujitsu (state and national champion), Kru in muay Thai

"Master Joe Varady, author of *The Art and Science of Staff Fighting*, has precisely hit the target again with this latest work, *The Art and Science of Stick Fighting*. This second book, in what is certain to be a long-running series in the Art and Science brand, provides the perfect balance between self-defense and sport methodologies. From stretching fundamentals to keep you safe and training, to detailed footwork, to strategies for effective combat and sport application, this book reaches all student levels from novice to master. Perhaps what is most enlightening are the parallels drawn in common training methodology to that of traditional open-hand training and fighting, making this work particularly useful to all martial arts practitioners. Moreover, the detail provided with regard to constructing training aids makes such training obtainable by absolutely anyone. *The Art and Science of Stick Fighting* is a wonderful book that intertwines historic references, personal experiences, and practical teachings all while providing an understanding of the commonalities among various stick fighting arts, thereby providing a sound foundation relevant to any martial style."

—**Master Michael J. Gallagher**, USA Taekwondo National Weapons Champion, owner/operator/instructor of Generations Taekwondo, executive board member for the Universal Systems of Martial Arts Organization, 2015 inductee of the Philadelphia Historic Martial Arts Society Hall of Fame, 2018 inductee of the Pennsylvania Karate Hall of Fame, Pennsylvania state officer for the World Taekwondo Masters Union

"Master Joe knows his stuff. In this book, *The Art and Science of Stick Fighting*, he distills years of experience in both sport and combative stick fighting to give the novice or experienced practitioner a practical step-by-step guide to get the most out of their training, to help improve their technique, and maximize their competitive edge, be that in the ring or on the street."

—**Neil McLeish**, second-degree black belt Doce Pares eskrima, second-degree black belt kapatiran olisi y baraw eskrima, first dan black belt Bushi kempo jujitsu

"I have known Joe Varady for many years. Joe is like a fine wine: he just keeps getting better with age, and this new book reflects that perfection. From the depth of explanation of techniques to the quality of the drawings and clarity of the photos, this book is in every sense a complement to his first book and should be in every martial artist's library. The way he blends East and West and his understanding of the techniques is unmatched. Joe's skill at teaching makes it a pleasure to learn from him. I have had the honor of watching Joe in action, and this book is very much a work of love and from his heart. I applaud Joe Varady. Great work. You are truly an asset to the world of martial arts."

—**Dave Dickey**, author, founder of Live Steel Fight Academy, founder of *Live Steel Magazine*, lifelong martial artist, two-time nominee for the Martial Arts Hall of Fame

"*The Art and Science of Stick Fighting* by Joe Varady is an incredibly well-organized and systematic instructional guide on the use of medium-length striking weapons for both sport and self-defense. After a short introduction and warm-up guide, the material is presented in nine levels: Foundation, Long Range, Crossing the Gap, Middle-Range Offense, Middle-Range

Defense, Close-Range Infighting, Single-Stick Sparring, Short Stick versus Other Weapons, and Empty-Hand Defense against the Stick. Each level provides concepts, principles, techniques, drills, and sample workouts to build competency in the art of stick fighting. As a bonus, Varady also includes information on both commercial and homemade training equipment. In its entirety, this impressive tome provides an outstanding curriculum for self-study, or for class instruction to be used by the instructor looking for a well-organized and systematic approach to teaching stick fighting. I predict *The Art and Science of Stick Fighting* will be a welcome and much-used text in many martial artists' libraries."

—**Alain Burrese**, JD, martial artist, author, survival specialist

"Joe Varady is a top weapons expert in our style, Cuong Nhu martial arts, as well as in the greater martial arts world. Master Joe's comprehensive new book, *The Art and Science of Stick Fighting*, will add to the knowledge and aid the practice of the beginner, midlevel, and advanced martial artist. Any martial artist wanting to start training with weapons or looking to add sticks to their practice will easily follow the instruction and drills in this book. The trained stick fighter will find this book to be a great reference and is certain to find some new insights to their training."

—**John Burns**, ninth dan Cuong Nhu martial arts, head instructor at Berkeley Cuong Nhu Karate, Berkeley, California, fifth dan aikido

"*The Art and Science of Stick Fighting* is a must for martial arts practitioners at any level. Master Varady organizes the book so that you feel like you are on a journey of discovery first and learning second.

"The book is full of well-organized, content-rich sections supported with illustrations, pictures, and tips, along with 'nuggets' of information to improve the reader's experience. Of course, in order to be able to fight or defend someone with a stick, you will want to understand the whys in order to defend and counter effectively. Master Varady methodically walks you through each lesson, along with the rationale of why a specific way is most effective. He organizes the sections logically to make learning easier by starting with the basics: range, distancing, footwork, etc. For example, the section Long-Range Defensive Tactics is structured in a progressive order that allows you to learn and remember when to use it the next time you practice with your partner. Furthermore, sections are intentionally named in a way to help you remember key principles and tactics in order to know what to employ and when to employ them. Another gem in the book is a section on how to build training targets, dummies, and even target sticks to simulate a 'real' fight as closely as possible.

"I strongly recommend *The Art and Science of Stick Fighting* as one of the most comprehensive books for martial artists. Even if you don't plan to learn how to fight using a stick, at least you would want to know how to defend against someone with one. In fact, it should be considered as one of the key reference sources for successful weapons training and defending."

—**Grandmaster Bao Ngo**, tenth-degree Cuong Nhu, author of *Cuong Nhu Martial Arts Training Manuals* and *The Bao Way Self-Defense* DVD series

"*The Art and Science of Stick Fighting* is clear and easy to understand as compared to other books I have read on same topic. Reading this book had provided me greater insight in stick fighting techniques and strategies. It was almost as if I had Master Varady right next to me and instructing me through those nine levels. Each level provides details for developing solid foundations, applicable techniques, and logical strategies that can be adopted in other short- and middle-range weapons and also empty-hand fighting. This book will add great value to martial artists of all levels."

—**Alan Shen L. Cheung,** grandmaster, ninth dan shorinji ryu karate do, seventh-degree black belt Universal Kenpo System, and fifth-degree black belt American kenpo karate; 2007–2008 coach North American Federation of Martial Arts Team USA martial arts team; founder of the Universal Systems of Martial Arts Organization; 2007 NAFMA Nationals first place in stick fighting and stick forms; 2008, 2016, and 2019 NAFMA Nationals grand champion adult black-belt weapons; 2009 and 2013 World Karate Union Championships grand champion black-belt weapons and forms; 2004 inductee of the Action Martial Arts Magazine Hall of Fame and World Karate Union Hall of Fame; 2014 inductee of the Philadelphia Historic Martial Arts Society Hall of Fame

"Joe Varady has taken stick fighting to a new level of learning for anyone that trains in the martial arts. His detail on the principles, concepts, and processes of the art of the short stick is truly remarkable. Master Joe knows how to take the best from many arts and evolve them into what works for effective and realistic training. His photos are precise in details and applications, and the book is a must read for any serious martial arts student."

—**Kirk Farber**, seventh-degree black belt Cuong Nhu martial arts, executive director and founder of Fitness and Character Education (FACEKids), and author of several books, including *The Soft Style Training Manual*, *Teach the Teacher Operation Manual*, and *Partner Operation Manual*

"I got to know Master Joe Varady at the 2014 World Eskrima Kali Arnis Federation World Championships in Hungary. We quickly realized that we shared many similarities in martial arts and attitudes of mind. During the championships we had to fight against each other and Joe proved to be a splendid fighter. Our friendship grew stronger during my numerous teaching visits to his school, notably in 2017 when my team and my two children joined me during a visit to Pennsylvania. Joe's new book, *The Art and Science of Stick Fighting*, includes all that is needed to learn stick fighting, complete with theory and practical exercises for both beginners and advanced practitioners.

"I want to wish my friend all the best and I am looking forward to more training together."

—**Grandmaster Perry Zmugg**, owner and founder of Body Fight Art Center, Zmugg, Austria

JOE VARADY

The Art and Science of Stick Fighting
A COMPLETE INSTRUCTIONAL GUIDE

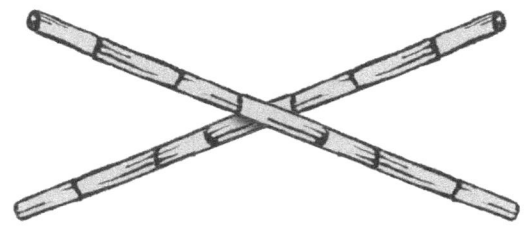

YMAA Publication Center
Wolfeboro, NH USA

YMAA Publication Center, Inc.
PO Box 480
Wolfeboro, NH 03894
800 669-8892 • www.ymaa.com • info@ymaa.com

ISBN: 9781594397332 (print) • ISBN: 9781594397349 (ebook)

This book set in Adobe Garamond and Frutiger

All rights reserved including the right of reproduction in whole or in part in any form.
Copyright © 2019 by Joe Varady
Cover design by Axie Breen
Typesetting by Westchester Publishing Services
Photos by Andrea Hilborn
Illustrations by the author

20200409

Publisher's Cataloging in Publication

Names: Varady, Joe, author.
Title: The art and science of stick fighting : a complete instructional guide / Joe Varady.
Description: Wolfboro, NH USA : YMAA Publication Center, [2016] | A companion volume to the author's "The art and science of staff fighting" (YMA Publication Center, c2016). | Includes bibliographical references and index.
Identifiers: ISBN: 9781594397332 (print) | 9781594397349 (ebook) | LCCN: 2019920364
Subjects: LCSH: Stick fighting—Handbooks, manuals, etc. | Single-stick—Handbooks, manuals, etc. | Staffs (Sticks, canes, etc.)—Handbooks, manuals, etc. | Hand-to-hand fighting—Handbooks, manuals, etc. | Self-defense—Handbooks, manuals, etc. | BISAC: SPORTS & RECREATION / Martial Arts. | SPORTS & RECREATION / Fencing.
Classification: LCC: GV1141 .V37 2020 | DDC: 796.8—dc23

The author and publisher of the material are NOT RESPONSIBLE in any manner whatsoever for any injury that may occur through reading or following the instructions in this manual.

The activities, physical or other wise, described in this manual may be too strenuous or dangerous for some people, and the reader(s) should consult a physician before engaging in them.

Warning: While self-defense is legal, fighting is illegal. If you don't know the difference, you'll go to jail because you aren't defending yourself. You are fighting—or worse. Readers are encouraged to be aware of all appropriate local and national laws relating to self-defense, reasonable force, and the use of weaponry, and act in accordance with all applicable laws at all times. Understand that while legal definitions and interpretations are generally uniform, there are small—but very important—differences from state to state and even city to city. To stay out of jail, you need to know these differences. Neither the author nor the publisher assumes any responsibility for the use or misuse of information contained in this book.

Nothing in this document constitutes a legal opinion, nor should any of its contents be treated as such. While the author believes everything herein is accurate, any questions regarding specific self-defense situations, legal liability, and/or interpretation of federal, state, or local laws should always be addressed by an attorney at law.

When it comes to martial arts, self-defense, and related topics, no text, no matter how well written, can substitute for professional, hands-on instruction. These materials should be used for **academic study only.**

Printed in USA.

Acknowledgments

I would like to thank the Old Gang: Steve Wolk, Don Walz, David Lipscomb, John Aversa, and Chris Hall; my Cuong Nhu instructors, especially Dong Ngo, Quynh Ngo, and Bao Ngo; Neil McLeish for our epic battle in Hungary; Dave Berzack for designing the "Striking Point"; and Carol Riley for her editing prowess.

Special thanks to my talented and dependable production team: Madeline Crouse, Andrea Hilborn, and Brian Lesyk; and, as always, to my wonderful wife, Kathy, for always putting up with my crazy obsessions.

Models: Joe Varady, Madeline Crouse, Kathy Varady, and Brian Lesyk

Photo credits: Andrea Hilborn

Cover photo: Andrea Hilborn

Photographer: Andrea Hilborn

Table of Contents

Foreword	xi
Preface	xiii
Introduction	1
Overview	1
Why Learn Stick Fighting?	3
A Brief History of Stick Fighting	5
Traditional versus Progressive	8
Getting Started	9
Warming Up and Cooling Down	11
Warming Up and Stretching	11
Training Equipment: The Jump Rope	15
Cooling Down	18
LEVEL 1: The Foundation	21
Choosing a Stick	21
Holding the Stick	23
Stances	26
Basic Striking	28
Ready Positions	35
Types of Strikes	36
Range and Distancing	37
Footwork	39
Training Equipment: The Floor Pattern	45
Twirling: Figure Eights	46
Power	48
Training Equipment: The Tire Dummy	56
Level 1 Workout	60
LEVEL 2: Long Range	63
The Outside Game	63
Controlling the Distance	64
Training Equipment: The Evasion Bopper	65
Long-Range Defensive Tactics	66
Long-Range Offensive Tactics	72
Training Equipment: The Target Stick	82
Feinting	84
Twirling: The Six-Count Flower	85
Training Equipment: Striking Point	86
The Long-Range Battle Plan	88
Level 2 Workout	92

LEVEL 3: Crossing the Gap	95
Entering Offensively	95
Entering Defensively	101
Level 3 Workout	106
LEVEL 4: Middle-Range Offense	107
Understanding Middle Range	107
Center, Centerline, and the Line of Combat	107
Targeting at Middle Range	108
Basic Middle-Range Combinations	109
Speed-Striking	110
Training Equipment: Weighted Clubs	127
The Middle-Range Battle Plan	130
Level 4 Workout	131
LEVEL 5: Middle-Range Defense	133
Checking	133
Blocking and Parrying	134
Middle-Range Disarms	147
Level 5 Workout	154
LEVEL 6: Close-Range	155
Infighting	155
Punching	155
Butt Strikes	156
Hubud	158
Hooking	165
Double-End Grip	166
Chokes	171
Training Equipment: Compression Dummies	174
Level 6 Workout	177
LEVEL 7: Single-Stick Sparring	179
The Moment of Truth: En Garde!	179
Safety Equipment	180
Training Equipment: Padded Sticks	181
Armor	182
Types of Matches	185
Controlling the Fight	186
Intensity	194
The Seven Principal Rules	195
Level 7 Workout	197
LEVEL 8: Short Stick versus Other Weapons	199
Mismatched Weapons	199
Stick versus Knife	199

Training Equipment: Padded Knife ... 204
Stick versus Staff ... 205
Training Equipment: Padded Staff ... 217
Stick versus Unarmed Opponent ... 218
Level 8 Workout ... 227

LEVEL 9: Empty-Hand Defense against the Stick ... 229
   Unarmed Defense ... 229
   Crossing the Gap ... 230
   Evasion ... 233
   Improvised Armament ... 236
   Level 9 Workout ... 238

Appendix: Training Equipment ... 239
   Jump Rope ... 239
   Floor Patterns ... 240
   Tire Bag ... 241
   Indoor Tire Dummy ... 242
   Evasion Bopper ... 243
   Target Stick ... 244
   Striking Point ... 245
   Weighted Clubs ... 246
   Arm Compression Dummy ... 247
   Neck Compression Dummy ... 248
   Padded Sticks ... 249
   Padded Knife ... 250
   Padded Staff ... 251

About the Author ... 252

Foreword

In the *Art and Science of Stick Fighting*, Master Joe Varady delivers exactly what his title suggests: a systematic, organized, and scientific approach to the use of a medium-length weapon in both self-defense and sport applications. The concepts, lessons, and training methods presented will enhance the knowledge of a very broad range of practitioners, from novices and enthusiasts to seasoned instructors.

Master Joe systematically breaks down core competencies of a weapons-based martial discipline, including how to move (stances and footwork), how to attack (grips and striking, both linear and circular), and how to defend (block, parrying, and disarming). He also explains how these skill sets are different for each of the different ranges of combat. After these concepts, extensions to a number of logical variations are presented, including use of the stick against other weapons, dealing with multiple opponents, and empty-hand defense against the stick.

There are also several additional and refreshing aspects to this work that set it apart from the existing body of literature. First, a multicultural history is presented that addresses commonalities between related martial arts systems from around the world, showing that the same realities and limitations of physics and human physiology were discovered by many serious practitioners of martial arts. This is often summarized in the martial arts world as "truth is truth." Along these same lines, an introduction to muscular anatomy and the nervous system is presented, which helps the reader understand the basis of these truths, as well as explaining the need for specific stretching and strengthening exercises used to facilitate development. Finally, following the presentation of ideas and theories, each level presents sample workouts and training that will reinforce those teachings. It is good to see that the text also acknowledges the importance of striking a heavy bag to develop power, as the bag doesn't lie, and your full-contact sparring shows everyone how much bag work you've done.

Over the past three decades, I have had the pleasure of training with Master Joe and observing his progress along the path from young, enthusiastic martial arts practitioner to veteran instructor. The Japanese term *sensei* is often translated as "teacher," but it is more correctly translated as "one who has gone before." Master Joe truly embodies that term. He has spent the long hours training and has extensively read the work of those who have gone before him. Never resting on his laurels, he constantly tests his skills and his ideas honestly, with no prejudice for or against any style. He regularly enters tournaments from different martial art systems (such as eskrima and historical Western combat) and continues to spar in his dojo with his students. Based on what he learns, he refines his approach and then tests it again.

I am honored that Master Joe has chosen to include in this book some of the techniques and concepts that he learned from me, such as speed striking and the associated letter system, programming, and tres-tres. To give credit where it is due, I wish to acknowledge

my teacher, Grandmaster Arnulfo "Dodong" Cuesta, and his teacher, Supreme Grandmaster Dioniso "Diony" Cañete of the Doce Pares Multi-style System of eskrima, for teaching me what I have passed on to Master Joe. The Filipinos are renowned in the martial arts world for the development of short-stick and knife training methods, and I have had the privilege of training under the guidance of these great teachers for over thirty years. One of my early karate teachers, Sensei Miguel Estrada, once told me that the best way for me to repay him for teaching me was to teach ten others. If I can count Master Joe as one of my ten, then I am on my way toward repaying that debt.

Grandmaster Steve Wolk
Doce Pares Multi-style System
Six-time world stick-fighting champion

Preface

Over the past three decades, I have trained in Eastern martial arts such as karate, kung fu, tae kwon do, judo, jujitsu, wing chun, and eskrima. I have also studied various Western martial arts such as boxing, fencing, long sword, sword and shield, and various methods of armored fighting. In addition, I like to research and write about martial arts training. I wrote six training manuals for my core style, Cuong Nhu Martial Arts, and I helped write a manual for my main Western martial arts school, Live Steel Fight Academy. My first book, *The Art and Science of Staff Fighting*, was published by YMAA in 2016.

Banging around with my favorite training partner back in 1993.

Clearly somewhat of a fanatic, I test my martial arts skills continuously. I competed in several eskrima tournaments in the early 1990s, during the time when I studied Doce Pares under the six-time world stick-fighting champion, Guro Steve Wolk.

In the 2000s, I tested my stick-fighting skills at Live Steel Fight Academy in matches against mixed weapons as disparate as the shillelagh and quarterstaff. I attended the

World Eskrima Kali Arnis Federation (WEKAF) National Championships in New York City in 2014, where I qualified for the US team. I then had the privilege of fighting in the World Championships later that year, traveling all the way to Hungary. I took home second place in full-contact staff and fourth place in full-contact double stick.

Team USA at the WEKAF World Championships, Hungary 2014.

The following year, in Jersey City, New Jersey, I took home a gold medal in full-contact single stick at the Doce Pares World Championships. Most recently, in 2018, I won first place in padded stick fighting at the WEKAF Nationals in Baltimore, Maryland.

I enjoy reading what others have to teach about the martial arts, and I have a large collection of books in my home library. I was surprised that I could find few books that talked about the actual strategies and tactics needed to become a successful stick fighter. The author Beverly Cleary once said, "If you don't see the book you want on the shelf, write it." So the stick was in my court. The next step, naturally, was to write the book that you are reading now, *The Art and Science of Stick Fighting*.

In this book, I present a methodical process for training to fight using the short stick. My book uses a multifaceted, interstylistic approach that is easily incorporated into any foundational martial art. It is designed to be absorbed in small chunks over time. If you keep an open mind, explore often, and train hard with the stick, you will increase your knowledge and develop your abilities to employ the weapon effectively in a fight. The result will be your own, personal stick-fighting method that is based on sound principles and good techniques.

> Lord Aki once said that martial valor is a matter of becoming a fanatic.
> I thought that this was surprisingly in accord with my own resolve,
> and thereafter I became more and more extreme in my fanaticism.
> —Yamamoto Tsunetomo, *Hagakure*

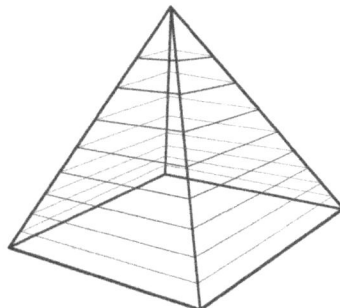

Introduction

The Levels

The *Art and Science of Stick Fighting* is a unique, non-style-specific approach to fighting with the short stick. Its curriculum is streamlined and divided into nine logical stages of training that allow the reader to quickly and methodically learn and develop the skills needed for fighting with the stick.

Whether you are just starting out or have been practicing stick fighting for years, there is something for everyone in this book. Whereas my last book, *The Art and Science of Staff Fighting*, featured an appendix that explained the physics of the staff, in this book I have tried to incorporate the science into the main body of the work, making it more pertinent and accessible to the reader. Like *Staff Fighting*, this book features detailed, systematic workouts and descriptions of how to make and use specific training equipment as you learn and master the art and science of stick fighting.

Level 1: The Foundation. Become one with your stick! Learn the basics on which everything else relies: a stable stance, basic footwork, and an effective guard. Once these basics are in place, you learn different types of strikes and how to practice them in a helpful, easy-to-learn striking pattern. The aim is to grow so comfortable wielding a stick that it is as though the stick has become an extension of your body.

Level 2: Long Range. Dominate the fight by mastering your outside game! Learn how to effectively apply the basic strikes, both offensively and defensively. Topics include striking, targeting, combinations, double striking, feinting, programming, evasion, and long-range disarming strikes.

Level 3: Crossing the Gap. Control the distance and you control the fight! Learn how to safely cross the gap from long range to middle range to keep your opponent guessing, and one step behind.

Level 4: Middle-Range Offense. Speed striking will teach you how to execute fast and effective combinations while checking your opponent's strikes at the same time.

Level 5: Middle-Range Defense. Learn how to block the opponent's attack and finish the job with a series of simple middle-range disarms that will leave your opponent wondering where his stick went.

Level 6: Close-Range Infighting. Things can get ugly on the inside! Learn the game of infighting with the short stick using devastating butt strikes, walloping double-handed striking, and throat-crushing chokes. End the fight with grappling and takedown techniques.

Level 7: Single-Stick Sparring. It's time to put your skills to the test by suiting up and bringing on the fight. Learn important guidelines for sparring, from light-contact up to full-contact training, how to construct your own padded weapons, and effective fighting tips that will up your game.

Level 8: Short Stick versus Other Weapons. What if your opponent does not have a stick? Learn techniques to counter all sorts of threats, from short-range weapons such as knives to long-range weapons such as staffs, spears, and even guns.

Level 9: Empty-Hand Defense against the Stick. Oh no, the worst-case scenario happens: your opponent has a weapon, but you do not! Learn the strategies and tactics that will help you not only survive but even beat the odds and emerge victorious.

Along the way, I'll also include information about special training equipment designed to help you perfect specific skills. Workouts at the end of each level outline the type of exercises and training that will help you achieve your goals.

While attackers may be of either gender, the pronouns *he* and *his* have been used in reference to opponents for the sake of simplicity. Similarly, while participants may be left- or right-handed, techniques have been demonstrated primarily from a right-handed perspective.

Stick fighting is a martial art, and martial arts are, by their very nature, intensely physical activities. Since it is difficult to learn the nuances of the martial arts solely from a book, I recommend seeking out and training with a qualified instructor. It also helps to have a dedicated training partner, or better yet, a group to practice with. However you end up training, always keep an open mind. Continually strive for a deeper understanding and a corresponding higher level of performance.

I admit that this book is by no means a comprehensive text on the topic of stick fighting. I'm not sure any single book could be. There are many stick-fighting styles and techniques that are worthy of study yet fell outside the scope of this book. However, I am confident that *The Art and Science of Stick Fighting* is a large step in the right direction. There is a lot here, and it will take a while to properly assimilate. The journey will take patience and perseverance on your part, but in the end, I think you will be very proud of your accomplishments. What do you say we get started?

> Vision without action
> is a dream soon forgotten.
> —Dr. Dong Ngo

Why Learn Stick Fighting?

There are many practical reasons to learn how to fight with sticks. Stick fighting is a healthy, competitive activity that has real-world applications. Stick-fighting skills are very practical for self-defense, while stick fighting also serves as a sport, offering both entertainment and fitness. It appeals to all types of people, of all ages and ability levels.

During a self-defense situation, it usually helps to possess more power than your opponent. Greater power can be achieved with greater physical size, muscular strength, and fighting experience. Weapons, such as short sticks, can also act as power multipliers. They increase your speed, force, and range, giving one person the ability to fight off much larger, even multiple, opponents. The odds of having your sticks with you to defend yourself are very low; however, your everyday environment contains many items similar to your sticks that can be used as effective, improvised weapons. Objects such as umbrellas, car antennae, curtain rods, plunger handles, walking sticks, baseball bats, and tennis rackets can be wielded in self-defense like a stick, thereby making it practical to learn how to fight with sticks. Concepts and skills from stick fighting apply to self-defense situations involving knives and weaponless defense as well.

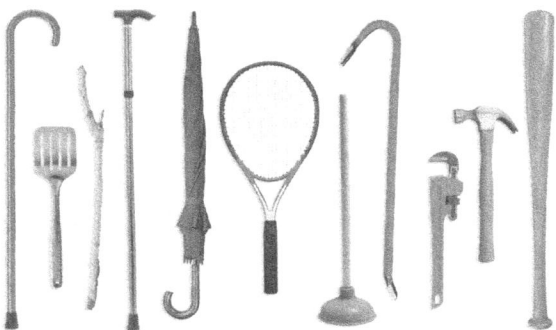

A sample of the improvised weapons available in your everyday environment.

There is an important distinction that needs to be made between self-defense and sport when it comes to stick fighting, and all martial arts for that matter. Sport fighting is meant to be similar to, but certainly not the same as, a self-defense encounter. Sport fighting is governed by clear-cut rules, and the contestants stand and fight in a safe, controlled arena until a winner is declared. On the street, your goal is to fight only as long as is necessary to escape to safety. There are no rules of engagement in self-defense except to do whatever is needed to survive, and the arena is never ideal. A serious, unwavering, and focused mind-set is critical in self-defense. Sport fighting provides the arena and the time for a fighter to focus on developing fighting skill sets that may help in self-defense. It provides the fighter an experience that develops personal discipline and fosters courage through a voluntary exposure to adversity. It is also a fun, safe way to get into shape, to improve your ability to think on the fly, and to test your spirit. It serves many purposes, of which training for self-defense is but one.

There is also an important distinction that needs to be made between a trained stick fighter and a person fighting with a stick. A fighter is called a fighter for a reason, and a trained stick fighter is a breed apart. A trained stick fighter has tremendous speed compared with an untrained stick fighter. Weapons move at a high speed, so training with them improves reaction time. Regular practice with weighted objects like sticks also helps develop overall body strength, coordination, and empty-hand speed. Ask any baseball or tennis coach, and they will tell you that speed is an acquired skill. Rigorous, repetitive training with a stick increases a stick fighter's ability to wield that stick faster and faster because his body becomes so comfortable moving and hitting with the stick that it requires less and less muscle energy. Untrained fighters, on the other hand, even those with greater raw power, will not be able to wield the stick to as great an advantage because their bodies will need to rely on muscle energy, making their strikes slower and weaker.

Just knowing how to swing a stick and to be able to swing it fast are not enough. Targeting and accuracy are just as important as speed and power, since a strike needs to hit a vulnerable target in order to inflict damage. A trained stick fighter not only knows how to hit with a stick but also knows where to hit for maximum effect. This knowledge and precision are developed with proper training and lots of repetitive practice. An untrained fighter lacks both the targeting and the accuracy needed to hit decisively and effectively with the weapon, especially in the heat of the moment, when he is trying to hit with maximum force for maximum effect.

A proper stick fighter's training regime is progressive, frequent, challenging, and physically strenuous. Stick-fighting practice provides cardiovascular exercise and all-around physical fitness. The best stick fighters achieve a level of physical fitness that a nontrained person usually does not have. The training that a stick fighter endures provides him with the stamina to keep fighting long after an untrained fighter has tired out. Perhaps even more importantly, stick fighting often leads to a lifelong path of health and fitness.

A Brief History of Stick Fighting

Stick fighting, for both self-defense and sport, has existed for many thousands of years. All across the globe, different cultures have shaped the way stick fighting is practiced, resulting in many different styles. Each of these styles has its particular strengths and weaknesses, and each of these styles has undoubtedly produced many capable and formidable fighters.

As humankind learned to work metal and make swords, stick fighting became sword fighting. Some blades, such as the short sword, were made exclusively as tools for killing, while others, such as the machete, were more utilitarian in nature. However, swords are both more dangerous and more expensive than sticks in terms of the cost of both weapons and safety equipment. Compared with metal swords, sticks are not only less deadly but also far cheaper and easier to obtain. This advantage has made stick fighting endure as a common alternative to bladed weapons in sword fighting practice, sport competitions, and self-defense.

Western stick-fighting traditions from Europe include those of the Irish shillelagh and French cane. While both evolved from walking sticks, they are very different in nature. The shillelagh is traditionally made from a stout knotty oak or blackthorn stick with a large knob at the top, and it was often used as a club or cudgel. Cudgeling was a type of duel fought with wooden weapons that was popular in Britain during the Georgian era (early 1700s to mid-1800s). Also known as *single stick*, the aim of the competition was to break the skin on the head, face, or neck so that blood was drawn. When the crowd saw blood, they would shout "A head!" and an umpire would determine whether the match was won. Competitors needed to have good endurance, as it could take quite some time to hit your opponent hard enough to draw blood. Cudgeling was one of the arts taught by James Figg at his amphitheater in London, and newspapers at the time reported on these matches as though they were mainstream sporting events. On Thursday, September 26, 1765, the *Gazetteer and New Daily Advertiser* ran the following article about a team contest:

> Monday afternoon a cudgelling match was fought on Wandsworth hill, for a laced hat, for the value of one moidore. The opponents on each side were nine, one part of which were named the London side and the other the Wandsworth side. Great dexterity was displayed during the contest by both parties, particularly by a dyer, a sugar cooper and a carpenter, on the London side; and by a maltster, a gardener and a farmer's labourer on the Wandsworth side. When, after the whole eighteen had undergone a very severe drubbing, each from his antagonist, fortune thought proper to bestow the hat on the countrymen, by a small pimple under the eye of one of the London side, breaking through his overstretching, from which sprung a little bloody tinged matter, which the umpire was held to be broken head.

In France, the cane became a popular weapon when knives and guns were banned in the 1800s. Modern-day French cane fighters compete against each other wearing padded suits and fencing masks, as do practitioners of the Portuguese art of jogo do pau.

Illustrations depicting techniques of canne de combat, French cane fighting.

In South Africa we find the art of donga, also called dlala 'nduku, which translates as "playing sticks." Participants usually wield two long sticks. One is used as the attacking stick while the other, the defending stick, is used as a shield. Ceremonial matches are full contact, and very little armor is worn. The transatlantic slave trade brought these traditions to places like Barbados, where "sticklicking" is still actively practiced to this day. African slaves also imported stick fighting to Trinidad, where it developed into a martial sport called bois. Bois uses thick sticks about four feet long and incorporates drumming and dancing. Don't let that fool you, however. Matches are full contact and no armor is worn. The fighter who draws first blood is declared the victor.

Left: A relief depicting stick fighting in Egypt. *Right:* Detail from a print titled *A Cudgelling Match between English and French Negroes in the Island of Dominica* by Agostino Brunias, 1779.

Asia also has its unique stick-fighting traditions. Among them is Japanese bojutsu, or "stick arts," which is most famous for its *rokushakubo* (six-foot staff) but also included instruction in the *jo* (four-foot staff) and *hanbo* (three-foot stick). In Okinawa, the *tambo* (short stick) was popular. The Filipino martial arts of eskrima, kali, and arnis are currently the most popular stick-fighting arts and are practiced in nearly every country in the world. Eskrimadors often fight high-energy, full-contact bouts with rattan sticks while wearing padded jackets, gloves, and barred helmets.

This list just begins to scratch the surface of the many stick-fighting traditions that can be found globally. Each is unique and has its own strengths and weaknesses. But they have certain commonalities as well. These common techniques certainly have different names and are not necessarily performed exactly the same way, but to get lost in the details would be to fail to see the forest for the trees. What is important are the universal principles behind these techniques that make them work. These commonalities are the essence of stick fighting, the things that every stick fighter should know, understand, and be able to use. They are the guiding principles that define the art and science of stick fighting.

Traditional versus Progressive

Traditional stick-fighting systems exist all over the globe. These systems each have their own unique history and methods of formal training. Schools and styles offer many benefits that are hard to find otherwise, such as instruction in an established curriculum, the community that comes with being associated with a group, and exposure to advanced practitioners who possess a deeper knowledge of their art.

This deeper knowledge includes advanced techniques and drills that are often complicated and therefore take far more coordination and skill to apply than the more basic techniques. It is exactly this challenging aspect that makes advanced techniques interesting and fun to practice. These techniques and drills explore the theoretical potential of what can be done with the stick. However, that does not mean they are always practical for fighting. Advanced techniques and drills usually depend on a very particular set of circumstances to be successful that are difficult to replicate in the confusion of the fight. This makes them very difficult, if not impossible, to apply against a noncompliant opponent, even for skilled practitioners with decades of experience. Practical techniques, on the other hand, have a high rate of success, even in nonscripted scenarios.

While I enjoy practicing and teaching advanced techniques myself, when it comes to fighting, I have found that it is usually best to keep it simple. At its essence, stick fighting is simply the act of neutralizing an attacker before he can incapacitate you. When you try to get too fancy, you start missing this very important point. Therefore, I have done my best to include only those practical techniques that I believe have a high rate of success, in both sport and self-defense.

The Art and Science of Stick Fighting does not present a style in the traditional sense of the word. It is a progressive, eclectic collection of highly successful stick-fighting techniques borrowed from many diverse sources. Most are universal concepts that can easily be applied to fighting with a variety of short weapons, both traditional and improvised.

> **Styles tend to separate men, because they have their own doctrines and then the doctrine became the gospel truth that you cannot change. But if you do not have a style, if you just say: Well, here I am as a human being, how can I express myself totally and completely? That way, it's a process of continuing growth.**
> —Bruce Lee

Getting Started

Before any serious undertaking, one should have a clear *perspective*. What is your overall *objective*? Well, I want to win a stick fight (duh!), but what exactly does that mean?

First, we need to define *winning*. There is actually a big difference between winning in a competition and winning in a self-defense situation.

Sport fighting refers to when you are in a ring facing another competitor. Sometimes the contact is controlled, and sometimes contests are full contact. The sticks may or may not be padded and the participants may or may not be wearing protective gear, but as long as there are rules, it is a sport. The goal is generally to hit the opponent as many times as possible without getting hit in return.

On the other hand, the goal of self-defense should be to survive the encounter long enough to either escape or neutralize your attacker. Either way, there is no score, and the winner is the guy who gets to go home. Therefore, if escape is an option, you should take it, especially if you have no third party to protect. While it may not sound like the courageous thing to do, the truth is that running is smart. A tactical retreat has served me well on several occasions that could have otherwise gotten ugly. A speedy departure may be all you need to discourage your attacker (unless he is *really* mad at you), and by keeping a proper perspective, you can achieve your goal with minimal danger to you. This does not imply that you will not have to fight, but quickly leaving the situation at your earliest opportunity not only ensures your personal safety but in many cases is also required by local preclusion laws.

Of course, there may be times when escape is not an option. Perhaps you are trapped or have a third party to protect such as a child or spouse. In some cases it may even be your duty or responsibility to confront an armed aggressor—for example, if you are a security or police officer. In such instances, the goal becomes to effectively neutralize the aggressor as quickly, and safely, as possible.

Our fighting methodology should be to achieve the objective (win a stick fight) through the application of scientifically sound strategy and tactics. Your strategy is your overall plan, such as to control the fight by controlling the distance. Your tactics are the specific techniques you use to achieve your strategic goal, such as using certain footwork patterns to stay out of your opponent's effective range, or using other footwork to quickly close the gap between you.

In an actual confrontation, your fine-motor control will likely be affected, resulting in decreased dexterity, so shutting things down fast can be the key to survival. There are many strategies that you could employ to achieve this. A basic but effective strategy is to stay out of range while delivering long-range shots that inflict enough pain to effectively take down the attacker's sensor grid, allowing you to stop the fight quickly with a powerful blow to a vulnerable target.

To wield the short stick effectively when fighting, you must practice until the stick becomes a natural extension of your body. Strive to strike sharply and block solidly at all times. Personalize your fighting style, working to integrate your short-stick skills with your chosen foundation art or primary method of self-defense. Realize that learning any new skill takes time. Learn gradually and take the time needed to master each level before moving on to the next.

This book is designed to share effective elements of stick fighting. My focus is fight functionality. The drills are mainly simple two- or three-step sequences, many predicated on the gross motor or adrenal state you're going to experience in a fight as well as the most likely responses from your opponent. While I have had the privilege of being exposed to the techniques and tactics of several different styles of fighting with the short stick, I have purposely avoided adhering to the teachings of any one system, instead choosing to present techniques that are common to many of them. These common elements are often the most effective ones. Just as every word in the English language is built from the same twenty-six letters, so too, all stick fighting seems to be built on a small handful of techniques that reflect those principles. Temporarily setting the constraint of style aside allows you to open your mind to the core techniques presented in *The Art and Science of Stick Fighting*.

The following strategies, tactics, and techniques are the results of many decades of study, not only by myself but also by the many talented and knowledgeable teachers I have had the privilege of studying with over the last thirty-plus years, and by their teachers, and their teachers before them. The techniques have been tested and proved effective; however, words and pictures can only serve to educate. It is up to you to study and practice until you understand and can apply them.

Then go study and practice some more.

> **A journey of ten thousand miles starts with a single step.**
> **—Lao Tzu**

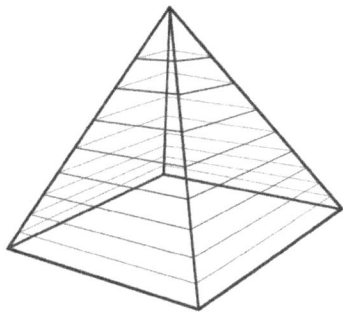

Warming Up and Cooling Down

Warming Up and Stretching

There are more than ten million sports injuries every year, but many of them could be avoided by implementing a proper warm-up. This produces a two- to three-degree rise in core body temperature that can last for up to forty-five minutes, preparing your muscles for strenuous activity and helping to prevent injury. A well-designed warm-up routine accompanied by some light stretching can also be extremely beneficial to your overall performance, so long as the activity is suitable to the sport and not performed too vigorously. If you warm up, you will have looser muscles, making you faster, stronger, more agile, and less prone to injury.

Think you can ignore or rush through your warm-up? Well, let me tell you a precautionary tale. It was April 2018, and I was fighting in the World Eskrima Kali Arnis Federation Stick Fighting East Coast Nationals in Baltimore. So far I was having a great day. I was undefeated, having already taken gold medals in staff and padded stick fighting, and was well on my way to adding a third gold medal to that list, this time for knife fighting. I won my first fight and was halfway through my second when I suddenly heard a pop and staggered. I felt as if someone had just nailed me in the calf with a stick, hard. I looked around to see who had hit me, but it was just me and my opponent. I actually asked the ref, "Who hit me?" but he just shrugged and answered, "Nobody." I finished that fight in extreme pain, but I won. I got some ice on my calf, but by the time my final match came up, I could barely stand on it. I fought that last fight on one leg, and although I gave it my best, I still lost four to six. When I went home, I looked up calf injuries. A class 3 calf sprain was described as being accompanied by an audible pop and feeling as if someone has stabbed you in the calf. That sounded about right.

I don't mind losing to a superior opponent, but I do mind losing to my own stupidity. I had trained hard for that tournament and was well prepared, but all my training came to naught because I had forgotten to do one basic thing: warm up. Sure, I had warmed up when I first arrived at the tournament, but that was over five hours before, and after standing around all day, my legs were getting cold and stiff. I did do some quick stretches before my match, but obviously it was not enough. I missed stretching my calves, and when I needed my body to perform the most, it broke under the strain and cost me a gold medal, not to mention the fact that it took several annoying months to heal.

This is why all good coaches include preworkout techniques specifically designed to increase performance and decrease injuries. Physically, the benefits of warming up include increased flexibility, muscle stability, and range of motion. Warming up also increases your mental alertness and psychological readiness. This is partly because aerobic exercise releases endorphins that can actually put you in a positive mood, making you feel more prepared and ready to perform.

The primary goal of your warm-up activities should be to increase your body temperature a few degrees. The amount of exercise needed to get to this point varies depending on your cardiovascular conditioning level, but it is recommended that you exercise until you observe light to mild sweating in normal ambient conditions.

Research shows that warming up by slightly increasing your body's temperature with physical movement can actually enhance your physical performance. A proper warm-up causes your blood vessels to dilate, reducing their resistance to blood flow and thereby minimizing the strain on your heart. The increased blood flow not only decreases muscular stiffness but also increases oxygen and nutrient delivery, improving muscular endurance and increasing your ability to sustain peak performance for as long as possible. Warming up also helps to prevent overheating by promoting the dissipation of body heat through sweating.

This increase in temperature allows muscles and tendons to become more extensible, making stretching muscles and tendons easier and more effective. The heat also augments the sensitivity of your nerve receptors and increases the transmission speed of your nervous impulses, meaning your muscles can contract with more force and relax more quickly. This results in enhanced speed and strength, making you a better stick fighter. By improving the muscle's elasticity, you also decrease the risk of pulling that muscle. Warming up can further decrease your risk of injury by increasing the range of motion of your joints.

Your first goal should simply be to increase your body temperature. You need to do five to seven minutes of light to moderate activity until you break a light sweat. The activity could be any type of light cardio or plyometric training—jogging, stationary bike, treadmill, shadow boxing, and so on. The best activity for stick fighters, however, is probably skipping rope, since it activates practically all of the same muscles you will use when fighting with the stick. Whatever the activity, you should be looking to increase your heart rate to 55–60 percent of your maximum. To calculate your personal maximum heart rate, subtract your age from 220. This is the upper limit of what your cardiovascular system can safely handle during physical activity. For example, a forty-year-old would have a maximum heart rate of 180. For the same person, the target heart rate for a warm-up would be about 100 to 120 beats per minute.

After your body has been warmed up, you should go through a light stretching routine. When you stretch at the beginning of your workout, you generally want to concentrate on performing dynamic stretching. Dynamic stretching takes each limb gently through its full range of motion, gradually increasing reach and speed. These motions include swings and circles with your arms and legs, as well as gentle twirling and striking with the stick.

You may be surprised to hear that, while light, dynamic stretching does not decrease performance, heavy, static stretching does. Static stretching involves holding a position for extended periods of time. Holding a stretch for longer than thirty seconds can cause a muscle to become less responsive and stay weakened for up to thirty minutes. Therefore, since traditional static stretching is still needed to address or improve certain areas, only hold these stretches for twenty to thirty seconds at the beginning of your workout. A foam roller can be a useful tool to help work out areas of stiffness and immobility. A quick foam-rolling routine can improve range of motion without decreasing muscular activation or force.

The following warm-up stretching routine is meant to be general and preventative, not individual or prescriptive. Specific limitations can be addressed through precise drills and stretches that are best prescribed by a sports therapist on an individual diagnostic basis.

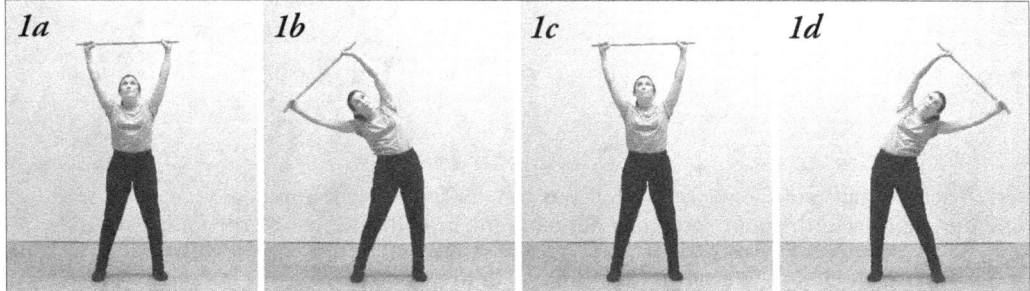

Begin gripping your stick in two hands and holding it high over your head (*1a*). Lean to your right to stretch your lats and obliques (*1b*). Return to the top position and lean backward slightly as you reach high (*1c*). Lean to your left to stretch your other side (*1d*).

Hold the stick straight out in front of you, reaching forward as far as you can (*2a*). Look over your right shoulder as you turn your upper body to the right for a twisting stretch that extends from your ankle all the way up to your neck (*2b*). Hold the stick straight out in front of you again, reaching forward as far as you can (*2c*). Look over your left shoulder as you turn your upper body to the left (*2d*).

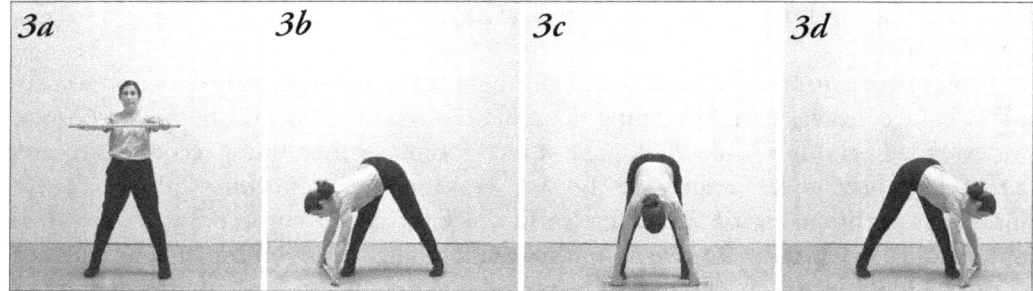

Return to the front-facing position (*3a*). Turn to your right and bend at the waist, reaching down to your right side (*3b*). Bend forward at the waist to stretch your back and hamstrings (*3c*). Turn to your left and bend at the waist, reaching down to your left side (*3d*).

Reach across your chest with your right hand and hook your right arm with your left from underneath to stretch your triceps and deltoids (*4a*). Switch sides and stretch the other side (*4b*). To warm up your wrist and forearm, hold the stick out in front of you with the tip pointing toward the ground. Rotate the stick back and forth through a 360-degree rotation clockwise and then counterclockwise (*5a and 5b*). Switch hands and repeat.

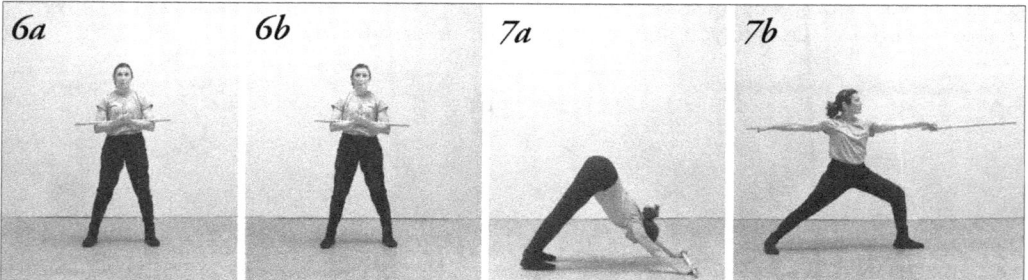

Rest your stick in the crooks of your elbows as you grasp the back of your left hand with your right so that your fingers are grasping the base of your palm and your right thumb is pressing against the base of your pinky finger. Turn your hand inward, pinky toward your center, to stretch your wrist (*6a*). Repeat on the other side (*6b*). The "downward dog" position from yoga stretches your calves (*7a*), while "warrior two" helps to ready your body for lunging. Keep the heel of your front foot in line with the arch of your rear foot (*7b*).

Training Equipment: The Jump Rope

Stick fighting requires good cardio, light footwork, and sharp pivoting for fast, explosive striking. This requires good leg strength and endurance. However, not just any leg workout will help you accomplish your goals for stick fighting.

While squats are great for developing leg strength, they are not done fast enough or for a long enough period of time to mimic the constant quick bursts of speed required for fighting. Running does a somewhat better job, especially at developing your cardiovascular endurance, but the heel-toe motion used when running is unlike the metatarsal-based stepping utilized when fighting. This results in slower, heavier steps that not only waste energy but are also easier for your opponent to read.

On the other hand, fighters who jump rope have a nice, relaxed bounce and move with a calm slickness. Jumping rope develops your ability to make the many quick, tiny contractions required to move and strike effectively in a stick fight. The act of having to clear the rope on every pass requires mental concentration and focus. Physically, the entire activity requires quick, coordinated reflexes and agility. This is why regular training with the jump rope will make you a more powerful and energy-efficient fighter.

Jumping rope may be difficult and tiring at first, but this is usually due to excessive tension in the body. The motions will become more automatic as you develop the "muscle memory" (actually neural pathways in the brain) to jump without thinking about your movements. As your motions become more relaxed, you will be able to jump longer while expending less energy. This relaxation is crucial in a stick fight, where, depending on the situation, you may have to swing your stick repeatedly over and over for a considerable length of time without getting tired. Once you have achieved a fair amount of skill with the jump rope, you will be able to throw hundreds of powerful strikes without getting tired. This is something that other leg exercises cannot teach you.

Jumping rope is actually fun once you get the hang of it. The extreme physical activity causes your body to release endorphins, hormones secreted within the brain and nervous system that activate the body's opioid receptors, causing an analgesic effect. In other words, they make you feel good.

There are also so many different ways to jump rope that it is hard to get bored. The most basic jump is the two-foot jump. Hold one end of the rope in each hand, letting the center hang down in front of you. Step over the rope so it is now behind you and you are standing in front of it. Then swing the rope over your head and jump over it as it passes under your feet. You don't have to jump high. In fact, this is why the activity is often called skipping rope. Jump off the balls of both feet, just high enough to clear the rope before landing softly and evenly back on the balls of both feet.

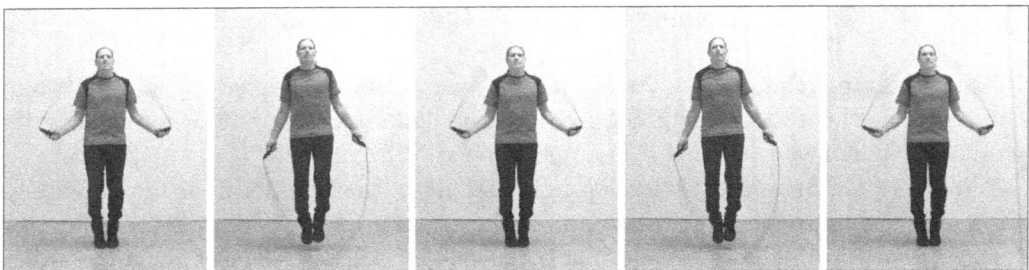

The standard two-foot jump.

The many challenges presented by skipping rope keep the activity fresh and entertaining. Try crossing your arms in front of you as you jump or passing the rope under you twice in a single jump. You could also alternate feet as you jump. As you swing the rope over your head, land on one foot instead of two. Switch feet on every pass of the rope. Try switching on every other pass, or every third. Try jumping ten seconds on each foot, gradually increasing the time you can spend jumping on one foot. Try high stepping, where you raise one knee to waist level at the same time that you jump with the other foot. Other variations include the side-to-side, front-to-back, straddle jump, toe tap, heel tap, double jump, and crisscross, to name but a few. Detailed instruction in each of these would be outside the immediate scope of this book, but I recommend checking out some of the many fine instructional videos available on sites like YouTube.

The crisscross.

Skipping rope is a great way to burn calories, and the more you weigh, the more calories you burn. At a slow to moderate pace, a person weighing 130 pounds can expect to burn about five hundred calories per hour, whereas a 200-pound individual could expect to burn more than eight hundred calories doing the same activity. Jumping at a more vigorous rate would of course burn even more.

There have been many studies done over the last fifty years comparing the training responses to rope skipping and jogging. Some studies suggest that just ten minutes of even moderate skipping can be equal to thirty minutes of jogging. In one study, researchers had one group jump rope for ten minutes a day while another group jogged for thirty minutes. After six weeks, both groups showed comparable levels of cardiovascular fitness. To be fair, other studies dispute this, but there is certainly enough evidence out there to demonstrate that skipping rope is an effective training method. In fact, it activates many of the same muscles used when stick fighting.

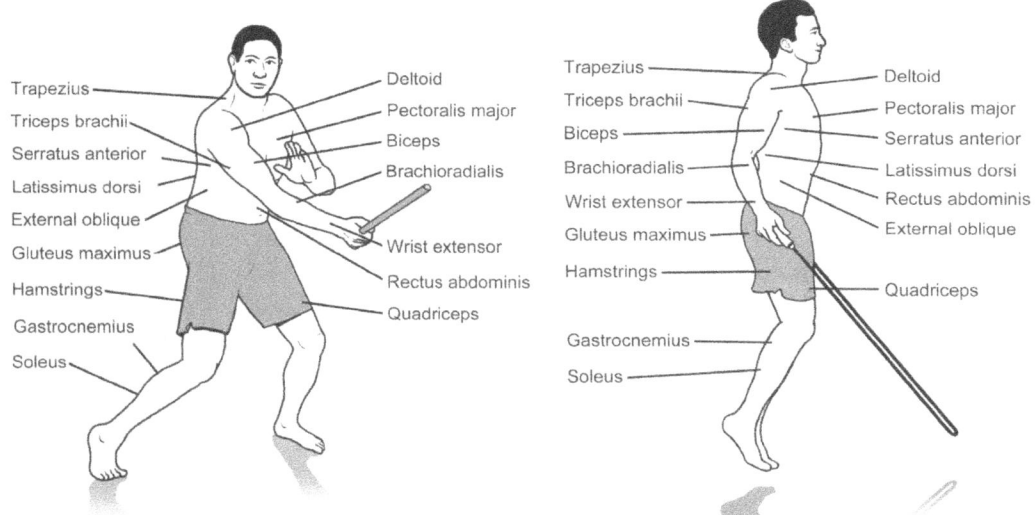

Muscles activated when swinging a stick   Muscles activated by jumping rope

Since the jump rope is a small, lightweight piece of training equipment, it is convenient and easily portable. And since all you need is a small space, it can be done almost anywhere, even if you don't have a rope! Or perhaps you do not have the ceiling clearance to jump inside. Either way, simply go through the motions of skipping rope, acting as though you actually had one in your hands. It may not be as fun as actually jumping rope (and you may look a little strange doing it), but the results you get can be nearly the same.

Making Your Own Jump Rope

While jump ropes are relatively inexpensive and easy to find, if you do not have one available, you may wish to make your own. The first step is to select the material for your jump rope. You can use any of a variety of materials, such as actual rope, leather, or even an old electrical cord.

Different materials will have different effects on the speed and durability of your rope. Braided nylon rope is slower but doesn't hurt very much when it hits you. On the other hand, a leather or electrical cord jump rope, while great for speed, can feel like a whip when it hits your skin.

To personalize your jump rope, measure the length from the top of your chest to your feet, then cut your rope to twice this length. General guidelines are that an eight-foot rope would be a good length for someone between five foot two and five foot six, while taller people (five foot six to six foot two) would be more comfortable with a nine-foot rope. People taller than six foot three should go with a ten-foot rope. A longer rope will take longer to rotate, which can be beneficial for you if you are new to jumping rope. As you get more experienced and want to maximize your speed, you will want to have as little excess rope as possible. It's best to have a little extra length to begin with, because you can make adjustments to shorten the rope later as needed.

You can make jump rope handles using commonly found items around your home, such as PVC or wooden dowels. Heavier handles will give you more upper-body benefits than lighter handles. To make the handles, cut two pieces of material into equal lengths, about six inches long (these could be longer or shorter depending on your preference). Drill a hole through one side of each handle, making sure that it is wide enough for your rope. Dowels should be drilled all the way through on a slight angle.

You might consider adding some beads to your jump rope. The beads add a little weight to the rope, changing its feel and performance. They also make a sound when they hit the ground, which some jumpers use to keep a good rhythm. If you are using beads, you will need to slide them onto the rope before you attach your handles.

Feed each end of your rope through a hole in one of your handles. Then tie a secure knot at each end of the rope so that the ends will not slip back through the handles. Use a lighter to carefully singe the ends of nylon rope to prevent them from fraying.

Try out the jump rope to test the length. If it seems too long, adjust it by pulling the unwanted length of rope through the handle and holding onto it or knotting it temporarily, then try using it again. When your rope seems to be a good length for you, tie a knot at one end and cut off the excess with a pair of scissors.

See the appendix at the end of this book for blueprints and more precise instructions on creating your own jump rope and many other types of equipment to aid in your training.

Cooling Down

A cooldown is the opposite of a warm-up, and it is just as important. To understand why, let's take a look at how your body's autonomic system works. When you train and fight intensely, your body shifts from its normal resting parasympathetic biorhythms into fight-or-flight mode, activating your body's sympathetic system. This increases your heart rate, dilates the bronchi in your lungs, and slows your digestion, among other things. These changes enable your body to work at peak performance. However, a number of negative effects can result if you do not take the time to bring your body back from this state.

WARMING UP AND COOLING DOWN 19

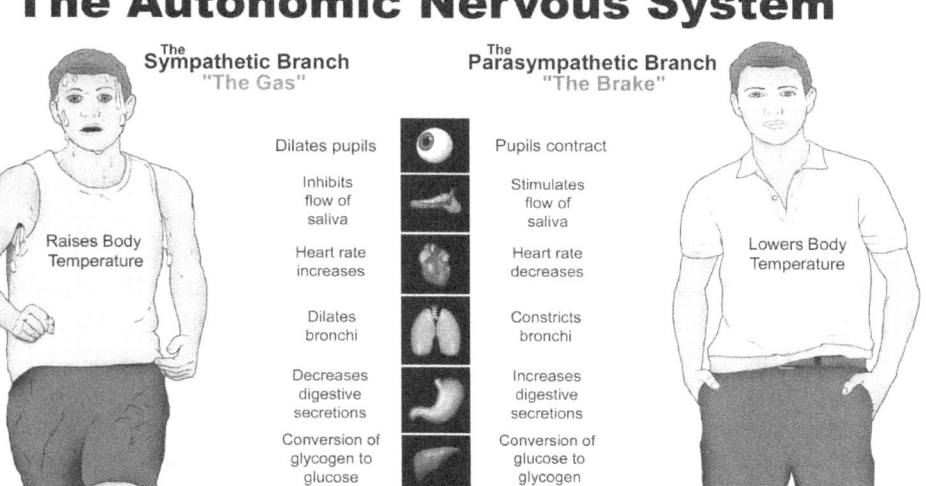

The cooldown period reduces your breathing and heart rate to normal levels, lowers your body and muscle temperature to preexercise conditions, and effectively turns your digestion back on.

At the end of the workout, you want to gradually reduce your heart rate. A sudden stop to exercise without cooling down can lead to blood pooling. Your heart is constantly fighting against gravity to pump blood throughout your body. This is normal. During extreme exercise, your muscles contract and help to force the blood through the vessels and back to your heart. When you suddenly stop exercising, your muscles are no longer contracting and assisting with the flow of blood. Gravity can then cause the blood to pool in your legs, which may adversely lower your blood pressure and result in dizziness and fainting.

Once you have taken a few moments to lower your heart rate, you should stretch to loosen, lengthen, and strengthen your muscles. Static stretching, holding postures for extended periods of time, causes tired muscles to relax, let go, and lengthen. In fact, when your muscles are tired, they relax and lengthen more easily. When stretching, you will improve your results by gently working with one part of your body at a time. Take care not to hyperextend your joints or force a stretch to the point of pain. Allow your mind and body to merge, thus enabling you to effectively relax each muscle individually by recognizing the tension held within it and then consciously releasing it.

Prolonged static stretching (more than thirty seconds) should be saved for the end of your workout, as it can temporarily decrease your potential muscular output. However, you need this type of stretching at the end of your workout because it will help shorten your recovery time by dissipating lactic acid away from the muscles where it has been concentrated during exercise. Stretching at the end of a workout helps to move this lactic acid into the bloodstream and return your body to its preexercise, baseline values. This is especially important because the lactic acid can change the pH levels of your cells, making them more acidic and decreasing the effectiveness of enzymes involved with cellular metabolism.

Cooldowns should last at least five to ten minutes. The result is a quicker and more complete recovery after exercise, better preparing your body for its next round of training.

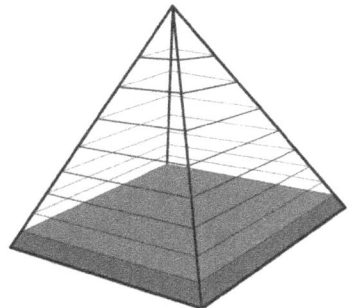

LEVEL 1
The Foundation

Choosing a Stick

You have many options when choosing a stick. You could choose hardwood or rattan, long or short, heavy or light.

Although the techniques in this book can be applied to a wide variety of lengths and types of stick, I demonstrate mainly with kali sticks, rattan sticks about twenty-eight inches long. This is a versatile length for the average-size person, long enough for good reach while still short enough to allow for quicker manipulation than a longer, heavier stick (at six foot two, I am a little taller than average, so I can comfortably wield a slightly longer stick and cut my sticks to around thirty-one inches).

A longer stick has an obvious reach advantage, while a shorter stick usually has less weight and, thus, a speed advantage. Heavier sticks hit harder and are better for blocking. However, their mass makes them slower. Heavy sticks are good for developing the muscles used in manipulating sticks. Lighter sticks are faster, generally don't hit as hard, and can break when put under the stress of a hard strike or block. Lighter weapons are usually preferred for forms and free fighting.

The maximum length of the stick depends on your height. When you hold your stick in a natural grip with your arms at your sides, the tip should reach just below your ankle. Anything longer and you start to risk hitting the ground when you twirl or strike. The stick should be about one inch in diameter. You want it to be sturdy, but not so thick that you can't wrap your fingers all the way around it.

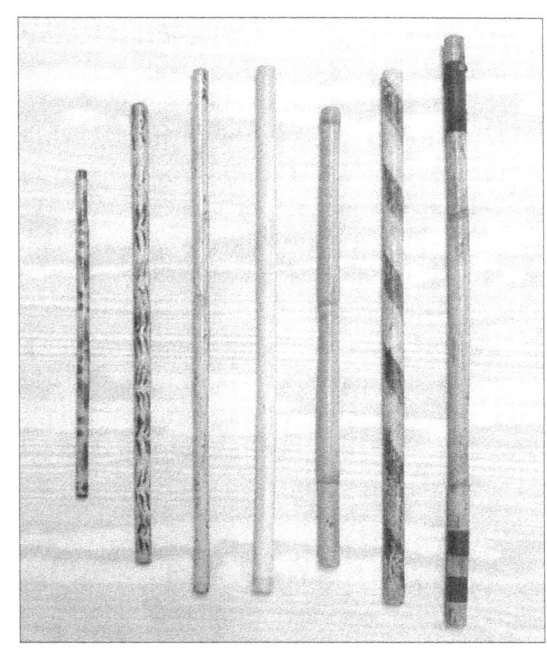

Sticks come in many sizes, lengths, and weights.

I recommend practice weapons made from rattan. Rattan looks like bamboo but is actually a vine-like plant that grows in Southeast Asia. Unlike bamboo, it is solid, yet it is not nearly as heavy as wood. This makes rattan easy to train with because it is light and more forgiving when you accidentally hit your training partner (hey, it happens). As the rattan is struck over and over, the fibers begin to separate and eventually the stick might lose its rigidity, but it will not shatter or splinter, leaving a sharp end, as regular woods have a tendency to do. This makes it preferable to wood in many ways.

Rattan is fibrous and does not splinter like wood.

Wood makes an ideal material for a heavy stick. Heavy sticks are good for developing strength and hitting hard. When selecting a wooden weapon, you want it to be durable and resist breaking. Therefore, one of the most important factors to consider is hardness. Most people know that there are two distinct kinds of wood: hardwood and softwood. However, these designations don't refer to the actual hardness or softness of the wood. Hardwoods come from deciduous trees (the kind that drop their leaves each fall), while softwoods typically come from evergreen trees (those that have needles and keep them year-round).

The actual hardness of a particular kind of wood is determined by the Janka hardness test, in which scientists see how much weight is needed to drive a small steel ball into a sample of wood. This test still does not necessarily predict how well suited a wood is for impact, but it is a starting place. The Janka ratings go from five hundred to five thousand pounds of force. The species that are optimal for martial arts have a Janka hardness in excess of two thousand pounds of force. These include exotic woods like purpleheart and Brazilian cherry. North American woods that rank high on the scale include black locust, persimmon, sycamore, and dogwood. Hickory and ash are not recommended because they have low Janka ratings, making them more prone to shattering. White waxwood also has a low Janka rating, but it resists breaking because it has a high modulus of elasticity (how much a stick can bend and still bounce back into its original shape). Tigerwood is a good overall choice, as it not only is hard and has a high elasticity but also has an interwoven wood grain for good shock absorption. All of these types of wood and many more are available online.

As of the time of this writing, Lowe's and Home Depot stock four-foot-long solid laminated bamboo paint-roller extensions for about seven dollars each. With a diameter of seven-eighths of an inch, they are lightweight and extremely durable and break clean with no splintering. All you need to do is cut them to length, give them a light sanding, and rub in a few coats of linseed or tung oil as a finish.

Whatever the material you use, carefully inspect your weapon before each workout by running your hands gently along its length, feeling for any splinters. Remove or tape over them before use. A shiny protective lacquer finish can cause a stick to slip out of your hand, especially if you are sweating. To prevent this, you should lightly sand off any lacquer finishes on your sticks.

Remember that it is the quality of your martial training that is of paramount importance, not the specifications of your weapon. If you are ever forced to defend yourself or your loved ones, the odds are that you will not have your regular weapons readily available. Instead, you will have to improvise and effectively wield whatever weapon may be at hand, be it long or short, light or heavy, sharp or blunt. Therefore, you must attempt to improve your odds by training with a variety of weapons at a variety of ranges.

Holding the Stick

Stick fighting literally begins with learning how to properly hold the stick. This is important because the way you grip the stick goes a long way to determining how fast and hard you can hit with the weapon.

There are basically three ways to hold the short stick with one hand: natural grip, middle grip, and reverse grip. The middle and reverse grips are used primarily during infighting and therefore will be dealt with in more detail in Level Six: Close-Range Infighting. For long- and middle-range fighting, I recommend the natural grip because it gives you a longer reach and the ability to deliver more powerful strikes than you typically can in either the middle or reverse grip. For these reasons, the natural grip is the instinctive way most people hold and use a stick.

24 THE ART AND SCIENCE OF STICK FIGHTING

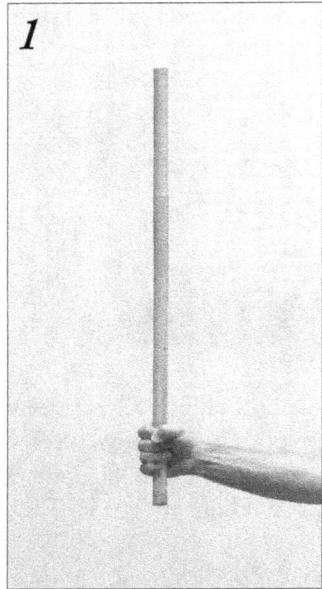 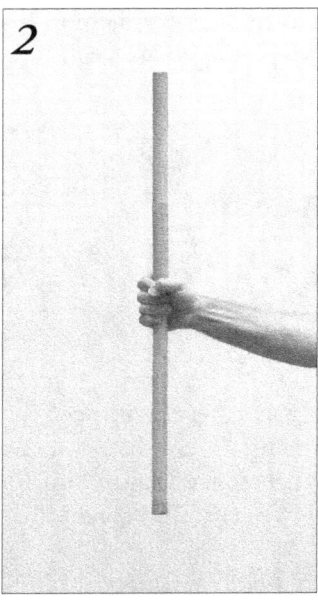 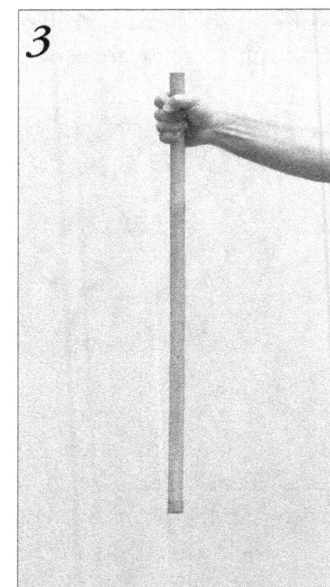

Regular grip Middle grip Reverse grip

Hold the stick at one end so that it extends outward from the thumb side of your clenched fist. The butt of the stick should extend one to three inches from the bottom of your hand. This gives you enough of an end to strike with, but not enough that your opponent could get a good grip on the bottom, which would allow him to control the tip of your weapon and also put him in an advantageous position to potentially disarm you.

Grab the stick with your fingertips, then close your thumb over them, taking care to make sure your thumb is not sticking straight out. Grasp the stick firmly, but not too tightly, as excessive tension will slow down your strike. More advanced fighters will often use a more relaxed grip that allows them to maximize the whip of their stick at the end of a strike, but be forewarned that a loose grip makes even the best fighters more prone to being disarmed. Speaking of which, there are variations on the natural grip that have the thumb pressed against the shaft of the stick, but failure to lock your thumb over your fingers also makes you extremely susceptible to being disarmed.

Your stick can be held in any of a number of positions in relation to your body. While there may be no superior ready position, it is good to lead with the stick in your dominant hand, especially when you are first learning. We'll discuss more advanced fighting positions, such as the rearguard and two-hand guard, later in this book. The basic guards are the middle and high guards, pictured here.

LEVEL 1: THE FOUNDATION 25

The Middle Guard: The middle-level guard is a very natural way to hold the stick. It is also a versatile position, good for both offense and defense. From this position, you can deliver a variety of strikes, and, since the stick is being held vertically in front of you, it can cover the maximum amount of your body with the least amount of effort. Your empty hand should be held ready but not overextended.

The High Guard: Another common ready position is the high guard. This position offers good protection for your head, especially from a right-handed opponent. It also offers offensive capabilities, as the guard itself acts as a chambered ready position for a number of strikes.

Your guard should never be static but rather always moving, smooth, and flowing. This makes you less predictable and keeps your opponent mentally occupied trying to guess your next move. Do not just randomly flow from one position to another. Consider strategy and tactics. Defensively, you might want to keep your stick perpendicular to your opponent's weapon to make it harder for him to strike you. If your opponent's stick goes high or low, you stay with him. Offensively, since it is easier to detect motion from stillness than it is to detect motion from motion, a flowing, ever-changing guard is a deceptive way to hide your strikes from your opponent until it is too late for him to block or evade them.

Whatever the position of your stick, your empty hand should be actively seeking and checking your opponent's weapon hand. However, be careful and don't overextend your guarding hand; when the opponent's weapon arm is not in range, your guarding hand should be held close to the body in a ready position.

Stances

Stances are ways of posturing that promote the proper alignment and structure of the body. Keeping your body weight balanced over a stable base allows you to fight more effectively. There are five basic stances that you will commonly employ: the ready or fighting stance, forward stance, lunge, back stance, and cat stance. Stances should never be static but rather flowing in response to your opponent and the ever-changing situation of fighting.

In order to move and strike powerfully, your upper and lower body must move in concert. Since your spine acts as the center axis for your body, strive to keep it straight but relaxed. This is the most economical way to move because there is a minimum amount of rebalancing to be done before you can effectively strike again.

"The basic fighting stance."

Fighting Stance

The basic fighting stance is a semicrouched position that prepares you for fighting. Also called the ready stance, it is a good neutral position because it allows for quick movements in all directions. Stand with your feet about shoulder width apart, one foot slightly ahead of the other, with your weight distributed evenly between both feet. Crouch slightly by bending your knees and hollowing out your body. Stay light on the balls of your feet. This loads both legs for quick, springy stepping. Keep both hands up and ready at all times.

Forward Stance and Lunge

The forward stance gives you more range and puts more power into your strike, so it is generally used to maximize your reach when attacking. To assume a forward stance, start from a ready stance and slide your front foot forward until your stance is about twice your shoulder width from front to back and most of your weight is on your front foot. In the final position, your back leg is straight (but not locked out) while your front knee is bent.

The forward stance is a good stance to use when you are on the offensive, but you must be ready to retreat or move to the side at a moment's notice. Therefore, keep the majority of your weight slightly forward, on the balls of the feet.

The forward stance.

A long forward stance is called a lunge. In using it, take care not to overextend yourself. Although your weight is mostly on the balls of your feet, keep your feet flat on the floor and do not let your lead knee extend past the toes of your front foot.

When you lunge, you need to be able to recover quickly to a more mobile, less exposed stance. Push off the ball of the front foot as you strongly contract your adductors (inner thigh muscles) to pull your feet back together quickly.

The lunge stance.

Back and Cat Stances

The back stance is predominantly used to evade your opponent's strikes. It is a good way to quickly move your body back and out of the range of an opponent's strike.

To assume a back stance, shift your weight backward so that most of it rests on your back leg and only a little rests on the front. Stay low in your back stance, coiled like a snake ready to strike. Always keep both knees flexed, because a straight front leg can easily be broken by a strong kick or strike to the knee.

You can pull your lead foot back into a very short back stance that is called a cat stance. With only about 10 percent of your body weight on the front foot, the cat stance lacks the stability of the longer stances, but your back leg is spring-loaded for quick movement in any direction.

Use the cat and back stances to hover just outside your opponent's effective striking range until you see an opportunity to spring forward and attack.

The back stance.

The cat stance.

Basic Striking

To be an effective stick fighter, you will need to learn how to become one with your weapon. Drilling these nine basic strikes will begin your study of proper body mechanics, specifically your body's relationship to the stick and the floor. You will learn about the space you occupy, the space in front of you, and the space around you. Drilling in the fundamental strikes teaches you distancing, range, striking surfaces, and tip control. You will also learn how to deliver power by moving from your core.

There are nine basic strikes. Practice each strike separately at first, checking to make sure you follow the same path each time you strike. Strive for precision as you swing the stick, slowly at first, gradually working up to hard, fast whipping motions. Use a mirror or video camera to check yourself.

Proper positioning of your body, weapon hand, and feet is vitally important for effective striking. Your body's mass and momentum, not just your arm and shoulder muscles, should power your strikes. Pivot on the balls of your feet to get the power of your hips and shoulders into your strikes. However, do not turn your body so much that you expose your flank and leave yourself open to a counterattack.

The nine basic strikes can be practiced using the following pattern. It begins with an open ready position (open because the attacking arm is chambered on the same side of the body) and starts with a downward diagonal strike from right to left because that is the most common angle of attack.

Begin each strike from a fully chambered ready position and fully commit to the delivery of each one, going through the full range of motion for each strike. Shorter strikes are faster and usually more practical for fighting, but you must first understand the mechanics of each swing on a large scale before you can begin to economize the overall motion, minimizing the preparatory and finished positions while still maximizing your speed and power.

The Nine Basic Strikes: Strikes 1 and 2: Start from an open ready position, with the stick held in a natural grip in your right hand and the tip of the stick over your right shoulder.

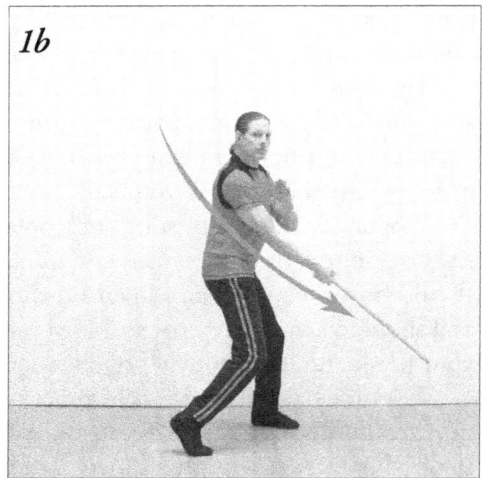

Make a diagonal downward forehand strike from right to left.

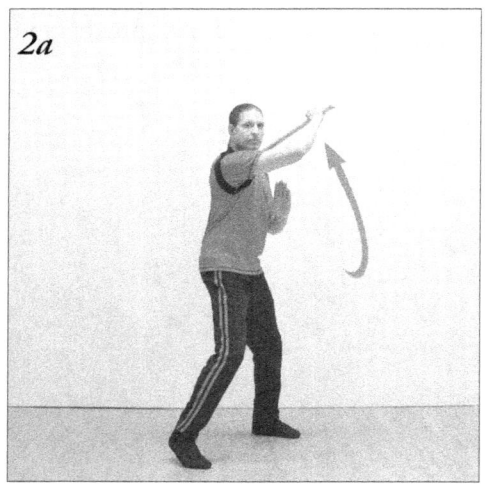

Continue strike 1, following through to a high closed ready position with the stick over your left shoulder.

Make a diagonal downward backhand strike from left to right.

LEVEL 1: THE FOUNDATION 31

Strikes 3 and 4: Continue your swing until you reach the middle-level open ready position.

Strike horizontally from right to left.

Continue through to the middle-level closed ready position.

Strike horizontally from left to right.

Strikes 5 and 6: End in the low open ready position.

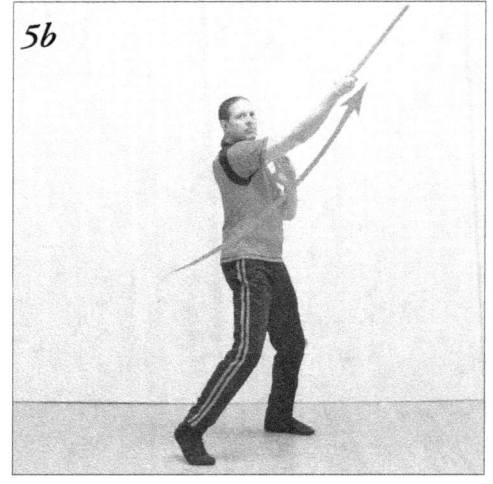

Strike diagonally upward from right to left.

Continue to a low closed ready position.

Strike diagonally upward from left to right.

LEVEL 1: THE FOUNDATION

Strikes 7 and 8: Continue your swing, bringing the stick around your head and into a high overhead ready position.

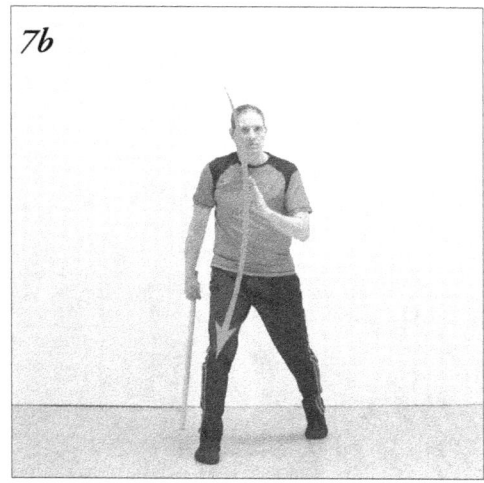

Strike vertically downward through the centerline.

Turn your hand over so your palm is facing up.

Strike vertically upward through the centerline.

Strike 9: Continue until you reach a middle-level open ready position with the tip of the stick aimed forward at your opponent.

Thrust to the center with the tip of the stick.

There are three levels: high, middle, and low. High strikes target the head and neck, while low strikes target the knees and legs. At middle level, all strikes should pass through a six-inch target at solar plexus level, and you should angle your diagonal strikes to cut through your opponent from shoulder to hip. Strive to make your horizontal strikes flat and your vertical strikes straight up and down. Forehand strikes originate from an open ready position, whereas strikes that start from a closed ready position are classified as backhand strikes.

There is a logical rationale behind this particular pattern of strikes. First, the strikes flow smoothly from one into the next, providing you with an example of how the strikes are used consecutively and in combinations. Strike 1 (diagonally downward from right to left) is the habitual method of attack that most people will revert to when fighting with the stick, therefore you will use and encounter it very often. The horizontal strikes are the next most common, followed by the less common diagonal upward and vertical strikes. The final pattern forms the shape of an asterisk and demonstrates how to smoothly flow between the nine different strikes.

This is only the pattern used for learning the nine basic strikes. After you have learned how to execute each strike individually and how to flow smoothly between them, it is time to start practicing the strikes in different orders as well. For example, you could practice reciprocal diagonal strikes (paired strikes that cut back along the same angle). After performing strike 1 (diagonally downward from right to left), you could immediately cut back with a number 6 strike (diagonally upward from left to right). This is an effective combination because it attacks both sides of the body in quick succession and is therefore difficult to block.

When you have mastered striking with the right side, or just become fatigued and need a break, switch to the left grip and repeat the pattern using the mirror-image strikes (e.g., a right-to-left diagonal strike in the right grip becomes a left-to-right strike when using a left grip). Although the strikes are demonstrated in the natural grip at middle level, each strike can also be performed in middle or reverse grip and to any level: high to the head and neck, middle to the torso, or low to the legs (when striking low, drop your body by bending at the knees, not by bending at the waist). Stand in one place when practicing until you gain

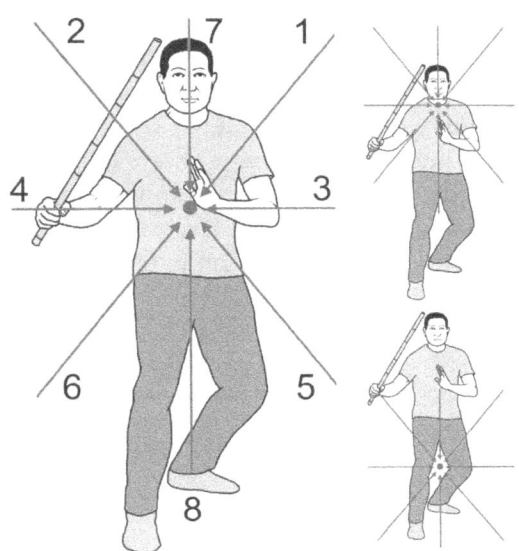

The different targets for each angle of the nine strikes applied to various levels.

a good understanding and execution of each strike. Then begin practicing the strikes while incorporating the different types of strikes and footwork described later in this level.

Ready Positions

Now that you know the nine basic strikes, work on increasing the speed at which you can execute powerful consecutive strikes. To accomplish this, it is important to understand how to efficiently reload after every strike. Each of your strikes should start from a chambered ready position (see positions 1a, 2a, 3a, etc.). A ready position lines up your body and weapon to deliver your strikes with the most effective mechanics possible. By initiating your strike from a position conducive to the angle at which you intend to strike, you can begin to maximize the amount of mass and momentum you put into the strike at the earliest opportunity.

To understand the importance of the ready positions, let's take a look at an analogy using guns. A double-action firearm requires you to first chamber a round and then pull the trigger to shoot, while a semiautomatic firearm not only fires a bullet each time the trigger is pulled but also performs all the steps necessary to prepare it to discharge again, making it much faster to shoot.

Like a semiautomatic firearm, you can maximize the speed at which you can deliver consecutive strikes by finishing each strike in a ready position so that you are immediately prepared to strike again. These ready positions facilitate smooth transitions between your strikes. None of the ready positions limits the choice of strikes that you can deliver.

If your stick is chambered across your centerline, you are in a closed ready position. If your weapon is held on the same side of your body, you are in an open ready position. Untrained fighters almost always initiate their attack from an open ready position. The closed and open positions can each be further subdivided into high, middle, and low guards depending on the level of your stick. In any ready position, your free hand should assume a guarding position in front of you.

Types of Strikes

There are three ways of striking with the stick. Each type of strike serves a different purpose. All of the nine basic strikes can be performed as a snap strike, full strike, or double strike.

Snap Strikes

Snap strikes are fast, but they typically lack the power of a full strike. Snap strikes hit their target, then return to a ready position without continuing through the target. Your finished position does not necessarily have to be the same ready position that the strike originated from, but it is usually on the same side of the body. The snap strike's weakness is that your stick has to come to a complete stop before it can change direction; starting the stick's movement and then stopping it each time takes time and energy, both to accelerate and to decelerate the stick.

Full Strikes

The full strike focuses all of your body's mass and momentum into a single, committed attack. Not only are full strikes very strong, they are also the instinctive way that most people attack with a short weapon. The basic strikes are usually performed as full strikes that follow completely through the target.

Double Strikes

Double strikes utilize a twirl to strike twice along the same angle with a single swing. Double strikes are deceptive, as the weapon passes the target twice in a single swing. Both passes could be used as strikes, or the first pass of the weapon could act as a feint or draw to create an opening to target with the second pass of the stick, which is usually the more powerful of the two since it follows completely through the target and thus can be fully committed to.

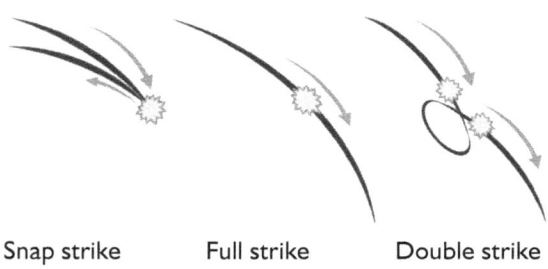

Snap strike   Full strike   Double strike

LEVEL I: THE FOUNDATION   37

Range and Distancing

Range is how far you can reach with your weapon. There are three general ranges: close range, middle range, and long range. Long range is the distance you can reach while lunging and reaching forward with the tip of the stick. Middle range is the distance you can comfortably reach with your stick held in natural grip. When you can touch your opponent's body with your hand, you are in close range. Each of these ranges has its own set of strategies and tactics and an arsenal of effective techniques that we will examine in more depth in later levels.

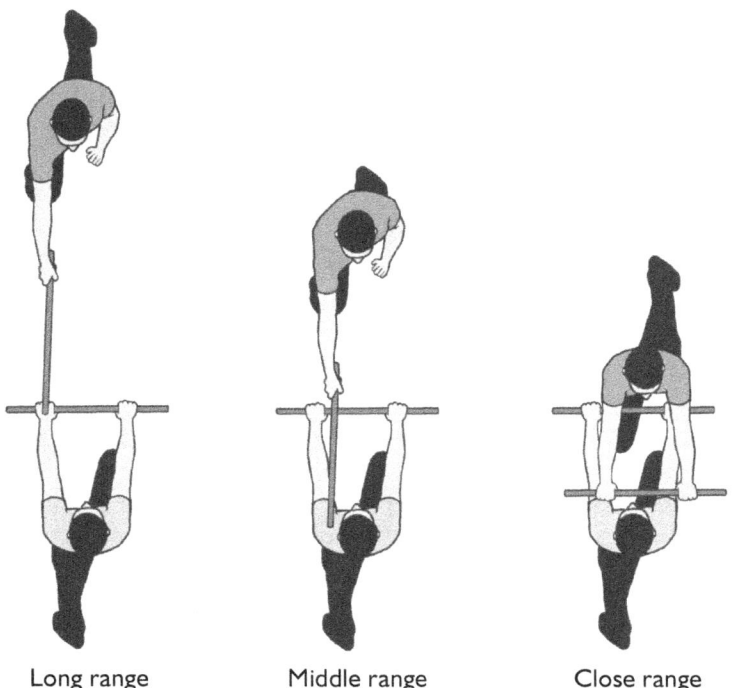

Long range   Middle range   Close range

Distancing is the space between you and your opponent. Range and distancing dictate what techniques you can apply effectively. You must develop a tacit understanding of the different ranges that includes the how, when, and why of moving from one range to the other. The goal is to unconsciously know how to properly distance yourself with (or without) a stick in your hand. Proper distancing usually means positioning yourself just outside your opponent's striking range. Strikes with the tip of the stick have the greatest range, and it is just outside this range that you will usually want to position yourself. This keeps you relatively safe while you look for the proper opportunity to close the gap and initiate your own attack.

The "circle of death" is the imaginary line around you that defines your effective range with your weapon—in this case, your stick. Defensively, you want to stay outside the opponent's longest range until you are ready to enter. Of course, you must stay at high alert, but since you can't effectively strike past your maximum range, minimal energy should be expended on any opponent who remains outside your circle; however, once an opponent enters your circle, he should be engaged at the earliest opportunity. Note that "engaging" the opponent also includes nonphysical techniques such as feints and evasive footwork, as well as immediate direct physical confrontation. After all, you want to fight smart, not hard.

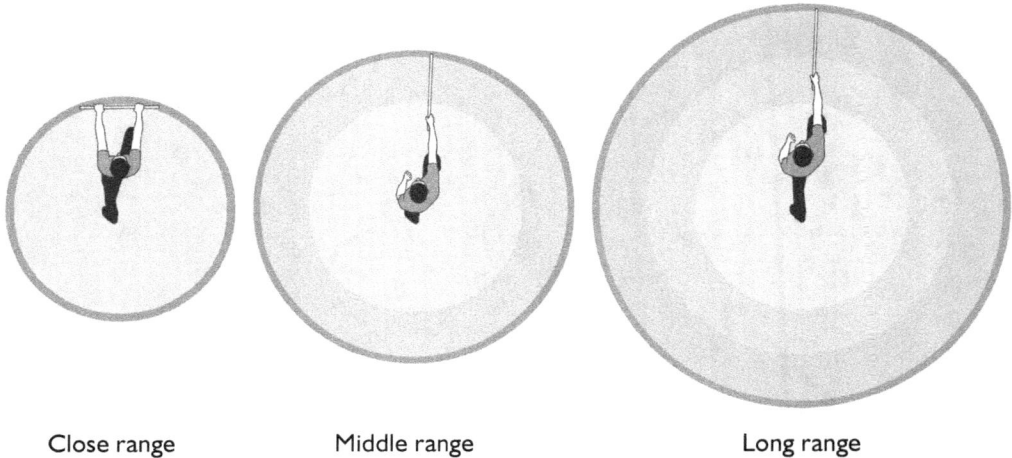

Close range   Middle range   Long range

To hit anything at a greater range than the lunge, the opponent will have to move his feet. By keeping your eyes on your opponent's body, you can learn to read his movements. This should give you ample opportunity to step back, maintaining the distance between you and the opponent and keeping you outside the effective striking range of his weapon. On the other hand, you might choose to angle forward, to pursue or close distance. The point is that footwork and distancing are interrelated skills that you must develop fully to fight effectively with any weapon. A skillful stick fighter controls the fight by controlling the distance, which is accomplished by reading the opponent's movements and then applying the appropriate footwork at just the right time.

Offensively, you don't have to wait for your opponent to enter your circle to attack him. Move your opponent into your circle by simply stepping toward him. If he tries to maneuver back outside your range, move so that he is back inside your circle, preferably directly in front of you.

Understanding range, distancing, and the circle of death goes a long way toward developing effective fighting strategies.

Footwork

Footwork is a term used to describe specific methods of moving your feet when fighting. Your fighting stance and footwork determine the effectiveness of your offense and defense. Good footwork is reactive to the opponent. For example, when the opponent moves toward you, you may choose to move backward the same amount, maintaining a safe distance between you and your opponent. More sophisticated footwork allows you to not only avoid your opponent's effective striking zone but also deliver your own attacks on his undefended flank.

As with stances, the general rule on footwork is to keep your body weight balanced over a stable but fluidly mobile base. This begins with a straight spine. A straight spine with stacked vertebrae requires minimal energy to maintain because it divides your body weight evenly and distributes it between your feet. This allows you to pivot your body quickly from side to side without having to rebalance yourself. A straight spine is also needed to make quick movements in any direction. If you tilt your spine, you not only unbalance yourself in the direction of the lean but also make it harder to move in the opposite direction.

By keeping "on your toes," you stay spring-loaded for quick movements and powerful striking. This does not mean your heels do not touch the ground, but the majority of your weight stays on the metatarsals, commonly called the balls of your feet. Smooth footwork is the result of not only pushing off with the ball of your supporting foot but also landing on the ball of the receiving foot. Heel stepping is slower because your heel lacks the musculature required to strike properly or even move again until the ball of your foot comes in contact with the ground. By landing directly on the ball of the foot, you are already loaded to move, or grounded to pivot and strike.

Take care not to make telegraphing movements that reveal your intentions before you step. Your natural inclination might be to shift your weight slightly onto your supporting foot to unweight your stepping foot, moving your body weight away from the direction in which you intend to step. This motion is counterproductive because you must then overcome this initial inertia and bring your body to a stop before you can begin shifting your weight back in the direction you originally intended to move. This makes you slow and telegraphs your movements to your opponent.

Use a mirror to watch yourself. Look for the small telltale signs you make before you move, then work to eliminate them. Don't just watch your feet; examine your head, shoulders, and arms for extraneous movements. Not only does this exercise allow you to do a good deal of self-correction, it will simultaneously teach you how to start reading your opponent's movements as well.

In order to better understand the fluid yet powerful footwork required for stick fighting, take a look at Western boxing. There are many great boxing videos on YouTube that focus exclusively on this very important aspect of fighting.

Shuffling

When fighting with a stick or other short weapon, it is customary to hold it in your lead hand. This gives you the best reach with your stick and makes it easier to keep your weapon between you and your opponent. Since you are strongest with your stick in your lead hand, shuffling is an effective footwork technique that allows you to maintain the same guard and stance while you move in, out, and around your opponent.

Shuffling is performed much like boxing footwork, with your lead foot taking a small step in the direction you want to go, quickly followed by the trailing foot. Begin by pushing off the ball of your rear foot as you reach forward with your front foot, landing on the ball. Immediately tighten your adductors, the inner thigh muscles that bring your legs together, to pull your rear foot back into a stable stance.

To move backward, take a small step back with your rear foot, followed by your front. Push off the ball of the front foot, not your heel. Reach with the ball of the rear foot, and as soon as it touches the ground, strongly contract your adductors to pull your front foot back into a stable, grounded stance.

Use this same method when stepping with your left foot to move left or your right foot to move to your right.

Always remember that powerful, controlled footwork is the result of pushing off with and landing on the balls of your feet, never your heels.

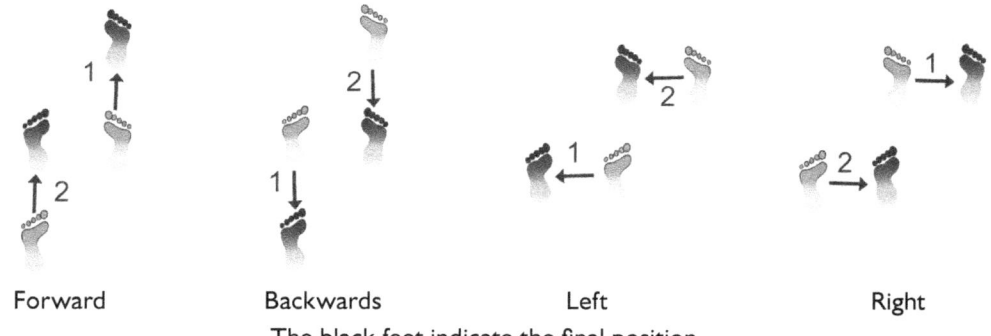

Forward　　　　Backwards　　　　Left　　　　Right

The black feet indicate the final position.

Circling In

Circling, also called angling, helps you avoid an opponent's strikes while still being able to deliver your own. When your opponent is maintaining distance in front of you, you can circle him as though he were on the inside of a circle that you were standing on, facing inwards. To circle, or angle inward, step forward on a diagonal to either your right or your left side. Which side you circle to depends mainly on your opponent. Immediately adjust your angle to keep your opponent on your centerline while moving off his centerline, making it harder for him to hit you effectively.

LEVEL 1: THE FOUNDATION   41

Circling In: You decide to circle in on your opponent.

Begin by moving your right foot forward to your right.

As soon as the ball of your front foot lands, your rear leg immediately follows and resets behind you.

In this example, I happen to deliver an overhead backhand strike, but you could do any of a number of defensive or offensive maneuvers.

   Your goal should be to remove your body from your opponent's effective striking zone. To do this, you will need to get off his centerline. Put simply, you do this by circling in such a way that you can no longer see through your opponent's legs. If your opponent is right-handed and wielding his stick in his right hand, this will entail moving forward to your left, into the opponent's acceleration zone. Your other option, circling to your right, is much more dangerous, as you would have to circle much farther, far enough to ensure you were well past the opponent's effective striking zone and into his deceleration zone.

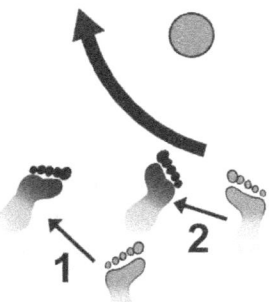
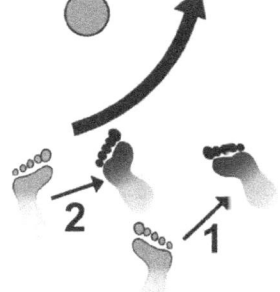

Circling in to the leftCircling in to the right

The black feet indicate the final position.

Circling Out

Occasionally an opponent will charge in, usually in an effort to close the gap quickly from long range to middle or even close range. When the opponent charges, avoid moving straight backward in an effort to maintain your distance. Your body is moved by pressing off the ball of the foot, so you move faster moving forward and pushing off the toes than you do moving backward, especially if you push back off your heel. This gives a charging opponent the advantage, as he can move forward faster than you can retreat, so it is often best to move off the line of attack. Circling out is an effective method of giving ground to an advancing opponent that allows you to avoid his strikes while still being able to deliver your own.

Visualize yourself retreating from an aggressive opponent. Instead of running straight backward, turn your body sideways as you retreat in a direction perpendicular to his incoming motion. Begin by sliding your rear foot backward on a diagonal to either your right or left side. Immediately adjust your angle to keep your opponent on your centerline while moving off his centerline, making it harder for him to hit you effectively. This motion of "opening the door" is analogous to the actions of a matador in a Spanish bullfight.

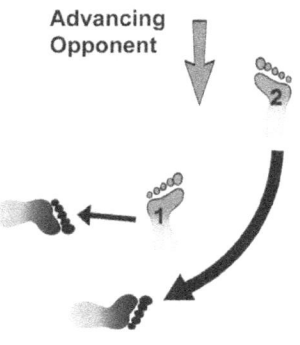
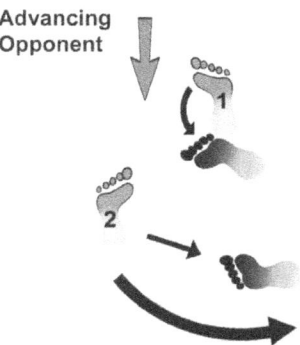

Circling out to the leftCircling out to the right

The black feet indicate the final position.

LEVEL I: THE FOUNDATION   43

Circling Out: Hold a guarded position as the opponent charges.

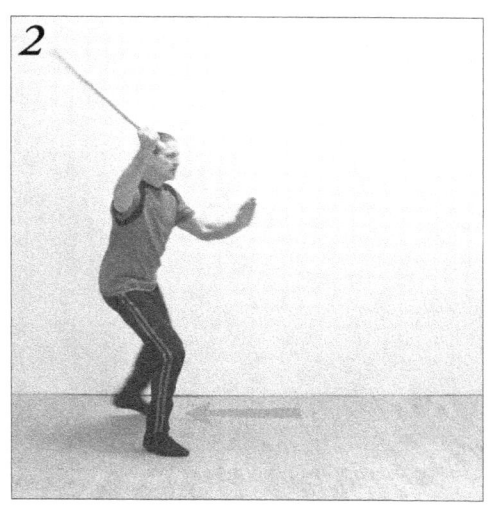

Give ground by stepping to the right and back.

Circling out as viewed from above.

Stepping

You can also do a full step, sometimes called a passing step, when one foot passes by the other, forward or backward. This not only covers more ground than shuffling but also allows you to switch your stance. In his classic treatise *A Book of Five Rings*, Miyamoto Musashi says that the most devastating strikes are performed with this type of footwork, and world heavyweight champion boxers Jack Dempsey and Mike Tyson proved it many times in the ring.

Stepping forward   Stepping backwards

The black feet indicate the final position.

Whether your weapon is a sword, a stick, or just a fist, the same concept applies because the stepping motion allows you to put more mass and momentum into your strike. Although there are footwork patterns that cross the feet when stepping to the left and right, I do not recommended them because they put you in a vulnerable position, albeit momentarily.

If you start the fight using a typical shuffling step, a well-timed full passing step is a good way to quickly advance on an unsuspecting opponent. Stepping is a key part of certain strategies, such as the rearguard defense taught in Level 2.

A Final Note on Footwork

How important is good footwork? Sit back and let me tell you a tale. It was the summer of 2014 and I was fighting full-contact double stick, representing Team USA. My opponent was the Australian champion Neil McLeish. Before the match even started, Neil's team had already looked me over and noticed a weakness: my left thigh was exposed through the slit in the skirt of my vest. As soon as the fight started, Neil began targeting my left thigh with big, full-power strikes. Between rounds, my corner man, Chris Snarr, told me to jam his strike by circling to my left. Much to my relief, Neil had a harder time getting my leg after that and finally gave up on it to beat me up in other ways. It was a great fight. After three rounds, it was a tie, so we had to go a fourth, but I ultimately lost the match in a split decision.

There are two important points to take away from this story. First, your footwork can make a huge difference in the outcome of a fight. It is possible that, if I had thought to simply circle to my left earlier, it might have made the difference in how the judges scored that first round and I might have won that fight. Therefore, you would do well to study and practice your footwork. The footwork patterns I've just discussed work well in certain situations. However, the dynamics of the fight are always changing. Therefore, when fighting, you must learn to read the situation and then apply the proper footwork to attain your immediate, short-term goal.

The second lesson doesn't have to do with footwork, but it is important, so I will include it here. While the force generated with the stick is considerable, definitely in the bone-breaking category, you cannot depend on any strike, or even combination of strikes, to stop a determined opponent. I had a super heavyweight champ beat on my leg for a full minute with an unpadded rattan stick and, although it hurt like hell, not only did I not go down, it barely slowed me down. You need to keep in mind that blows that you think would theoretically end a fight often prove to merely hurt and leave a nasty welt. When the adrenaline is flowing, it takes an exceptional blow with superb placement to stop a determined aggressor. You would do well to keep this in mind when you train.

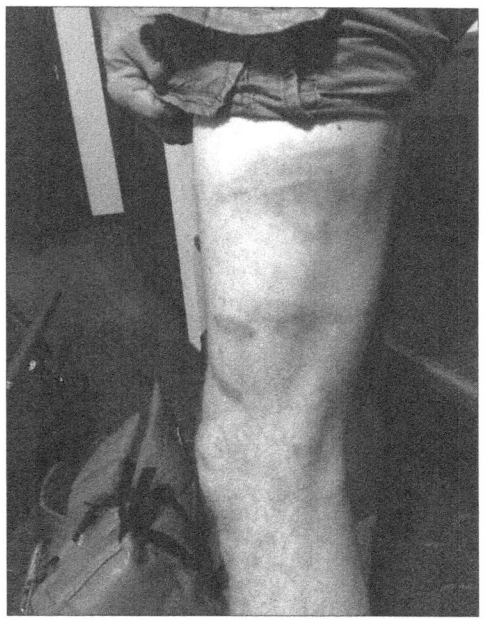

Some of the welts Neil left on my leg.

Training Equipment: The Floor Pattern

There is a classic saying, "Footwork wins fights," so it should be no surprise that a wide variety of methods have been developed for training effective footwork. Of these, the floor pattern is one of the simplest yet most effective.

Floor patterns give you a framework on which to practice your footwork. This will help develop quick, sure movement. Understanding the different lines and angles allows you to respond quickly and appropriately to your opponent's movements.

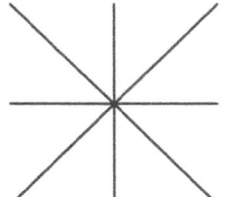 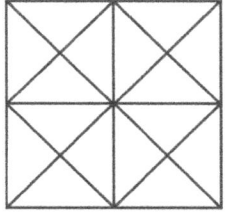  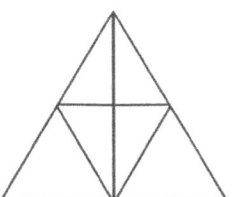

Some common floor patterns used for developing footwork.

The most basic floor pattern is the asterisk. Step forward, backward, and side to side, moving along the lines. Understanding the movements on this elementary pattern will help you unlock the combinations contained within the other, more complex patterns.

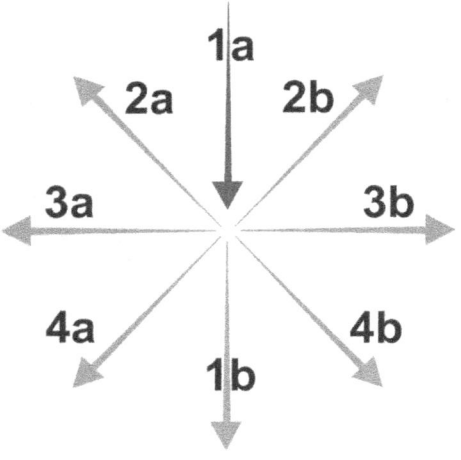

The Asterisk: Begin by imagining that an opponent is swinging or thrusting at you, with the vertical line representing his incoming movement (*1a*). You could move straight backward (*1b*), but since this keeps you on the opponent's line of attack and he can move faster forward than you can backward, this may not be the best option (not to mention that your opponent probably has initiative and momentum on his side). You can angle forward to the left or right (*2a and 2b*), move laterally to the left or right along the horizontal lines (*3a and 3b*), or angle backward to the left or right (*4a and 4b*). These movements make up your basic responses to an incoming attack.

Drilling on a floor pattern becomes a game of physical chess as you explore how to move in relation to an opponent. As you get the idea of angling in and angling out of an opponent's striking zone, you will realize that there is a forehand (palm up) and backhand (palm down) relationship to the patterns. Moving forward and left lends itself to a forehand strike, while moving forward and right lends itself to a backhand.

A well-worn floor pattern marked out with tape.

Don't forget charging right up the centerline (which you might forget if there is no tape line there). An overwhelming centerline blast with your momentum behind it can crash through your opponent's defenses and open up opportunities to insert your own rhythms into the aftermath.

Twirling: Figure Eights

Twirling is the act of putting together a stream of continuous, flowing strikes based on various natural, circular orbits. However, remember that you are still striking as you twirl. Chamber each strike by moving through the ready positions and visualize a particular striking point to help you maintain focus and power in your strikes.

Twirling can be used to deliver a quick flurry of strikes. It is easier to detect an incoming strike when it is initiated from a static position than to detect an incoming strike that has been hidden in a flurry of movement, so offensively, the motion can be used to hide your actual intentions. Defensively, the strikes can create a shield of sorts that may discourage an aggressive opponent from entering.

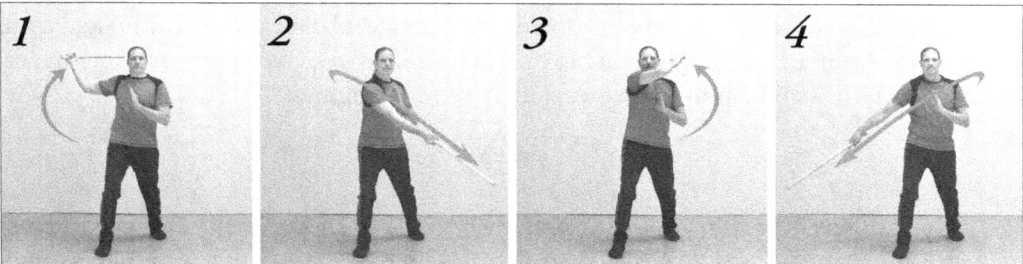

The Basic Figure Eight: The figure eight is a simple twirl that consists of two strikes, a downward diagonal strike from right to left (*1 and 2*), followed by another from left to right (*3 and 4*), forming an X in front of you. The shape could also be seen as a figure eight on its side, like an infinity symbol: ∞.

Advanced Figure-Eight Patterns

Once you are comfortable with the basic figure eight, try switching the direction of the flow by striking with upward diagonal strikes, a twirl commonly referred to as an upward figure eight. These patterns are horizontal figure eights. Vertical figure eights link upward and downward diagonal strikes, looping back at the top and bottom instead of on the sides. Finally, create diagonal figure-eight patterns by linking vertical and horizontal strikes together.

The figure eight covers a wide area in front of your body and can be used to hide your strikes or create a defensive shield that can momentarily ward off an attack.

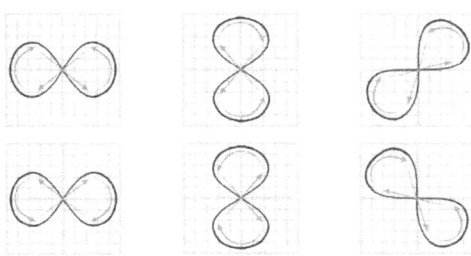

There are many different ways to perform a figure eight.

Normally, figure eights are performed with full strikes that continue through the target, but try performing the pattern with snap strikes and double strikes. Next, change up the levels, practicing targeting high, middle, and low. Finally, add the different types of footwork into your figure-eight practice. Your goal should be to combine all these movements into a single, free-flowing drill. Oh yeah, and don't forget that you have two hands!

Every drill you practice will add to your versatility and overall skill with the stick. Strive to acquire the ability to smoothly transition between all of your accumulated drills in a fast, free-form manner. The ability to link many different strikes seamlessly into unpredictable patterns will help to make you a more effective fighter.

Power

There are several reasons to learn how to hit hard with the stick. The first is pragmatic. Just a few powerful strikes in your arsenal can make you into a formidable opponent. Never forget that stick fighting is a violent activity where the goal is to neutralize your enemy. The shorter the fight, the less chance you have of being hurt, and a powerful strike has the potential to end a fight with a single blow. Since the stick is an impact weapon that creates blunt force trauma, striking with power is very important, much more than it is with a bladed weapon, such as a knife or sword, which requires very little force to cut or stab.

The second reason to learn power is mechanical. In order to strike with focused force, your entire body needs to move in concert. Striking hard with the stick requires muscular, skeletal, and respiratory coordination. Practicing for power gives you the opportunity to work out any weak spots in your kinetic chain. At first you will make large swings when trying to generate power. However, contrary to what you may think, it does not require a big swing to produce a powerful strike. Big swings are counterproductive to quick combinations and, since they are more easily blocked or avoided, are usually the trademark of the untrained fighter. Strive to strike along a shallow arc to the target.

The third reason to strike hard is that it is enjoyable and can be an effective means of reducing stress. It is also fun to experiment and see just how hard you can strike. These training experiences add to your overall skill level and technical knowledge of the capabilities of the stick. This, in turn, builds confidence both in your personal skills and in the practicality of the technique.

The Science of Striking

Calculating the power of a strike is tricky business, even for science-minded folk. There are many variables involved, including the type, size, and mass of the weapon, as well as the size, strength, and speed of the stick fighter. While the exact science is outside the scope of this book, I believe that even a brief, simplified overview can help us in understanding and personally mastering the mechanics of striking with a stick.

Since sticks are blunt trauma weapons, they are usually swung in an arc, a curved segment of a circle. However, it would be more accurate to say that a stick swing is composed of several circles of motion centered at different pivot points: one at the shoulder, another at the elbow, and one at the wrist. Biomechanics researchers have determined that, together, the three circles act as if they were one circle with the center located at about the middle of the forearm, so imagine a stick sweeping a circle with a center at that location.

Picture a vinyl record spinning on a turntable. As it rotates, a location on the edge of the record travels a distance equal to the circumference of the record while a point on the label traces a much smaller circle and travels a shorter distance in the same amount of time. Since both points are making the same number of revolutions per minute, the point on the outer edge must move faster than the point on the label in order to travel the longer distance in the same amount of time.

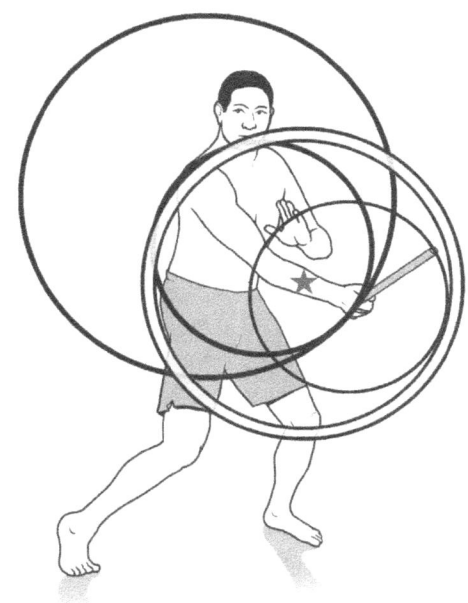

The different pivot points at the shoulder, elbow, and wrist equate to one circle with the center located at about the middle of the forearm.

The points are traveling (rotating) at the same angular rate (revolutions per minute) even though they are traveling at different linear speeds.

The same relationship occurs when striking with a stick. Locations toward the tip of the stick travel faster than those near the middle. Since power is the result of mass times velocity (speed) squared, speed is actually the deciding factor in the power of any strike. You want to strike as fast as you can, because that maximizes the kinetic energy of your strike. So how fast can someone swing a stick?

A 1998 article in *Christian Science Monitor* called "The Science of Slugging" showed that professional baseball players could swing a bat at about eighty miles per hour. Studies show that professional tennis players also top off at about eighty miles per hour. PGA golfers generate a higher head velocity, around ninety miles per hour, because of the weight of the head and the increased length of the club. Pro baseball pitchers throw one-hundred-mile-per-hour fastballs, but this type of all-out effort takes such a toll on their tendons and ligaments that sports trainers believe this may be the human body's upper limit for generating velocity.

Not everyone can swing a stick at eighty miles per hour, and those who can aren't able to do it consistently every time. Most strikes are probably half that speed. Although exercises such as weight training can help improve swing speed, research shows that everyone has their own top striking speed, dependent on body type, musculature, and so on, that is going to be difficult to exceed (fifty to sixty miles per hour, for example). The best you can do is train in proper body mechanics to maximize your natural potential. Just for fun, let's play with some numbers. I am going to simplify things as much as possible to make it easier to follow along. Since I don't want to get too tangled up in the details, these are only approximations, but they will give us a frame of reference for understanding the science of striking with a stick.

Let's start with the weapon. Stick lengths and weights vary, but let's say that you have the stick in a natural grip with twenty-five inches of stick extending out of your hand. You are so awesome that your swing has a speed of eighty miles per hour and hits with one hundred pounds of force (technically this should be measured in newtons, the unit of force in the International System of Units, but like I said, I'm simplifying here, so science guys, please bear with me).

For the sake of easy calculations, let's say that you make an inelastic collision with your target so that all of the energy of your strike is concentrated into one square inch at the tip of your stick. By dividing the power of your swing by the surface area of the impact (100 / 1), we can calculate the pounds of pressure per square inch that was delivered into your target. In this case, your stick would deliver a force of one hundred pounds per square inch.

As I showed earlier with the record player analogy, there can be huge differences in stick speed between the tip and the center of the weapon. Every two inches you move down the shaft, the stick is moving about five miles per hour slower, so it will not hit as hard. More importantly, by hitting with the shaft of the stick, you have distributed the force of the impact over a greater surface area, dispersing the energy of your strike, which results in a lower number of pounds per square inch.

If your strike hits just below the tip, let's say between the twenty- and twenty-three-inch marks on the stick, it will hit at about seventy miles per hour and ninety pounds of force. Furthermore, the energy will be spread out over about three square inches on the side of the stick, resulting in only thirty pounds of pressure per square inch, dramatically less than the one hundred pounds per square inch delivered with the tip of the stick. You can see this demonstrated by striking a large cardboard box. Strikes delivered with the tip of the stick will often punch a hole in the cardboard, while strikes that hit flat may leave a mark but usually cannot tear the material.

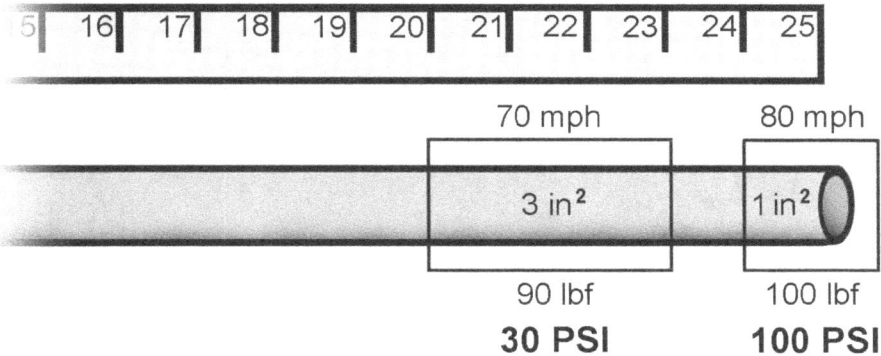

The physics of the impact based on what part of the stick you are striking with. *PSI* = pounds per square inch; *lbf* = pounds of force.

Although I used one hundred pounds of force in the foregoing example, the fact is that you can strike a lot harder than that. On an episode of National Geographic Channel's *Fight Science*, a television show dedicated to applying laboratory techniques to the study of the martial arts, they demonstrated that the short stick can strike with over one thousand pounds of force! That kind of force will easily crack a bone or crush a skull. Or could it?

A lot depends on the bone itself, its position in the body, and the angle of attack. The age, diet, and lifestyle of the bone owner also play a role. It is very easy to fracture a small bone, especially if the pressure is applied across the weakest point. As little as twenty-five pounds of pressure applied to one of your small bones, such as in a finger, can result in a fracture. Long bones, such as the femur, are much stronger and can withstand nearly nine hundred pounds of force before breaking. So the answer is yes, provided that your stick is heavy enough and hits correctly, your strike can break bones.

If you have played baseball or tennis, you are probably familiar with the concept of the "sweet spot." The sweet spot is more accurately called the center of percussion, or CoP. This is the spot on the bat, racquet, or stick that will transmit the greatest impulse into the target. Any impact causes a linear recoil (conservation of momentum) that results in the implement rotating about its center of mass (conservation of angular momentum). If you played baseball, you may have experienced how a hard hit creates a strong vibration that travels down the bat and actually stings your hands (illustration 1 in the accompanying figure). However, when the impact is directly on the CoP, these two motions cancel each other out and no reaction force is felt at the handle, thus its reputation as the "sweet spot" (illustration 2).

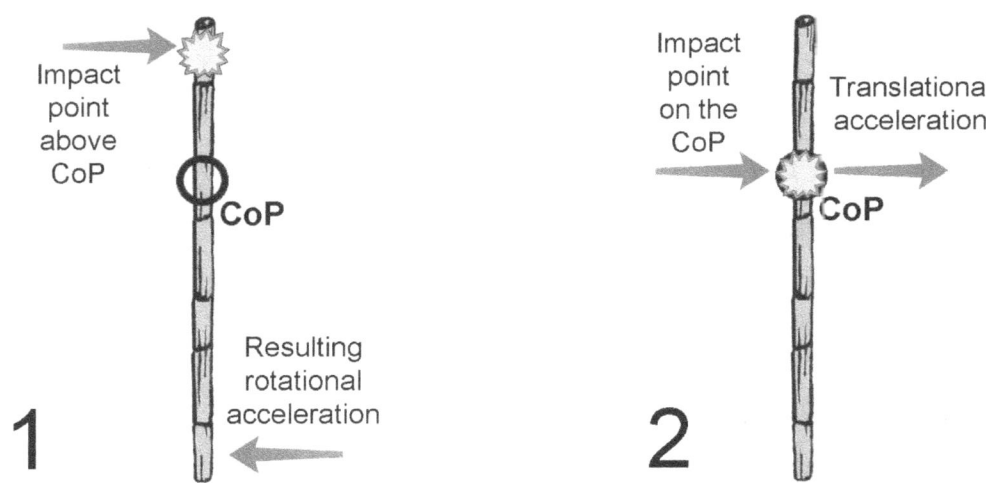

The results of impact on different parts of the stick.

The CoP is not actually a fixed point on the stick; rather, its location depends on exactly where you are gripping the stick, what kind of arc you swing through, how tight your grip is, and so on. You can get an idea of where it is by gripping the stick in your normal grip position, then hanging it with the tip down. Using a loose hold, so the stick swings freely in the hand, rapidly move your hand left and right a few inches, back and forth as quickly and smoothly as you can. Try not to let your hand move up and down, only side to side. Look down near the tip of the stick as you do this, and you will see one area that is barely moving as the rest of the stick rotates around it. That is the CoP and is the spot capable of delivering maximum power into your strike.

So where should you hit, with the tip or the middle of the stick? Barring that perfect tip shot that concentrates all your force into a very small area, the best result rests on a combination of power and speed; however, stick speed does play a greater role than power potential. As you move toward the middle of the stick, you have more power but less speed, and as you hit toward the tip, you have more speed but less power. Somewhere along that continuum, power and speed will be at a maximum combination. Although adrenaline and the quickly changing circumstances of a fight will make precision hard to achieve, training with it in mind will make it more instinctive to your body.

Can I Hit Something Now?

If you are anything like me, just reading that last section made you want to hit something. I have always been a fan of the maxim "It is more rewarding practicing the martial arts than reading about practicing the martial arts."

Powerful striking can only be accomplished by employing proper striking mechanics. By contracting only those muscles that add power to your swing, you stay relaxed, both physically and mentally. If you put too much emphasis on striking hard, you are likely to tighten up antagonistic muscle groups. Rather than add speed and power to your strike, these muscles actually oppose your desired motion and therefore slow you down. You will also likely shift more weight to the weapon side of your body in an attempt to get more mass into your strike, but this will only throw you off balance, further detracting from your strike.

To maximize your striking force, keep your spine straight, uniting your upper and lower body to activate the core. Your arms and legs can then act as extensions of your core. Moving from your central core does not mean simply moving around a single point. Rather, it implies moving your body as a single, coordinated unit. Staying relaxed and using your spine as the axis of rotation allows you to get the full mass and momentum of your body into every strike.

Watch a baseball batter hit a home run. He steps into the swing, then his hips twist to move his torso, and, finally, his arms swing the bat. A heavyweight boxer known for his punching power throws a cross by stepping his lead foot in, then turning his hips, which moves his upper body, then adding the final power to the punch with his pecs, deltoids, and triceps. If you look at old-school Okinawan karate masters and most kung fu styles, you will see this same sequential power build up: legs, then torso, then finally arms.

That being said, the secret to hard hitting is proper use of the hips. If your hip is three inches from your body's center, and the tip of your stick is forty-eight inches from your center, then any increase in hip speed will be magnified sixteen times (48 / 3) by the time it reaches the end of your stick! Therefore, increasing your hip speed is by far the most effective way to hit harder, and the key to maximizing hip speed lies in a subtle but very important hip lag. It is important to note that moving from your core does not mean you are limited to a single-unit energy transfer. To maximize speed, you need to lead your strike with your hip first, then have the strike follow an instant later. This one-two movement leads to greater acceleration and gives your strike a sharp whipping effect evident by the audible "whoosh" you will hear as your stick cuts through the air. You can generate even more speed on your strike by flexing your wrist just before impact.

54 THE ART AND SCIENCE OF STICK FIGHTING

Hip Power: This series of photos shows the important role that the hips play in generating power in the first two strikes. Begin in a high, open ready position with the stick chambered over your right shoulder.

Press off the ball of your front foot, driving your hips sharply from right to left and pulling your arm and weapon through the target.

As you complete the strike, turn your hand over.

Use the residual energy to carry the stick through to the next ready position.

LEVEL I: THE FOUNDATION 55

Strike 2 starts from a high, closed ready position with the stick chambered over your left shoulder.

Again, initiate the strike with a sharp rotation of your hips, this time from left to right.

The hip twist is powered by driving forcefully off the ball of your rear foot, turning your body from left to right as you swing the stick down and across your body.

Let your hand turn over naturally at the end of the swing to chamber for another strike.

Keep in mind that pivoting can be a double-edged sword. On the one hand, it allows you to generate a great deal of force by maximizing the amount of mass and momentum you are able to get into the strike. On the other hand, you must always be careful not to overrotate. Striking too far through your target will not only slow your ability to deliver a second strike but also expose your flank to your opponent's attacks. To avoid this, try to keep your front foot pointing at your opponent. Note how, in illustration 1c, the force of my strike has momentarily turned my front foot away. I am already recovering my alignment by illustration 1d, but any time you turn your center, you not only are turning your weapon away from your opponent but also putting yourself in danger of being flanked.

Be aware that power striking can also be hard on your body, specifically the muscles, tendons, and ligaments of your arm and shoulder. As is the case for the professional baseball pitchers who throw tons of fastballs, your body just can't be pushed that hard that often. While doing a high number of full-power repetitions when training is usually a good thing, progress cautiously to avoid unnecessary wear and tear on your body.

To develop striking power, you need to hit something, preferably very hard. As opposed to practicing against the air, striking a target that offers resistance enables you to practice combinations of moves in a more realistic manner. A striking dummy offers the same advantage to a stick fighter that a punching bag offers a boxer; it provides a target for developing focus, aim, power, and distance.

Training Equipment: The Tire Dummy

I went into a lot of detail on the pell in my last book, *The Art and Science of Staff Fighting*. Basically, a pell is a training device roughly in the shape of a person that is used for practicing hard strikes. The first pells were wooden stakes driven into the ground. However, repeatedly hitting any solid wooden post not only would be hard on your sticks but is also sure to take a toll on your body. Therefore, you should consider padding your pell. Not only will your sticks last longer, but it will also reduce the impact on your joints, and your neighbors won't complain about that loud "Clack! Clack! Clack!" noise.

While you could use a commercial heavy bag, they do not typically hold up well when left outside, and they sometimes rip when hit with weapons. I recommend making your own custom striking dummies. Rubber tires offer a very good choice of construction materials since they are durable and weather resistant and offer some give. Old tires are also easily obtainable in a variety of sizes; simply inquire at your local garage or tire service station and you can usually acquire as many as you need at little or no cost.

Constructing a Tire Dummy

Keep in mind that you may not need to construct anything. Your training equipment does not have to be fancy or complex. In fact, sometimes the most efficient solutions are the simplest. Simply loop a piece of heavy rope through the tire and look for a suitable hanging place, such as a tree limb or garage rafter (illustration 1 in the accompanying figure). If you want to get fancy, hang another tire below the first one for practicing low-line attacks (illustration 2). This type of tire dummy requires no cutting, drilling, or special tools, which means you can spend more time training, not building. Just hang it up and start thumping!

To make a more traditional heavy bag of tires, stack several tires. Drill holes in the sidewalls of each tire with a one-inch paddle bit, then thread them together with sturdy rope. Tie the rope off at the top and hang your tire bag from a sturdy support (illustration 3).

A stationary tire dummy can be made from an eight-foot log or similar long wooden post. For stability, your post should be at least four by four inches (you can screw two two-by-fours together). Dig a hole about two feet deep and toss a few inches of gravel in the bottom for drainage. Stand the post upright and secure it in place with quick-drying concrete. Drill some narrow guide holes in the tires and then screw them onto the post using sturdy lag bolts that penetrate deep into the wood.

A freestanding tire dummy may be more desirable since it can be moved. An outdoor version can be made cheaply using a concrete-filled tire to secure the post (illustration 4). To fill the tire base, duct-tape a plastic bag onto the inside of the bottom to keep the concrete from leaking out when you pour it. Set your wooden post in the concrete and support it temporarily so it won't move. The post will stay upright by itself within fifteen minutes and should be cured enough to move after an hour. Then you can screw your tires to the post using lag bolts.

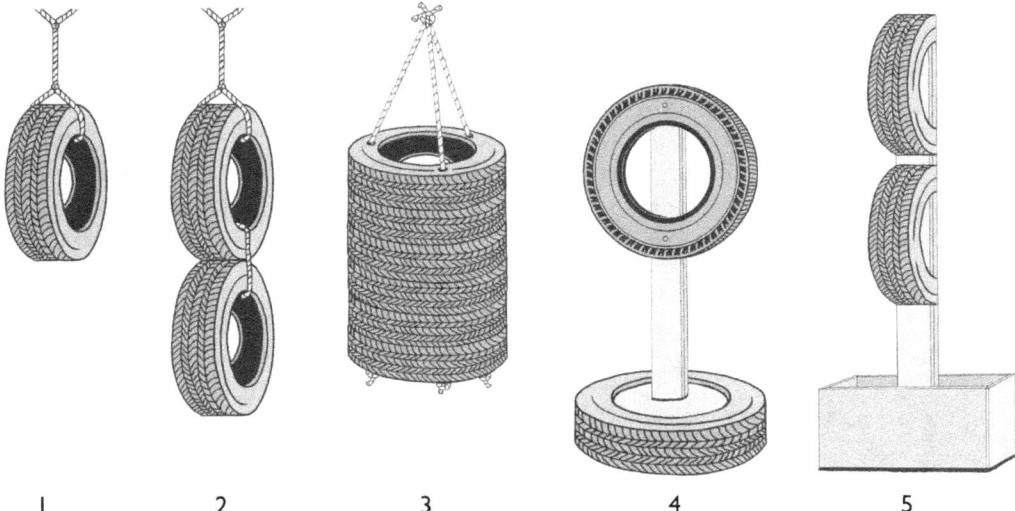

1   2   3   4   5

If you want to make a nicer-looking base, use a wooden box, but this will generally not weather well if kept outside (illustration 5). If you want to get really fancy, you can mount your tire dummy on a wheeled base. Cut a two-by-two-foot base out of three-quarter-inch plywood and screw heavy-duty swivel wheels in the corners. Mount your support post from below using lag bolts, then reinforce from above with shorter supports on each side. Attach your tires and you are ready to rock . . . and roll (get it?).

I've even seen a tire dummy with a spring-loaded arm that held a stick. While certainly not necessary, this type of addition could help in practicing checking an opponent's weapon while you strike. However, I suggest starting simple and working your way up. You want to spend your time practicing, not making the equipment (although that can be fun too). The good news is that tire dummies are relatively cheap and easy to make, so feel free to try new designs. It will keep your workouts fresh and exciting.

See the appendix at the end of this book for blueprints and more precise instructions on creating your own tire dummy.

Training with the Tire Dummy

Although your first reaction to having a target may be to see how hard and fast you can strike, remember that you are training your muscles to naturally execute each technique. Take time to evaluate your structure and alignment. Begin striking the dummy slowly with each technique until you know you are doing it correctly. Slow down whenever you feel clumsy or inaccurate in your strikes until you can resolve the issue.

Although you should eventually focus on power, not striking hard allows you to work on accuracy, proper body mechanics, and footwork. This can actually lead to faster progress and, ultimately, a deeper understanding of the alignment and structure behind your techniques.

When training for power, it is very important that you accelerate the stick through your target and not simply strike at the target's surface. Strike precisely with the tip of the stick to concentrate the power of your strike into the smallest area possible in order to maximize the pounds of pressure per square inch delivered by your strike. Consider the angle of impact on the target. In order to impart the most kinetic energy to a target, you have to hit it at a right angle. Anything else and the energy will be dissipated in directions other than the one you want.

For maximum power transfer, hit your target at a right angle (1).
Otherwise your strike will glance off the target (2).

Vary your attacks, practicing all techniques from all angles and to all levels. Strive to strike deceptively without telegraphing your intent.

A hanging bag has an advantage over a standing dummy because it moves dynamically and reacts to your strikes. A hanging tire can be made to move and will give more realistically when struck than a stationary tire dummy. To get more swing, hang your bag from a longer rope or chain. You can start the bag swinging at first, or simply let it swing in reaction to your strikes. The bag will "run away" at times, forcing you to give chase before it reaches the apex of its swing and charges back at you! Having a moving target is the best way to train for a moving opponent when you have no partner with whom to train.

Even if your tire dummy is stationary, you can still improve your footwork and movement by changing your angle of attack, moving in and out of range, and cutting and thrusting from opening to opening (high, low, left, right). In fact, strive to practice every technique you know on the dummy. Practice the accuracy of your strikes intermingled with thrusts and feints. Develop combinations, building from a simple, direct strike into a logical sequence of techniques. Take the time to properly develop each combination of techniques until they become reflexive actions, the result of muscle memory gained through countless repetitions.

Practice regularly. The tire dummy should be used daily to help improve your physical conditioning and stick technique. Spend time training while wearing all of the equipment you have to wear while fighting. If you wear a helmet and gloves when fighting, spend some time wearing them as you work the dummy.

You can also attach a weapon to your tire dummy by tying a long stick or staff to it. Or you could drill a hole in the wall of the tire using a paddle bit and then drive a stick or staff through the hole (for a tight fit, make the hole a quarter of an inch smaller than the diameter of the stick you want to use). A weapon attached to your tire dummy allows you to practice techniques that involve blocking or otherwise manipulating the weapon.

Continually modifying your training and equipment will help avoid the monotony and plateaus that can test the resolve of even the most dedicated athletes.

Level 1 Workout

Objective: This sixty-to-ninety-minute workout is designed to help you develop the strength, proper body mechanics, accurate targeting, distancing, footwork, and power needed to wield the stick effectively.

1. Warm-Up: 15–20 Minutes. Start with some light stretching. See the guide at the beginning of this book for a sample stretching routine. Follow this with five to ten minutes of jumping rope. You should be tired when you are done, but don't stop! Do some more light stretching until your heart rate returns to normal, then grab your stick and work through some basic footwork (advancing, retreating, side to side, and circling). Use a footwork pattern while you practice your figure eights (horizontal, vertical, and diagonal), first slowly and gradually speeding up. Intersperse different strikes into your twirls. Twirl, twirl, STRIKE! Twirl, twirl, STRIKE!

2. Targeting, Distancing, and Control: 15–20 Minutes. Perform the nine basic strikes on a target (heavy bag or tire dummy). Strike strongly and quickly, but do not actually hit the target. Instead, stop just short of contact, preferably one to three inches away. Practice each strike alone at first, then in combinations of two, building up to combinations of three to five techniques. Vary the levels and targets of your strikes. Once you have good control of your weapon, practice this drill with a partner, taking care to stop your strike before making contact! Target the lead hand, lead ankle, neck pocket (shoulder to top of ear), elbows, and knees. Thrusting targets include the face, throat, solar plexus, groin, thigh, and foot.

3. Power: 10–20 Minutes. Practice the nine basic strikes on a heavy bag or tire dummy. Use a sturdy stick and take care not to break it! Perform the strikes alone at first, then in combinations of two, building up to combinations of three to five techniques. Include footwork by starting at a distance, closing the gap, entering with feints and combinations, then exiting on a new angle.

4. Variety: 15–20 Minutes. Keep your workout fresh by switching things up. The nine basic strikes can be performed in many different combinations. Each strike can be performed in 3 different ways (snap, full, and double), making 27 different strikes. Each could also be aimed high, middle, or low, bringing the total to 81 strikes. Adding in the eleven types of footwork expands the list to 891 strikes. Of course you have two hands, so if you practiced every strike with your right and then your left, you would perform 1,782 different strikes. Whew, that's a lot . . . You'd better get practicing!

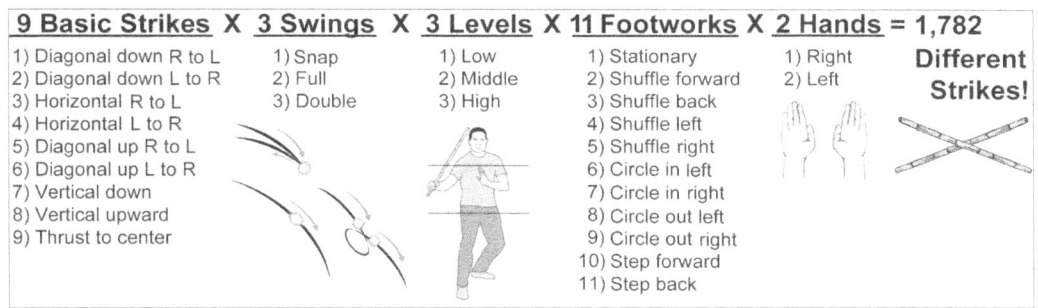

Be Creative: A regular training routine is important, but you also need to challenge yourself. As you get more comfortable with the basic strikes, try practicing in different conditions: in close quarters, in the rain, on uneven surfaces such as stairs, while sitting, or even lying on the floor. Substitute your stick with the improvised weapons that you find in your immediate environment, such as an umbrella, tennis racket, and so on.

5. Cooldown: 5–10 Minutes. Take a few minutes to take your body from fight-or-flight into rest-and-digest. Now is the time to use static stretching to increase your flexibility and break up the lactic acid that has accumulated in your muscles.

Follow-Up: When you are done, record each of your workouts in a training log. Include how long you trained and a short synopsis of the material you covered in the session. Set a goal for yourself, such as performing the foregoing workout ten times before moving on to Level 2. Stay motivated, remain disciplined, be consistent, and work hard. With practice, you will continue to improve your skills and deepen your understanding of stick fighting. You're just getting started!

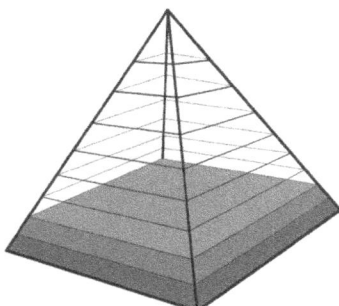

LEVEL 2
Long Range

The Outside Game

The fundamental long-range strategy, or "outside game," is to stay outside your opponent's effective striking range while targeting his outermost extremities. The most basic strategy with the stick is to simply attempt to strike your attacker without him striking you—that is, to "beat your opponent to the punch." However, if you and your opponent are similar in size, you will also have similar ranges (assuming you have matched weapons, of course). This means that if you can strike your attacker, chances are he can hit you as well. If you are similar in skill level, you can probably expect to win about 50 percent of the time. These are not good odds, whether you are fighting a match in a ring or against a hoodlum on the street.

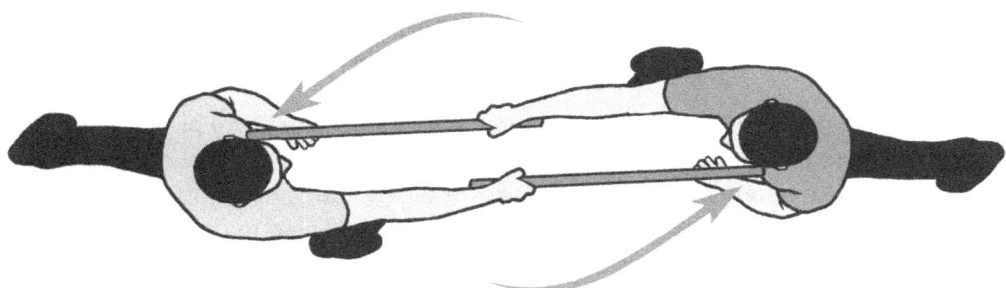

If you both target the head, neither has a tactical advantage.

However, when playing the outside game, you adapt your strategy slightly in order to increase your odds of hitting while not getting hit. Assuming that the attacker is targeting your head and body, you can effectively increase your own striking range by attacking the outermost targets on his body. The closest target will usually be his leading hand, followed by the knee of his leading leg. As you attack these primary targets (the ones that should be targeted first), your opponent will be forced to change positions, exposing secondary targets such as his elbows, body, and head.

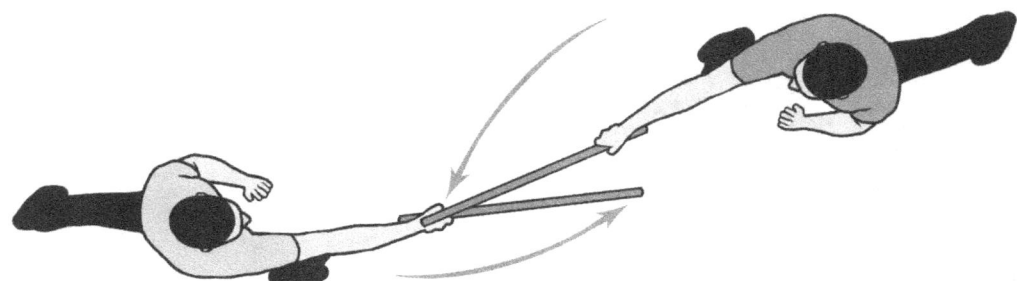

While your opponent targets your head, you target his hand.

There are two variations on this strategy. Defensively, you passively wait for the opponent to attack, then move just out of range and counterattack, usually targeting the weapon hand. Offensively, you can control the fight by striking preemptively. When properly employed, these two strategies can allow you to control most aspects of the long-range fight.

In chess, you often hear of masters planning several moves ahead in order to set an opponent up for a finishing move. This is possible in stick fighting as well. So how do you start thinking three or four moves ahead? First, you must control the fight by controlling the distance. Second, employ a series of logical, effective combinations that will allow you to predict not only how your opponent is likely to respond but also how to follow up effectively.

By developing effective strategies and tactics beforehand, you will be better equipped to deal with an opponent because you have a battle plan, just like the chess master. Your moves are no longer random techniques thrown haphazardly at the opponent. Instead, you are a tactician who employs a logical, systematic battle plan to control the fight and overcome the opponent.

Controlling the Distance

The long-range strategy is sometimes referred to as guarding by distance. Attacking from long range while staying outside your opponent's effective striking range requires that you control the distance; in this way, you can control the fight. Moving forward and backward is the obvious way of maintaining distance. Your opponent moves forward, you move back. Your opponent moves back, you move forward. Remember, while effective, moving straight backward can be dangerous because your opponent can charge forward faster than you can retreat. Circling to the left or right, on the other hand, puts you into a strategically more advantageous position than moving straight back and forth does. This is because, as you circle, you are not only controlling the distance but also controlling the line of combat.

The line of combat is an imaginary line that extends from your centerline to your opponent's center. Your strikes will be most powerful when you are aligned with the line of combat; when your opponent is right in front of you as opposed to standing off to one side. Only then can you maximize the use of proper body mechanics to generate maximum force. Therefore, keep your weapon centered on your opponent.

If you want your opponent directly in front of you in order to maximize your striking potential, it is also logical to assume that your opponent is seeking the same objective. While the most common method of controlling the distance is to move straight forward and backward, it would behoove you to move off the opponent's line of combat whenever possible in order to reduce his ability to strike you effectively. At the same time, remember to keep yourself centered on your opponent to maximize your striking potential. Circling is an effective method of achieving this.

Circling is a subtle method of controlling the distance in which you remove your body from your opponent's line of combat, out of his strike zone, and into either the acceleration zone or the deceleration zone. The initial stage of any strike is called the acceleration zone. Moving into an attack's acceleration zone can be beneficial because the strike is still building speed and momentum and has not yet reached its full power. Moving away from an attack, past the intended point of contact, puts you in the deceleration zone. This is the part of the swing where the weapon is no longer gaining speed but is actually slowing down and losing power. As you circle into these zones, maintain control of the line of combat by turning your body to keep the opponent centered in your own strike zone.

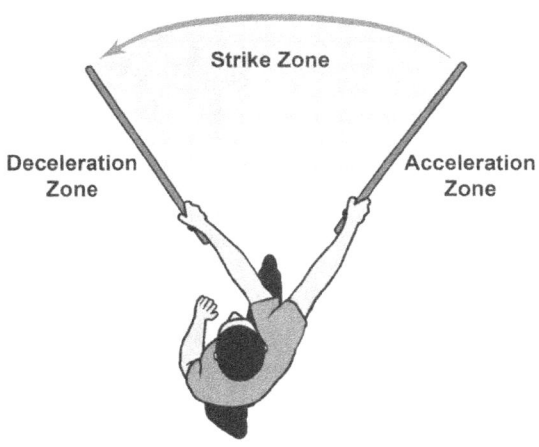

Training Equipment: The Evasion Bopper

The evasion bopper is an important piece of training equipment because it helps you practice evasion skills safely at high speed. You can make an evasion bopper by simply sliding a pool noodle onto a handle, such as an old stick, and securing it with glue or tape. Keep the unpadded handle short so there is no chance of you accidently hitting with it. The idea is to keep the striking half floppy, so you can swing it fast and hit hard, but since it does not hurt very much, if at all, you can overcome your natural fear of getting hit and instead concentrate all of your energy on learning to evade.

Have your partner swing the evasion bopper very slowly at first. Concentrate on getting out of the way of the evasion stick without getting hit. If you are unable to avoid the bopper, move your stick to block it so it does not make contact with your body (no striking!). As you get better, your partner can increase the speed of his attacks to keep it challenging.

Evade the strike, but keep your guard up and be prepared to block.

What is the appropriate speed for your partner to swing the evasion bopper at you? Studies have shown that an 80 percent success rate is optimal for learning. If you succeed consistently less than that, you begin to get discouraged and learning slows. If you succeed more than that, you don't learn as much because you are not being adequately challenged. Therefore, your partner should strive to swing the evasion bopper at a rate where you get hit about one time in five. Sometimes it will be more frequently, and sometimes less, but this would be a good average failure rate to maximize personal growth.

Long-Range Defensive Tactics

Each of the following long-range defensive tactics is presented in a logical, progressive order that makes them easy to memorize and employ. However, you should be able to vary these attacks, applying them as dictated by the specific conditions of your given situation.

When you think defense, the first thing that usually comes to mind is blocking an opponent's attack. While this can be an effective means of defense, it is not enough to merely block an incoming strike from hitting you. If you do not immediately do something to break the momentum of your opponent's attack, it is likely that he will keep attacking you until he finally succeeds in landing a blow. Therefore, it is important to take a strategic view of blocking. Blocks must be followed by quick, effective counterattacks.

When confronted with an armed opponent, it is to your advantage to disarm him at the earliest opportunity. A hand strike usually requires less power and does less bodily harm to your opponent than a head or body shot, yet still has the ability to end the confrontation.

This action, commonly referred to as defanging the snake, can be difficult to accomplish because the opponent's hand is a small target that he can quickly move. Rather than chasing the opponent's weapon hand around trying to hit it, increase your chances of striking it by waiting for him to commit to a strike instead. In that way, not only will you know where the opponent's hand will be at a given time, but, because he is committed to the attack, it will be difficult for him to avoid your counterstrike. Furthermore, if you strike his hand head-on as he is swinging at you, the resulting force will be far greater than if you had hit his hand when it was stationary.

The ability to strike your opponent's weapon hand consistently requires that you be able to read your opponent, see his attack coming, and plot the trajectory of his hand and weapon almost instantaneously in your head as you move to intercept it with your stick. Developing these skills takes practice.

Open the Door

This technique is best employed against an aggressive opponent. Maintain maximum distance, standing just outside his circle of death, but do not attack. Your passivity is intended to embolden your opponent into attacking you. When he enters your circle of death, evade his attack by maintaining distance and strike his weapon hand. Don't be content with a single counterattack. Use the multiple strikes to quickly deliver multiple strikes to the opponent's weapon hand and arm. Avoid moving straight back when you evade. Rather, circle out to remove yourself from the opponent's strike zone.

Opening the door: Let's look at the situation in which you and your opponent are standing just outside striking range.

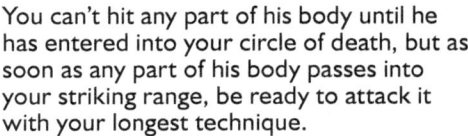

You can't hit any part of his body until he has entered into your circle of death, but as soon as any part of his body passes into your striking range, be ready to attack it with your longest technique.

Your primary target will usually be his lead hand.

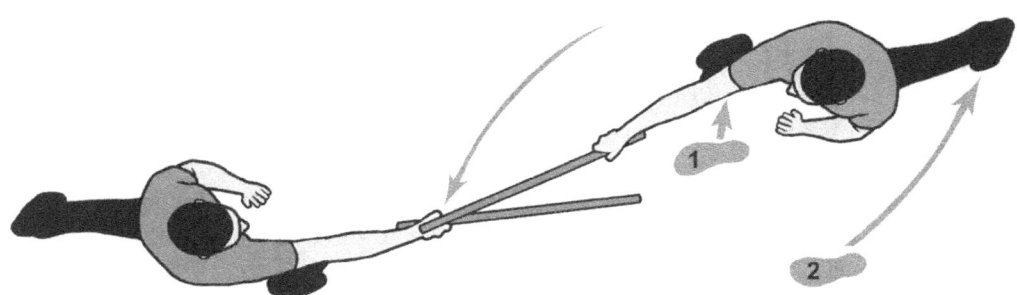

Opening the door as seen from above.

This strategy has a high rate of success because humans have a habitual method of attacking with a short weapon such as a stick; they instinctively grasp it in a natural grip with their dominant hand (90 percent of people are right-handed), draw the weapon back in preparation for a forehand strike, and then attempt to hit the opponent in the head with a downward diagonal strike (strike 1). Therefore, it makes sense that an untrained attacker or overly aggressive stick fighter will often overlook long-range targets in an instinctive, misguided attempt to hit secondary targets first, particularly the head.

Baiting and Drawing

A cautious opponent will not simply enter into your circle of death in an attempt to strike you; he must be enticed into making a rash move. Baiting and drawing are strategies common to Western boxing in which you purposely leave an opening in an attempt to get your opponent to attack you. While this may seem counterintuitive, it can be useful to create an opening for you to counterattack, and, since you are expecting the attack, you will be prepared to evade or defend.

Control the fight by subtly setting up your opponent. This can be done by drawing an attack. Begin by readying your mind to set the trap. You must be prepared to retract the bait before you even put it out. Next, leave an opening your opponent can exploit. As soon as he makes his attack, retract the bait and hit him where you know he will be vulnerable.

For example, since a right-to-left downward diagonal strike is one of the habitual methods of attack, there is a very good chance that you can draw a right high strike by leaving your head slightly exposed. Lure him into striking by gradually relaxing your guard. If this still draws no response, try extending your empty hand a bit or leaning your head forward slightly. Be careful not to be too obvious, as the opponent must believe your deception if you are to successfully draw him into taking the bait and attacking you. Make your motions look as though you are being careless and relaxing your guard, when, in actuality, this is only an act.

Never forget that when you attempt to draw an attack, you are placing yourself in a perilous position. When the opponent takes the bait, he will strike fast and hard, and he may take it the instant it is offered. Therefore, be fully prepared to react *before* you set the trap, ready to block or evade the instant your opponent strikes.

> Hold out baits to entice the enemy. Feign disorder, and then crush him. Pretend inferiority and encourage his arrogance.
> —Sun Tzu, *The Art of War*

Rearguard Defense

Even experienced fighters can fall for a trick guard, especially when it is suddenly and unexpectedly interjected into the heat of the fight. The rearguard is an invitational posture that tests the limits of baiting and drawing. It was the signature defensive stance of the nineteenth-century French stick fighter Pierre Vigny and was described in "L'art de la canne" (The Art of the Cane), an article first published in *la Revue Olympique* in 1912:

> The Vigny guard position is, in essence, a combat guard. The left arm is held in front as if bearing a shield; the right arm is raised at the rear, with the weapon held above the head, in a perpetual "spring hold."

When you are being attacked, quickly retreat with a swift guard change and bring your cane down powerfully upon the opponent's arm or hand. In doing this, you can be mathematically certain of reaching and damaging your target.

Early 20th century cane fighters demonstrate the Vigny guard.

Usually, the stick is held in a stick fighter's front hand because leading with your empty hand limits your range. Holding the weapon in your rear hand also seems to leave you more exposed to attack. However, this is exactly why the rearguard position is the perfect invitation to entice your opponent into attacking you.

Rearguard Defense: Stand just outside the opponent's range, with your stick held high behind you.

Hold your position until he is committed to his attack.

The opponent attempts to attack your exposed left flank.

Then make a full step backward with your front foot. This takes you out of the range of the opponent's intended strike and allows you to attack the exposed extended arm. Additionally, retreating puts you back into a regular guarded position.

When applying the rearguard defense, your stick does not have to be held high. You can also adopt a low rearguard defense (tail guard). When the opponent strikes, step back and meet his attack with an upward strike. As with all trick guards, you must take care not to overuse your ploy, or your opponent will catch on to your trick.

Tail Guard: The tail guard is a variation on the rearguard defense. Begin by adopting a left leading stance, dropping your stick behind you.

As the opponent takes the bait and closes the gap to strike you, step back to maintain distance.

Attack the opponent's weapon hand with strike 5.

Your goal is to disarm the opponent, defanging the snake.

Long-Range Offensive Tactics

Strategy and tactics are important, but different, things. Your strategy is your overall plan of action. The offensive long-range strategy is simple: attack by striking the closest available target at your longest range while still maintaining distance. However, saying it and making it happen are two different things. Long-range tactics, then, are the specific techniques you will use to accomplish that goal.

Practicing the following long-range offensive tactics in the order they are presented here will not only help you memorize them, but it will also help you to understand the logic behind the progression. The combinations start with a simple single swing and gradually work up to more sophisticated techniques. Each combination is its own attack, but together, they provide you with a general long-range offensive game plan comprised of progressively more-complex tactics that you can employ in quick succession to stay one step ahead of your opponent.

However, remember that this is only a general plan of attack, and not all opponents will always react the same way. Stay flexible and adapt these tactics to your given situation. Once you have assimilated this knowledge into your arsenal, you don't have to apply the attacks in any particular order and can vary the angles and targets as needed. Remember that effective long-range combinations include efficient footwork and target prioritization. Maintain distance and strike the closest available target.

In a self-defense situation, merely striking the opponent's weapon hand may not be enough to end the confrontation. Even if you are successful in disarming him, be prepared to continue striking until you have a chance to escape or the attacker is no longer a threat.

Targeting the Edges

The short stick is an impact weapon, so your targets need to be susceptible to blunt force trauma as opposed to bladed weapons that slice or stab and focus on vascular targets as well as internal organs.

Basically, a stick strike can be classified as either a distractor or a disabler. Distractors are those attacks that do not themselves debilitate the opponent, such as hand strikes or strikes that target the knees. These strikes create openings and opportunities for you to achieve your goal of landing a disabling strike to neutralize the opponent. As important as distractors are to your overall strategy, remember that alone, they are unlikely to dissuade a determined attacker. Therefore, you need to focus on using them to set up and land a solid disabling strike. Disabling strikes, such as solid strikes to the face or side of the neck, occur at middle range and inflict enough serious damage to prohibit the opponent from continuing the fight.

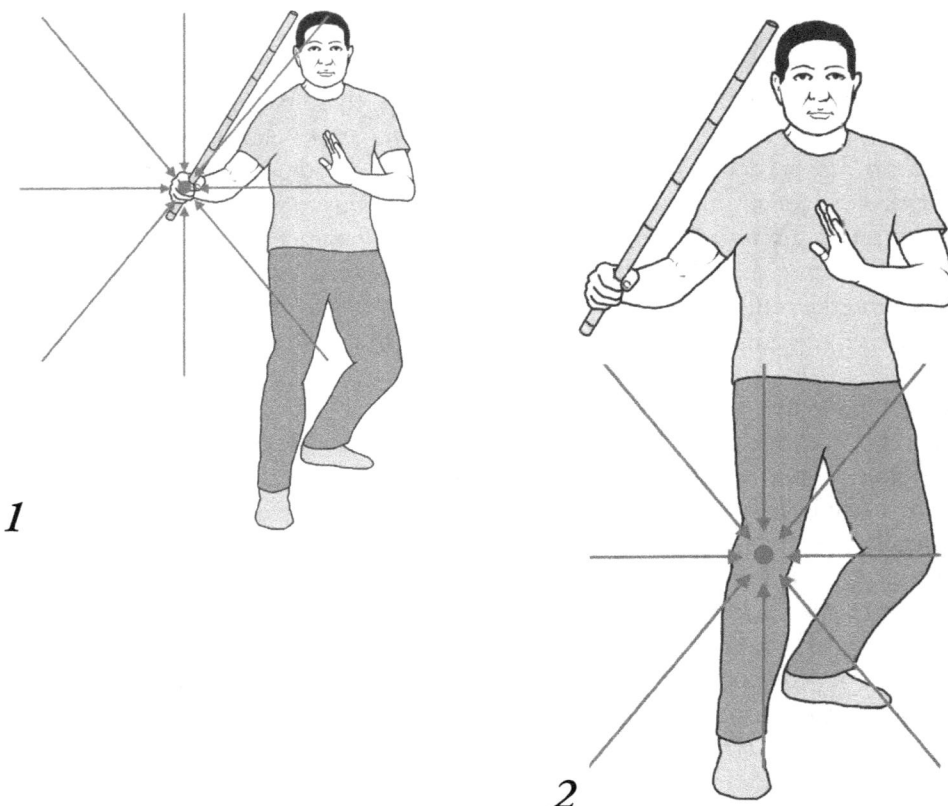

Attack from all angles when targeting the lead hand and lead knee.

Your primary target at long range is usually the opponent's weapon hand.

Strikes can also be classified as either structural attacks or attacks on the nervous system. Structural attacks aim to break and crush the muscles, bones, and joints of the opponent. Especially susceptible to attack are the knees, hips, shoulders, elbows, and hands. Nerve attacks cause pain, muscle failure, or even unconsciousness. They range from the "dead leg" that results from a strike (or repeated strikes) to the sciatic nerve on the outer edge of the thigh, to the knockouts that can result from a strike to the vulnerable carotid artery in the pocket of the neck, activating the body's vasovagal response. When vasovagal syncope occurs, your body overreacts to certain triggers that cause your heart rate and blood pressure to drop suddenly. This often results in dizziness and even loss of consciousness.

Other attacks could be classified as both structural and nervous attacks, especially thrusts to the extremely sensitive centerline targets such as the eyes, nose, throat, solar plexus, and groin.

When entering from long range, concentrate on the closest available targets. These are usually the hands and the knees. However, since hand and knee strikes are merely distractors, they may not cause enough structural damage to stop the opponent. Therefore, be sure to immediately take advantage of any opening you have created and move to a closer range to deliver a decisive disabling blow.

The Single Strike

Never underestimate the power of a single, well-placed strike. A single strike has the potential to disarm an opponent and end an encounter before an assailant even gets to swing at you. However, the ability to strike an opponent's weapon hand consistently requires timing, accuracy, and speed. The technique is simple and direct. Wait for the right opportunity, then suddenly attack the hand with a single, powerful, well-placed strike. This attack could be performed as a snap strike, full strike, or even double strike.

To be successful, it is important that you do not telegraph your intentions. Identify your target with your peripheral vision without looking directly at it. Be careful not to make any preparatory motions before your strike. Rather, lash out from wherever your stick happens to be at the moment. Since the shortest distance between any two points is a straight line, minimize your strike time by tracing a shallow arc to your target.

Single Strike: The opponent's hand is just on the edge of your striking range.

Suddenly lunge forward and strike the back of his hand with the tip of your stick.

Deliver a sharp, hard strike, with the objective of breaking the small bones of the opponent's hand and fingers (you should both wear hand protection in practice). Once an initial strike lands, be sure to follow up and quickly finish your opponent (a distractor followed by a disabler). If your opponent blocks, or you inadvertently hesitate for any reason and do not immediately counterattack, quickly return to your guarded position, ready to attack again. This applies to all the long-range combinations.

Consecutive Striking

Single strikes only give you one opportunity to hit your target. With consecutive striking, you link two or more strikes together, greatly increasing your chances for success.

Since stopping the stick and starting it again takes energy and time, conserve speed and momentum by making a tight turn that does not stop but rather flows quickly into a second full strike. Unlike a double strike that loops back to attack again on the same angle, a second consecutive attack can cut back on any angle.

Both your first and your second attacks should be part of the same swing. If you pause in the slightest, you are actually just executing two individual strikes. This is a one-two beat that your opponent can easily counter. Instead, rechamber and attack quickly on the half beat.

Consecutive Striking: Standing at the edge of your range, you see that the opponent's front hand is exposed.

Since attacking the lead hand at long range with the tip of the stick is a relatively basic tactic, do not be too surprised if your opponent is able to avoid your attack by simply moving his hand a few inches back, out of the range of your strike.

As soon as you realize he is pulling back to avoid your strike, make a tight turn and strike again from the opposite angle,

Only this time reach farther and aim your strike to hit a few inches farther down on your stick. That way, even if he moves back again, he may still get hit with the tip.

The Snap Strike Setup

Full strikes are powerful, but they follow a long arc through the target to the next ready position, giving them a relatively slow one-two count. This not only makes them easy to avoid but can leave you exposed to a quick counterattack, especially if your strike should miss and pass by its intended target. On the other hand, a snap strike returns quickly back to a chambered position on the same side of your body, ready to strike again. Snap strikes lack the power of full swings, but they are usually faster, so a snap strike followed by a second, deeper full strike should have a better chance of making contact with your intended target than two consecutive full swings.

Snap Strike Setup: Starting at long range, you see that the opponent's front hand is extended, making it a good target

So you lunge forward and snap strike, but the opponent pulls his hand back enough to avoid your strike.

Immediately return the stick to a chambered position

Execute a second, deeper strike to reach his hand.

Double Strikes

The fastest method to deliver a second strike is to employ a double strike, immediately looping back on the target with a second, deeper strike. This motion essentially gives you two opportunities to strike a target with a single swing. This attack is particularly difficult to defend against because the second strike is delivered on the half beat. When arcing into the second strike, pivot at the wrist and snap your hip to keep your stick moving, conserving as much power and momentum as possible for use in the second strike.

LEVEL 2: LONG RANGE 79

Double Strike: Hand-Hand: Starting from long range, you see that the opponent's hand is extended

So you strike to hit it, but your opponent avoids your strike by moving his weapon hand back.

Utilize a double strike to make another pass at the target without withdrawing your arm.

Your second pass must strike deeper, targeting the hand's new location with the second pass of the stick.

Double Strike: Head-Hand: Begin at long range.

Direct your initial downward attack at the opponent's head. Since you are maintaining long range, he should see this attack coming; in fact, you are counting on it.

When you see him begin to commit to the motion of the block, pull your strike back slightly, letting your stick pass his block without touching it.

Pivot at the wrist.

Loop back with a double strike.

On your second pass, target his weapon hand.

If you fail to draw a high block and the opponent instead leans backward to move his head out of range of your strike, simply loop back with a deeper double strike to the head. Just be aware that in attacking the head, you are entering middle range, in which case you should either switch to middle-range strategies and tactics or quickly retreat back to long range. When reestablishing range after a melee, exit on a different angle from the one you entered on to minimize the chances of your opponent following you with a counterattack. To that same end, it doesn't hurt to cover your retreat with a short, sharp snap strike.

LEVEL 2: LONG RANGE   81

Triple Strike: Hand-Hand-Head: This combination includes an element of programming. Building on the last combination, start from long range.

You attack the opponent's weapon hand, and he withdraws.

Loop back with a double strike attacking the hand again.

The opponent avoids that strike as well, but chances are that now he's retracted it too far, leaving his head exposed.

Continue advancing with a third strike.

Arc your third attack to the opponent's head.

If the opponent leans backward to move his head out of range of your third strike, loop back with an even deeper strike to his head. As the opponent leans back to avoid each attack, keep up the pressure, occupying the line of combat with additional quick strikes.

Again, by targeting the opponent's head, you are bordering on middle range, which has its own set of strategies and tactics. If you want to avoid middle range for the moment and continue to employ the long-range strategies, quickly return to a defended position at maximum range, ready to attack again.

Training Equipment: The Target Stick

Target sticks are important training tools for developing accurate stick strikes, similar to the focus mitts that boxers use to develop accurate punches. However, when working with weapons, a hand-held pad can be too dangerous for the holder because of the holder's close proximity to the weapon. For safety's sake, target sticks extend the holder's reach. While not intended for developing hard strikes, target sticks can provide easily movable targets that will help you develop accurate distancing and precise aim.

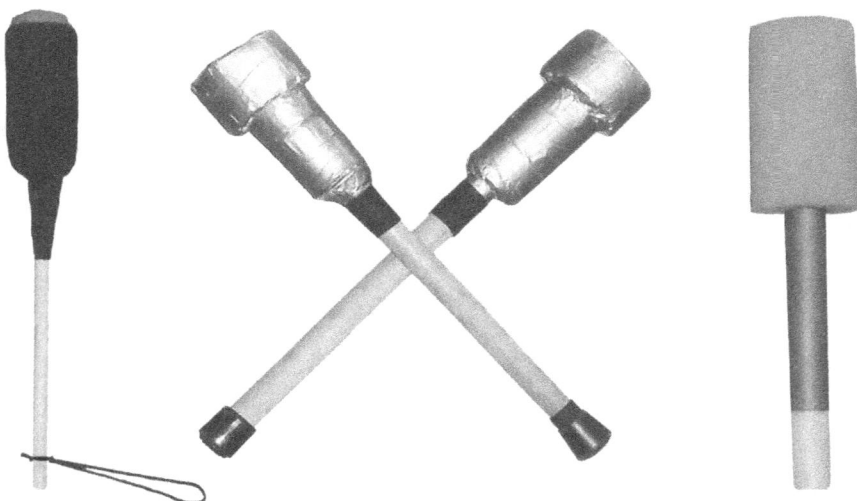

Examples of different target stick designs.

To make a target stick, start with a handle (this is a good use for a broken or beaten-up stick). Long sticks are better, about two feet, as you want to keep your hands well out of range of your partner's strikes, especially early on in his training. Wrap the top half of the stick with some sort of padding. An old piece of carpet will work, but tends to be heavy. Foam rubber, especially in the form of foam pipe insulation, is a light, convenient, and durable material to use. Whatever padding you use, make the end relatively thick so it will not be too hard to hit. Wrap it in several layers of duct or athletic tape for durability. Finally, you should put a wrist strap on your target stick so it does not accidently fly out of your hand.

Have your partner hold one target stick while you hit it with each of the basic strikes. Take special care not to hit your partner's hands. Just in case, though, your partner should still wear some sort of protective hand gear. Start out slowly until you can hit the target easily, then gradually add speed. If you see your accuracy begin to diminish, slow down until you can hit the target stick consistently before speeding up again. Work up to free targeting, with your partner moving one or even two sticks around at random for you to strike. Target holders should retreat, advance, and circle as they slowly change the levels of the target sticks.

Work on gradually minimizing the extent that you chamber for each strike. If you intend to strike with the tip of the stick, it is counterproductive to put that tip behind you to chamber. This is a habit because it is necessary for learning power and proper mechanics, but it actually serves to increase the time it takes to make the strike and telegraphs your intentions to your opponent. Instead, learn to strike by moving the stick from wherever it happens to be directly to the target. Concentrate on your form and don't strike too hard. Keep in mind that the purpose of the target sticks is not to develop power but rather to develop fluid, accurate strikes.

Strike the targets from all angles and all levels. Strive to hit with the tip of your stick.

You can get creative in your choice of materials for target sticks. I have used all sorts of improvised target sticks with great success. In fact, the black target on the left in the picture of different target stick designs is just an empty plastic water bottle on a stick covered in tape. You are limited only by your imagination and the resources you have at hand. See the appendix at the end of this book for blueprints and more precise instructions on creating your own target sticks.

Feinting

Feinting, also called faking, is an excellent way to create an opening to score a hit. It begins with an attack that appears to be a committed technique but is actually a fake intended to be easily perceived by the opponent in order to draw a block. As the opponent reacts to this first technique, redirect your strike to attack from a new angle while the opponent is still committed to defending against the first. This will make it difficult for him to quickly change his initiated plan of action. If timed properly, your second strike will come in on the half beat (as opposed to a full one-two count), giving your opponent practically no time to react.

The basic strikes can be used in matched pairs for feinting from opposite angles. For example, strikes 1 and 2 work well together as a feint-strike combination. You could apply this same tactic with almost any pair of strikes that come from different directions. You will find that some work better for you than others.

Feinting: Lean forward with a number 2 left-to-right downward diagonal strike. It is important that the opponent perceives your attack as a genuine threat and responds by using his stick to defend his upper right-hand quadrant.

However, halfway through the motion, around the time your opponent is thinking that he will be able to block your strike, redirect your stick around his defenses as you suddenly change the angle of your attack to a number 1 right-to-left downward strike to the head instead

When feinting, do not make contact with your opponent's stick, but stay committed to your attack until he is committed to defending against it. It is crucial that you do not stop the momentum of your feint to pull back or pause, as this would only break your final strike into two moves. Instead, flow from a number 2 strike into a number 1 strike midswing. Watch yourself closely in the mirror or on video to see what you look like. Make corrections and continue to hone your technique until you can perform this feint and strike seamlessly.

Remember, if your opponent does not defend against your initial strike, then your feint should become an actual strike!

Twirling: The Six-Count Flower

The six-count flower is a simple twirl made up of three double strikes. You can use it to help develop smooth and fast double strikes. You can also use it as an effective offensive combination without any modifications at all!

The Six-Count Flower: Start with a number 1 strike, swinging diagonally downward from right to left toward the center of your body.

Halfway through the strike, arrest the motion of your arm and pivot at the wrist to deliver a second strike from that same angle.

Loop back with a number 2 backhand strike, swinging diagonally downward from left to right.

Pivot at the wrist to deliver a downward vertical strike.

Stop your stick with the tip facing downward, low to your outside, and reverse the motion, striking vertically upward.

Pivot at the wrist to loop into a second vertical upward strike, returning you to your starting position, from where you can repeat the pattern.

Pivot on the balls of your feet and engage your hips. Practice until your strikes flow smoothly into each other. Practice your accuracy against a target stick. Don't hit hard, because that's not what the target sticks are intended for. Instead, work on perfecting your distancing, accuracy, and tip control.

Practice your power by striking another stick (not a padded target stick). Have a partner hold it horizontally in front of you and as far away from his body as possible. Always aim for the tip of your partner's stick, imagining that he is grabbing the weapon at that end. This not only works your accuracy but also keeps your strikes as far from your partner's actual hand as possible. Even so, your partner may still want to consider wearing hand protection.

If you are the partner holding the target stick, don't just stand there. Be part of the exercise. Physically, use it to train your grip and arm strength. Switch hands when you get fatigued. Mentally, this is a chance for you to work on your powers of observation. Pay close attention to how your partner's shoulders and body move as he strikes. This information will serve you well later, when you are learning how to read your opponent.

Training Equipment: Striking Point

The striking point is a great tool for solo practice to develop focus and precision when striking with the stick. It is simple and inexpensive to construct, and the "BOINGGGG" you get with a good strike is very gratifying.

LEVEL 2: LONG RANGE 87

You'll need a flange, a circular piece of metal with four screw holes used to attach a steel pipe perpendicular to a flat surface. Use a flange adapter or coupler piece to connect your spring to the flange. Find a compression spring that fits snugly in the coupler, situating itself with the thread. Finally, mount a tennis ball on the end of the spring by cutting a slit just wide enough to fit on the spring (the smaller the hole, the better).

The materials cost less than twenty dollars. Construction is easy if you can find parts that fit together nicely. As with all the training equipment I present, easy-reference construction plans appear in the appendix at the end of the book.

The Long-Range Battle Plan

Let's look at how you can combine the long-range offensive and defensive strategies and tactics I've mentioned into an effective overall plan of attack. There are an incredibly large number of possible combinations that one could employ, but it would take several books to explore them all. Bruce Lee referred to something he called "choice reaction time." He believed that the more options you have to choose from, the longer it will take you to make a decision. If you only have a few options to select from, the act of mentally choosing a course of action should be faster, resulting in an overall faster reaction time.

Luckily, you have already covered all the basic techniques that you will need to get started. All that remains is to put what you have learned into a tactical flowchart to form a ready-to-use long-range battle plan.

Fight psychology is different in sport from how it is in self-defense. In a combat scenario, you will need to finish the opponent as quickly and safely as possible, so staying at long range may or may not be the best choice.

In a sporting match, it often makes sense to start out slow, then ramp things steadily up from there, so starting with an outside game makes sense, as long as it is working for you. After all, if it ain't broke, don't fix it, right? It is strategically better to start defensively and work up to offense tactics. If you start out aggressively implementing offensive techniques, not only do you lose an important opportunity to feel out your opponent early in the fight, but should you decide to change to defensive tactics and suddenly fall back, stop attacking, and set a trap for your opponent, chances are he'll become suspicious and it will be that much harder to lure him in.

Start by employing the defensive strategies and tactics. Let him charge in, then you circle out and counter. Bait him to draw a strike so you can target his hand. That way, when you do switch to the offensive tactics, it will be that much more surprising. Switch to employing offensive tactics only after the opponent has grown wary of your defensive tactics and stopped entering to attack.

Hopefully the results of your defensive tactics will be effective enough to have made a psychological impact too, and now, after having his best attacks countered, the opponent is becoming demoralized, or at least far less aggressive. Either one suits the purpose of breaking his momentum. The proper time to start employing more aggressive tactics is when the opponent becomes hesitant and unsure how to proceed. If the opponent is preoccupied with having to defend against your sequence of ever more sophisticated combinations, he should have a difficult time mounting an effective offense of his own, allowing you to control the fight.

I've provided two prototype battle plans. The first one, just discussed, is presented in a simple, linear fashion that unfolds sequentially. The second is a more complex flowchart that contains the same tactics but assembles them in such a way as to represent several possible courses of action, as well as specifying when to apply each one. The linear plan is simple, making it easy to memorize and implement. However, it lacks the versatility of the more complex flowchart, which plots out different reactions based on reading the opponent's demeanor (aggressive, defensive, or neutral). Both plans have their merits. Studying the linear battle plan and the complex flowchart will give you a deeper understanding of the strategies and tactics of the outside game and ultimately allow you to create new battle plans based on your own personal successes.

By developing strategies beforehand, you will be better equipped to deal with an opponent because you have a battle plan, just like the chess master. Your moves are no longer random techniques thrown haphazardly at the opponent; rather, they become tactics in a systematic, logical plan to control and overcome the opponent.

Of course, if you have any fighting experience at all, you know that it never goes as smoothly as all that. However, having some plan is much better than having no plan. The art lies in being able to read your opponent in order to apply the different strategies and tactics at the appropriate times.

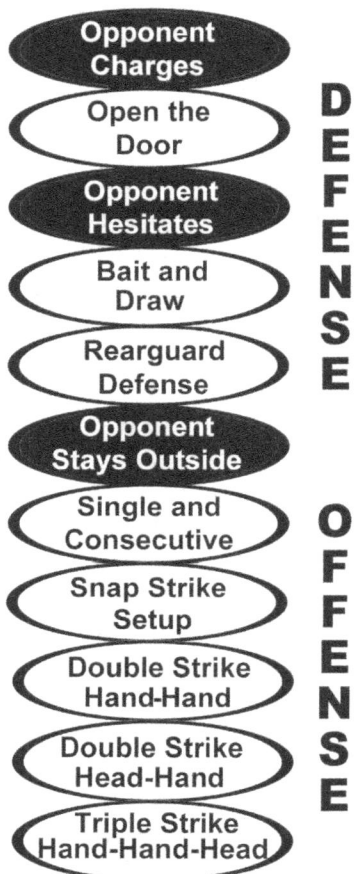

The long-range battle plan organized as a simple flowchart.

If you fail to plan, you are planning to fail.
—Benjamin Franklin

No battle plan survives first contact with the enemy.
—Helmuth von Moltke the Elder, chief of staff of the Prussian Army

A more complex flowchart depicting the long-range battle plan.

Level 2 Workout

Objective: This sixty-to-ninety-minute workout will help you acquire the skills you will need to apply the long-range battle plan effectively.

1. Warm-Up: 15–20 Minutes. Start with some light stretching. See the guide at the beginning of this book for a sample stretching routine. Rather than jump rope, have your partner swing an evasion bopper at you. Work on your footwork to keep out of range. When your partner advances, avoid moving straight back. Instead, circle out to either side. Warm up your arms and upper body by swinging your stick where you see that an imaginary opponent would be, but remember that you are practicing long-range footwork, so if your swings come close to your partner, you are way too close. Staying out of range is your top priority, but you won't be able to evade the stick every time. If you see that you cannot get out of range in time, you can duck or block gently with your stick to avoid being touched. When you get winded, take a break with some additional light stretching until your heart rate returns to normal.

2. Accuracy and Distancing: 15–20 Minutes. Use two pieces of pool noodle to have a controlled sparring match with only two targets, the opponent's lead leg and weapon hand. No headshots! This practice will teach you how to stay at range while targeting the opponent's lead hand. This should be good cardio training, taking the place of jumping rope in this workout.

3. Partner Drills: 15–20 Minutes. Slow things down a bit by practicing the linear version of the long-range battle plan one step at a time with a partner. Work through variations on each tactic. Later, you can move on to the more advanced flowchart. Keep in mind that this is *not* sparring, it is drilling, so keep things slow and controlled. Leave believable openings to lure your partner in, then have him attack as he would in a fight, but at half speed. If your baiting is too obvious, your partner should tell you so.

Practice everything at half speed. Moving slowly allows you to concentrate on refining your techniques. Moving quickly and instinctively does not allow for analysis and evaluation during the execution of each technique, when the most potential for progress and improvement exists. Use this time to learn how to see, feel, and flow with the stick. Speed will come later of its own accord, and, when it does, your techniques will be fast without the appearance of being rushed. Even though you should both be moving slowly and with good control, it is recommended that you both put on protective gear. At this point, gloves and a helmet should suffice.

4. Power: 10–20 Minutes. Perform the six-count flower twirl using a partner's stick to develop power. Have your partner hold his stick out for you, with the tip held well away from him for his protection. Target the top six inches of your partner's stick as though that were the end where his hand was holding the stick. Work up to striking fast and hard, performing all six strikes before flowing seamlessly into the drill again. Repeat with your left hand.

5. Cooldown: 5–10 Minutes. Take a few minutes to shift your body from fight-or-flight into rest-and-digest. Now is the time to use static stretching to increase your flexibility and break up the lactic acid that has accumulated in your muscles.

Keep It Fresh: As you get more comfortable with these skills, try practicing in different conditions: in the rain, on uneven surfaces such as stairs, while sitting, or even while lying on the floor. Substitute your normal training sticks with improvised weapons such as an umbrella, tennis racket, and so on.

Solo Training: Many of the exercises in this workout are intended to be performed with a partner. However, you still need to train even if a partner is unavailable, so modify the exercises as needed. Sometimes you will have to visualize your opponent instead of actually having someone in front of you. Mirrors can help you in this regard. For accuracy, use a striking point in place of a partner-held target stick. Often a tire dummy or heavy bag can substitute for a training partner. If it is suspended by a rope or chain, swing it to imitate the movements of a live opponent.

Follow-Up: Don't forget to record each of your workouts in your training log. If you still haven't started one, now would be a good time. Include how long each training session lasted, as well as a short summary of what you did. Keep pushing yourself by setting new goals. Use these goals to stay motivated and to keep your training fresh and exciting.

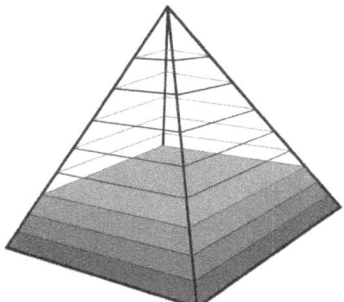

LEVEL 3
Crossing the Gap

Entering Offensively

Even though you may prefer to fight from long range, there will be times when you will want, or need, to go to middle range, where you can use your free hand to check your opponent's weapon hand. Perhaps you are not winning at the outside game, or maybe your primary strategy is to skip over long range altogether to engage the opponent at middle range. Perhaps it is a self-defense situation in which you need to disarm and neutralize the attacker quickly and do not have time for an extended long-range confrontation, in which case you could transition directly to close range. Whatever the reason, you will still have to move through the opponent's long-range zone before you can engage your opponent at a closer range. This is called entering or crossing the gap.

When moving to middle range, you are most vulnerable to attack while crossing the gap. Your goal is to cross safely into the middle-range striking zone without getting hit in the process. There are several ways to accomplish this. Although these are not the only ways, and they are by no means foolproof, the following methods do have a high rate of success across a variety of situations.

If you are already actively engaged in the long-range game, entering offensively is only a matter of proper timing, as you must wait until your opponent is in a poor position to strike you. The opponent can inadvertently put himself in a bad position by overcommitting to a strike that ends up missing its target, leaving him temporarily unable to counter. The opening will be very brief, so you must be ready to spring inside as soon as his strike goes by.

You can increase your odds of success by controlling the action. Use the technique of baiting and drawing to entice your opponent into making a big swing. Leave an opening that your opponent cannot resist. When he takes the bait, move his intended target just out of the way. Provided that your opponent was sufficiently committed to his strike, his momentum should carry his weapon past the target. Immediately enter through the resulting gap in your opponent's defense.

Flower Transition

You can enter offensively, using rapid-fire strikes to cover your approach. Use the flower twirl to attack the opponent's lead hand, getting progressively closer until you end up at middle range.

Entering with the Flower: Begin your attack at long range, targeting the opponent's weapon hand. As expected, the opponent withdraws his hand to avoid your first strike.

Use a double strike to loop back deeper with a second attack, which he attempts to avoid by retreating yet again.

He is now out of position and unable to launch a substantial attack, giving you an opportunity to transition to middle range as you strike a third time with a backhand strike.

Twirl to the outside into a fourth strike as your free hand moves to check his weapon hand.

Stop your downward momentum and reverse your motion into a fifth strike vertically upward under the chin.

Loop around one last time to catch your opponent with a sixth strike upward into the groin.

Blitz Attack

Blitzkrieg, German for "lightning war," is a strategy by which the attacking force uses a short, fast, powerful attack to break through the opponent's lines, displacing their defenses in order to deliver a decisive blow. That is exactly what this simple but effective combination does.

You can use a striking technique known in sword fighting as a beat to disrupt the opponent's defenses. Beating entails hitting the opponent's weapon in order to open the line of combat. To beat the opponent's stick, hit it with a quick, sharp snap strike, so you can execute a second attack on the half beat. For maximum effect, strike to the weakest part of the opponent's stick, hitting as close to the end of his stick as possible. Hitting the middle of the stick doesn't work as well because the stick is structurally stronger there, so there will be less movement of the opponent's weapon. Don't overcommit when executing a beat, since you will have but an instant to take advantage of the opening you have just created.

The Blitz: Begin squared off at long range.

Step your rear foot forward on an angle as you move to strike the opponent's weapon.

Beat his weapon with a sharp strike to open his defenses.

Twist back and deliver a horizontal backhand strike to the opponent's neck or head area.

Programming

The human mind can be very predictable. Our brains have a natural tendency to look for patterns, and you can use this knowledge to trick your opponent into doing what you want him to do. This is called programming. Programming is an exceptional method of setting up your techniques, maximizing the probability of eluding your opponent's defenses in order to land a decisive, disabling strike. This is accomplished by first getting your opponent to expect a certain attack, then quickly changing the angle of your attack halfway through the technique.

To begin, deliver a strike to any open target. If it is blocked, retreat to your ready position, only to attack the same target again, in the same manner, a moment later. Each time, observe how your opponent counters your technique and quickly determine where he is open in that instant. The third time you attack, your opponent will subconsciously expect the same attack you have thrown previously. Use that expectation to your advantage by feinting with the initial technique before striking where your opponent has left himself open.

Again, timing is important. You must remain committed to your feint until you perceive that the opponent has committed to a specific defense, then quickly and smoothly change your strike to an unexpected, and therefore undefended, angle. Do not strike on a one-two practice count, as this allows your opponent an opportunity to adjust and counter your technique. Instead, strike on the half beat—not one-two but rather one–one and a half!

Programming: Lean forward with a sharp number 2 left-to-right downward diagonal snap strike. It does not matter if the opponent's head lies just out of your reach; it is only important that he perceives your attack as a genuine threat and responds by using his stick to defend his upper right-hand quadrant.

Immediately return to your start position.

Deliver a second snap strike to the same area to reinforce the point to your opponent that he is under attack from that direction.

Quickly pull back to your ready position. (4)

By now your opponent should be well programmed to expect an attack from your left. Begin your third strike in exactly the same manner as your first two in order to draw a block from the opponent as he moves to protect his right side.

However, halfway through the motion, around the time your opponent is thinking that he will be able to block your predictable strike, redirect your stick around his defenses as you suddenly change the angle of your attack to a number 1 right-to-left full downward strike to the head instead.

The Leaping Grasshopper

Just because you are stick fighting does not mean that you should get so fixated on using your weapon that you forget to use the many other tools at your disposal. For example, never forget that you have legs! Do you come from a kicking art? Then try to incorporate kicking into your stick fighting. Low-line kicks, those delivered below the waist, have a very good chance of scoring when you are in range, particularly because they are so unexpected.

The Leaping Grasshopper: This is an unorthodox, and therefore unexpected, means of crossing the gap. The technique begins just outside striking range.

Raise your rear knee and kick forward.

Use the momentum of the first kick to suddenly leap forward with a second front kick.

Your kicks do not have to be higher than knee level, as they are not intended to be genuine attacks.

They only need to draw the opponent's attention low as you leap forward.

As soon as you see that the opponent is moving to block his low line, strike to the right side of the opponent's neck with the intention of rendering him unconscious.

Entering Defensively

Studies of historical injury patterns show that the left side of the head is targeted far more often than the right, and that the great majority of blows come from a downward direction. This is in accordance with the habitual method of attack for a right-handed person. Whether it is Roman gladiators (Head Injuries of Roman Gladiators" *Forensic Sci Int.* 2006 Jul 13;Vol 160(Issues 2–3), Pages 89–236.) or medieval soldiers, the majority of injuries sustained in combat are found on the left side of the skull. In his 2016 research paper on the 1461 Battle of Towton, which occurred in England during the Wars of the Roses, Michael Cahill writes, "The majority of the blunt force wounds were delivered to the front left side of the skull indicating that these individuals partook in face to face combat against right handed assailants."

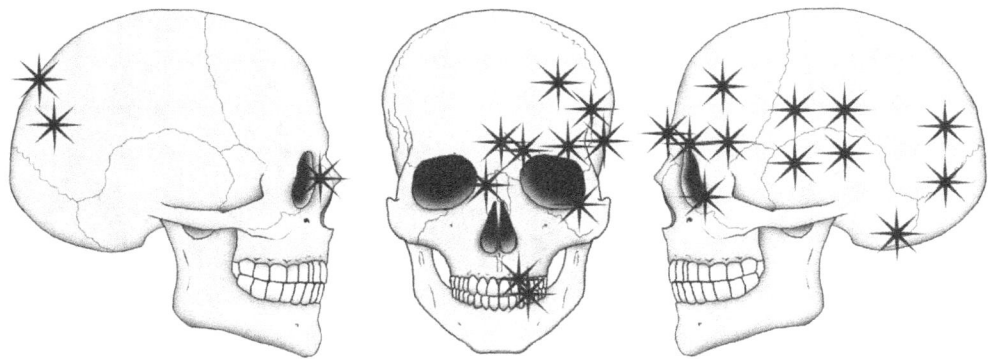

The locations of different blunt force trauma injuries suffered by numerous victims who died in the Battle of Towton, Britain, in 1461. Note the concentration of injuries on the left side of the head.

Roof Block Cover

The historical data is clear: in combat, most strikes are delivered on a downward angle to the left side. You can expect to encounter similar trends in a stick fight. Therefore, when crossing the gap defensively without having already engaged the opponent, your primary concern should be blocking your upper left-hand quadrant. This is often accomplished with a high block, also called a roof block or upper block, in which the stick is held over the head on a diagonal with the tip by your left shoulder.

One of the most important elements of crossing the gap with a block is speed. The less time you spend in long range, the less opportunity your opponent will have to hit you on your way in. The quickest way to cross the gap is to use a full passing step. Full steps are how humans regularly walk and run, so they are naturally a faster means of moving forward than shuffling.

The Roof Block: Start at long range across from your opponent. Drop your guard slightly to draw a high attack.

Lean forward as you use a roof block in your upper left-hand quadrant and check his weapon hand with your empty hand.

As you step forward, flow from your defensive position into an offensive attack, striking with a number 2 strike to the pocket of the opponent's neck. This strike has a good chance of activating the opponent's vagal response, making him light-headed or even knocking him unconscious.

Immediately loop back into a horizontal strike targeting the opponent's solar plexus. Get your hips into this strike and attack with the intention of convulsing his diaphragm, thus knocking the wind out of him.

Slide your left hand down and grasp the opponent's stick as you shift your hips back to your right and swing over his arm, targeting his temple with the tip of your weapon.

This should result in a full disarm.

Stay unpredictable by varying your attacks so that they come from all angles and all levels. For example, as you cross the gap with a roof block to protect your head, you can use the motion as a windup for a forehand strike. This can be delivered to any level. For example, you could follow up with a downward diagonal number 1 strike from above that targets the opponent's left neck pocket; a number 3 strike that rips horizontally from right to left across his abdomen, targeting his diaphragm; or a low strike to the inside of the opponent's lead knee.

Targeting the Knee: Start at long range across from your opponent.

Begin your motion with a lean forward as you block your upper left-hand quadrant and seek his weapon hand with your empty hand.

Cross the gap quickly, using a full step. As you check the opponent's weapon hand, bring your stick around your head.

Deliver a downward diagonal strike to his lead knee.

The Uppercut

A less obvious counter comes on an upward angle, striking from right to left, targeting just under the opponent's jaw. Since this strike is effective at hitting anywhere from his ribs to the side of the head, you have a wide margin of error, increasing the functionality of the technique.

The Uppercut: Start at long range across from your opponent.

Begin your motion with a lean forward as you block your upper left-hand quadrant and seek his weapon hand with your empty hand.

Check his weapon hand as you whip the stick around your head into an upward diagonal strike.

Strike the opponent under the ridge of his jaw.

The Smackdown

This is a fantastic self-defense technique! If the opponent can't see you, he will be much less of a threat, so instead of attacking with a mere palm strike, use a tiger claw. The tiger claw is a hand position that involves tensing your fingers so the tips point forward. The concept behind the tiger claw strike is simple: strike the opponent's most vulnerable target, his eyes, at the earliest opportunity. Since you use all five fingers to attack both of your opponent's eyes, you have ten chances to score, giving this technique a particularly high chance of success. An eye strike may take speed and accuracy to be successful, but it does not require a great deal of power to momentarily incapacitate any attacker.

LEVEL 3: CROSSING THE GAP   105

The Smackdown: Draw a high strike by exposing your head.

Charge in, covering your upper left-hand quadrant. Remember to cross the gap quickly, using natural, full walking steps.

Use your stick to block the opponent's strike, but instead of using your free hand to check the opponent's weapon hand, use it to deliver a tiger claw strike to the opponent's eyes as your palm hits his face.

Push his head backward and break his structure, weakening his ability to defend or counterattack effectively.

Level 3 Workout

Objective: This sixty-to-ninety-minute workout will help you learn how to cross the gap safely.

1. Warm-Up: 15–20 Minutes. Start with some light stretching. See the guide at the beginning of this book for a sample stretching routine. Follow this with five to ten minutes of jumping rope, followed by some more light stretching until your heart rate returns to normal. Then, grab your stick and work through some basic movements such as figure eights (horizontal, vertical, and diagonal), and the six-count flower. Remember, you are still warming up, so work slowly and take this time to perfect your technique.

2. Crossing the Gap: 40–60 Minutes. Stand across from your training partner, each of you armed with a stick, just outside his effective striking range. Take turns offensively crossing the gap, entering using different tactics such as the six-count flower, programming, or the leaping grasshopper. Next, practice defensively crossing the gap using a roof block as cover. Remember to practice less obvious counters such as the uppercut and smackdown, and work through variations on each tactic. Again, resist the urge to start sparring. Keep things slow and controlled.

Practice everything at half speed. Moving slowly allows you to concentrate on refining your techniques, as opposed to moving quickly and instinctively. Speed will come later of its own accord, and, when it does, your techniques will be fast without the appearance of being rushed. Even though you should both be moving slowly and with good control, it is recommended that you wear protective gear; gloves and a helmet should suffice. It is natural that, as your skill increases, you will both speed up. This is fine, just be careful not to hit your training partner excessively hard.

If you don't have a partner (possibly because you kept hitting him excessively hard), use your tire dummy or heavy bag as though it were an opponent and visualize his reactions as you practice.

3. Cooldown: 5–10 Minutes. Take a few minutes to take your body from fight-or-flight into rest-and-digest. Now is the time to use static stretching to increase your flexibility and break up the lactic acid that has accumulated in your muscles.

Follow-Up: Don't forget to record each of your workouts in your training log. Keep pushing yourself by setting new goals. Use these goals to stay motivated and to keep your training fresh and exciting.

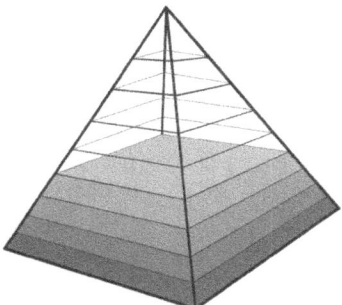

LEVEL 4
Middle-Range Offense

Understanding Middle Range

The middle range can be defined as the distance at which you can touch any part of the opponent's body with your free hand. Once you can touch your opponent, you can begin to check his weapon. Furthermore, you can use your tactile senses to monitor his general body movements and even read his intentions. This especially applies to touching your opponent's weapon hand.

Like stick fighting at long range, fighting at middle range has its own unique set of strategies and tactics. While strikes at long range are usually delivered in short bursts every few seconds, at middle range you can deliver strikes to the target at a much faster rate. For a trained stick fighter, delivering five hits a second is not uncommon.

Because you are close enough to actually make body-to-body contact, at middle range you can use your off hand to check the opponent's weapon. This can effectively neutralize his attack, allowing you to attack him with impunity.

Center, Centerline, and the Line of Combat

In order to grasp the subtle dynamics of stick fighting, it is necessary to understand the concepts of center, centerline, and the line of combat. For the sake of this discussion, let's consider the spine as the body's *center*. Your *centerline* is an imaginary line that runs bilaterally straight down the center of your body and extends in a vertical plane in front of you. The *line of combat* is an imaginary line that connects your center with your opponent's center. It represents the most direct path of attack (illustration 1 in the accompanying figure). You can attack most effectively when your centerline is aligned with the line of combat because your opponent is right in front of you, allowing you to maximize the effective use of both your weapon and your free hand. Therefore, it is usually best to keep your centerline turned directly toward your opponent. However, if you are standing directly in front of each other, then neither of you holds a tactical advantage (illustration 2).

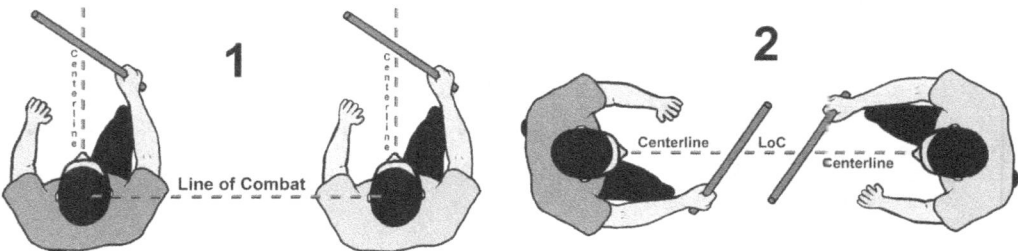

Therefore, try to stay off your opponent's centerline. A quick shuffle step counterclockwise to the opponent's left (your right) places you in his deceleration zone, taking away his ability to strike you with maximum force (illustration 3). Immediately realign your centerline to the line of combat to place your opponent in the middle of your strike zone (illustration 4).

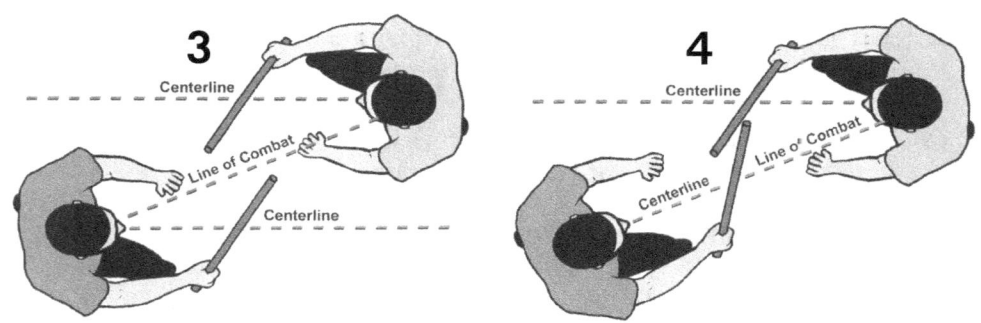

Likewise, circling clockwise to the opponent's right (your left) places you in his acceleration zone, which should have the effect of jamming his attack.

Targeting at Middle Range

Although each strike is generally performed along a prescribed line, your targets will vary, and they will not always be in the same positions. Therefore, you need to understand that each basic strike is also capable of attacking at slightly different angles. For example, a downward diagonal strike can target the temple, the pocket of the neck, the point of the shoulder, the elbow, or the hand. Upward diagonal strikes can attack the knee, the sciatic nerve, the hip, the ribs, or the elbow. Downward vertical strikes can be used to attack the crown of the head, the face, the clavicle, the point of the shoulders, or the hand. Upward vertical strikes can strike the groin, the hand, or up under the chin.

Horizontal strikes can strike a number of targets stretching from temple to knee, including the elbow and the hand. Thrusting strikes can be used to effectively attack the face, the throat, the solar plexus, or the groin.

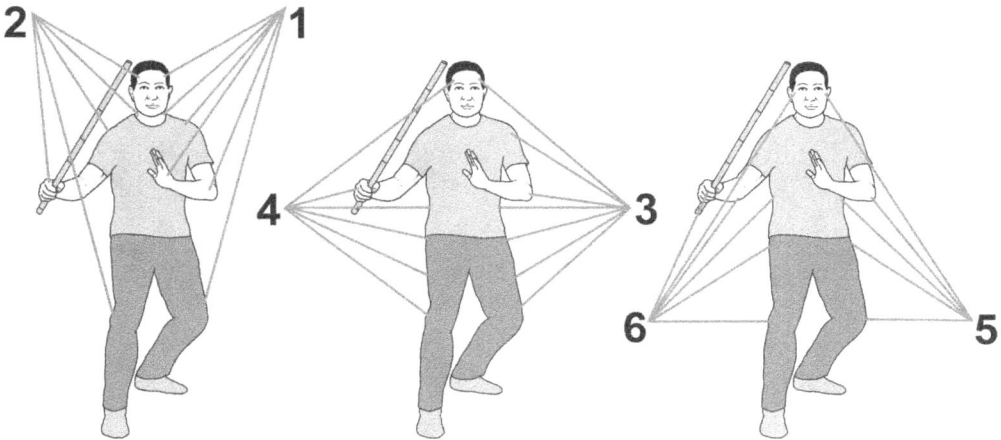

Each strike is capable of angling toward any one of a number of targets.

Continue attacking available targets from all angles, at all levels, with all the techniques in your arsenal until the opponent has been neutralized. Whenever possible, read the situation and employ restraint, applying the minimum amount of force needed to control the situation. While difficult for the beginner, this becomes more feasible as your ability with the stick increases.

Basic Middle-Range Combinations

It is rare that a single strike will disable your opponent, so you should attack in well-thought-out combinations. Combinations are prearranged series of moves that you practice to apply later in fighting. Some combinations are more effective than others. Each move in a combination should have a specific application. Effective combinations have a higher chance of success because they have a higher degree of functionality.

You've been practicing combinations already with the basic strikes. Consecutive full strikes with the stick can be effective in the prescribed order, so it is a good place to start. Strikes 1 and 2 can be used to attack the right and left sides of your opponent's body in quick succession, as can strikes 3 and 4. However, your goal should be to put a variety of different strikes together quickly into effective combinations, so do not limit yourself to the basic pattern. Shorter combos consisting of only three or four strikes will be easier to remember and implement during a fight. Whatever the combination, each strike should create an opening or otherwise set you up for your next attack.

High-Low Combo: You notice the opponent is guarding high.

Draw a high block by attacking with a number 2 snap strike to the opponent's right high line.

Once he has committed to a high defense, smoothly switch to a number 4 full strike to his right low line.

Check his weapon hand with your free hand as you immediately cut back and strike with a number 3 horizontal strike to his left side.

Speed-Striking

    I owe a lot of my stick fighting knowledge to my eskrima teacher, Guro Steve Wolk. Steve first introduced me to these combinations when I had the privilege of training with him in the early 1990s. At the time, Steve was working very hard training for the World Eskrima Kali Arnis Federation World Championships, and these patterns were his secret weapons. He would work them on the heavy bag for hours. We timed him working his patterns, and he could easily strike six times a second or more for extended periods of time. His efforts obviously paid off, because over the years he won six world championships.

    Guro Steve had a letter name for each pattern based on the shapes your stick makes as you perform the strikes. Some patterns look just like they are tracing the letter they are named for, but others do not. The letters were just a convenient way of referencing

LEVEL 4: MIDDLE-RANGE OFFENSE 111

each combination, and I have never found a better method. It is with Guro Steve's permission that these patterns are included here, appearing for the first time in print.

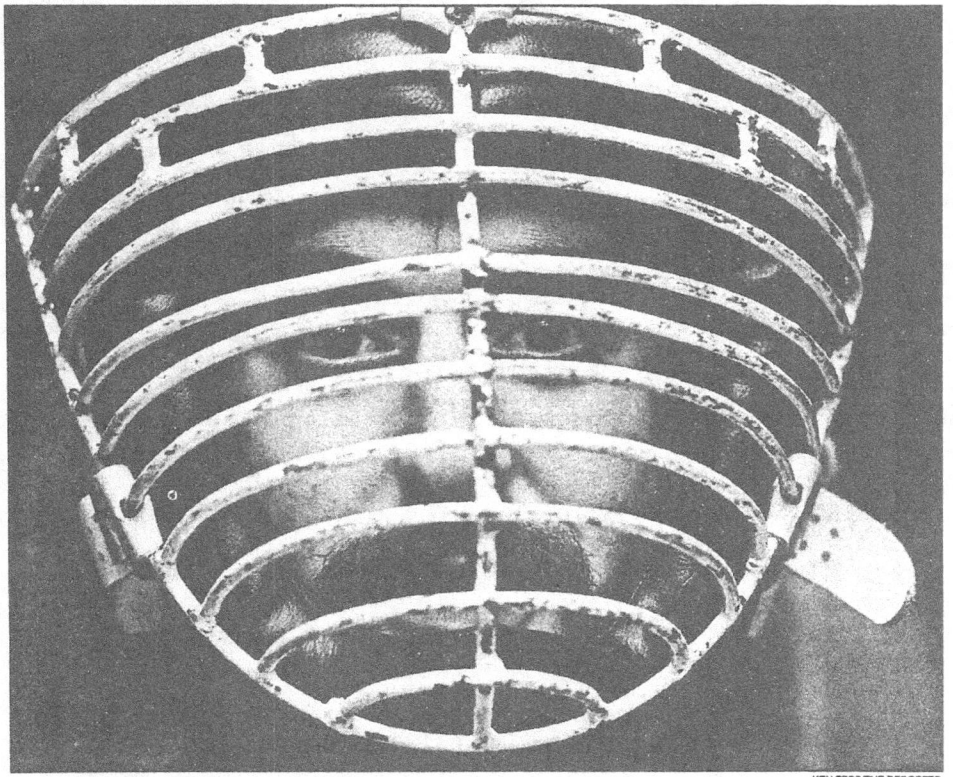

THE REPORTER — FRIDAY, OCTOBER 20, 1989

Local chemist hard at work on top stick-fighting formula

KEN ZEPP/THE REPORTER

MASKED MAN: Steve Wolk of Hatboro peers out from behind the protective mask he wears for stick fighting.

The Helicopter Strike

The helicopter strike is an extremely quick method of striking. The pattern consists of a series of overhead horizontal snap strikes that feed into each other in such a way that you can deliver many strikes very quickly to opposite sides of your opponent's head. The key to performing this technique properly is to keep your hand in one spot and pivot at the wrist by moving your elbow from side to side in front of you.

112 THE ART AND SCIENCE OF STICK FIGHTING

Solo Practice: Pivot at the wrist and strike with an overhead horizontal backhand snap strike. (1) Recoil into a second overhead horizontal snap strike to the opposite side. (2)

LEVEL 4: MIDDLE-RANGE OFFENSE 113

Striking a Target: To develop strong, fast helicopter strikes, practice to a partner's stick held vertically in front of him.

Strike the tip of his stick with the tip of yours.

At no time should you come close to hitting your partner's hands.

Even so, your partner might be wise to wear some protective hand gear, especially in the beginning levels of training. When you don't have a partner, you should practice by hitting a heavy bag or tire dummy.

With a Partner: One way to apply the helicopter strike is to leave your head exposed in order to draw a strike.

When your opponent takes the bait, block his strike with a number 1 overhead block.

Check his weapon hand, clearing the high line so you can pivot at the wrist and strike him with an overhead horizontal snap strike to the left temple.

Use the force of the impact to bounce into a second quick snap strike to the other side of his head. You often will be able to deliver this strike several times before your opponent can begin to counter you.

You can use helicopter strikes to specifically target the opponent's temples. The temple is one of the weakest parts of the skull and is easily broken. The inner surface of the temporal bone houses the branches of the middle meningeal artery and vein. If the bone is fractured, it could sever one of these vessels, causing bleeding between the brain and the skull. Depending on the strength of the strike, it can cause dizziness, unconsciousness, or, in some cases, death.

S Pattern

This pattern loosely resembles the letter *S*. The concept is simple but effective: draw the opponent's guard high with helicopter strikes, then suddenly switch levels and strike low. The secret to making this a fast and powerful combination lies in twisting your hips with each strike.

We've already learned how devastating the initial attacks to the temples can be. The final strike in this combination targets the opponent's diaphragm. Strike just under the rib cage on a slight upward angle to what most people would refer to as the solar plexus. However, this is technically incorrect, as the solar plexus, or celiac ganglia, is actually a meshwork of autonomic nerves located around the coeliac trunk that is well protected from any strike. When people say they got hit in the solar plexus, what they really mean to say is they were hit in the epigastric region, the area located just below the chest. This is a painful hit that can cause the diaphragm to spasm uncontrollably. Since your diaphragm controls your lungs, this can cause temporary difficulty breathing. Depending on the angle and power of the strike, injuries could also include bruised or broken ribs.

Solo Practice: Strike with an overhead horizontal backhand snap strike from right to left.

Pivot 360 degrees at the wrist into a second snap strike from left to right.

LEVEL 4: MIDDLE-RANGE OFFENSE

Finish with a number 5 right-to-left horizontal strike.

With a Partner: To apply the S combination, begin at middle range. Check the opponent's hand with your free hand as you deliver an overhead horizontal snap strike to the opponent's left temple.

Use the force of the impact to bounce into a second quick snap strike targeting the opponent's right temple.

Now that you have drawn the opponent's attention high,

Suddenly change levels and rip across his abdomen with a strong number 4 horizontal full strike. Generate power by pivoting your hips into the strike.

T Combo

The helicopter strikes can be an effective attack, but there will come a time when you will have to retreat to regroup. Keep your perspective; don't stay on the inside too long. Since stick fighting is a very demanding activity, if you have several rounds to fight, you will want to pace yourself. You can avoid burning out by momentarily retreating back outside the opponent's range. The T combination is a great way to cover your withdraw.

A good strategy is to close the gap to deliver an intensive burst of strikes on the inside, then get out on an angle quickly without being hit. Befuddle your opponent on the outside as you get a little breather before closing in for another middle-range combination. Changing the range like this allows you to control the fight by keeping your opponent guessing.

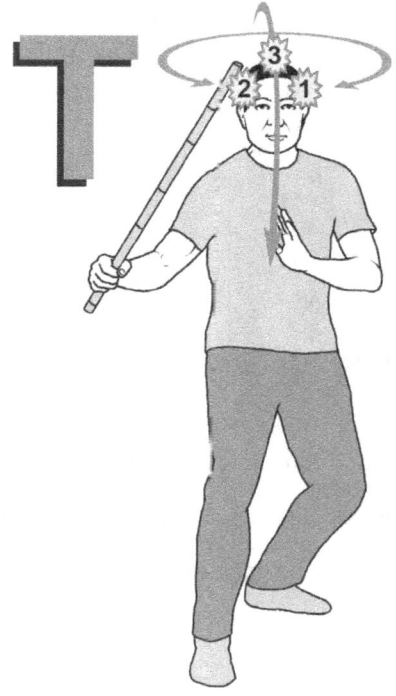

LEVEL 4: MIDDLE-RANGE OFFENSE 119

Solo Practice: Strike with an overhead horizontal backhand snap strike from right to left.

Pivot 360 degrees at the wrist into a second snap strike from left to right.

Finish with a number 7 vertical downward strike.

With a Partner: Begin the T combination at middle range, striking with a horizontal snap strike to the left temple,

Then bouncing into a second quick snap strike to the other side of his head.

You suddenly get a grip on his stick and hop backward, yanking it out of his hand. As you do, cover your exit with a number 7 vertical downward strike.

Light impact to the dome of the head, while painful, is usually not serious because the skull is made of hard, thick bone designed to protect the brain from injuries. However, a strong blow to the crown of the head can cause a concussion. A concussion occurs when the brain, which floats in cerebral fluid, bumps hard against the inside of the skull. This can result in the rupturing of blood vessels. The increased flow of blood to the bruise triggers a neurometabolic cascade that can cause dizziness, confusion, or even loss of consciousness. If the skull fractures, the bone could penetrate the brain, resulting in even more traumatic brain injury.

U Pattern

Another effective combination is the U. In this combination, you strike both high and low and to both sides of the body in quick succession.

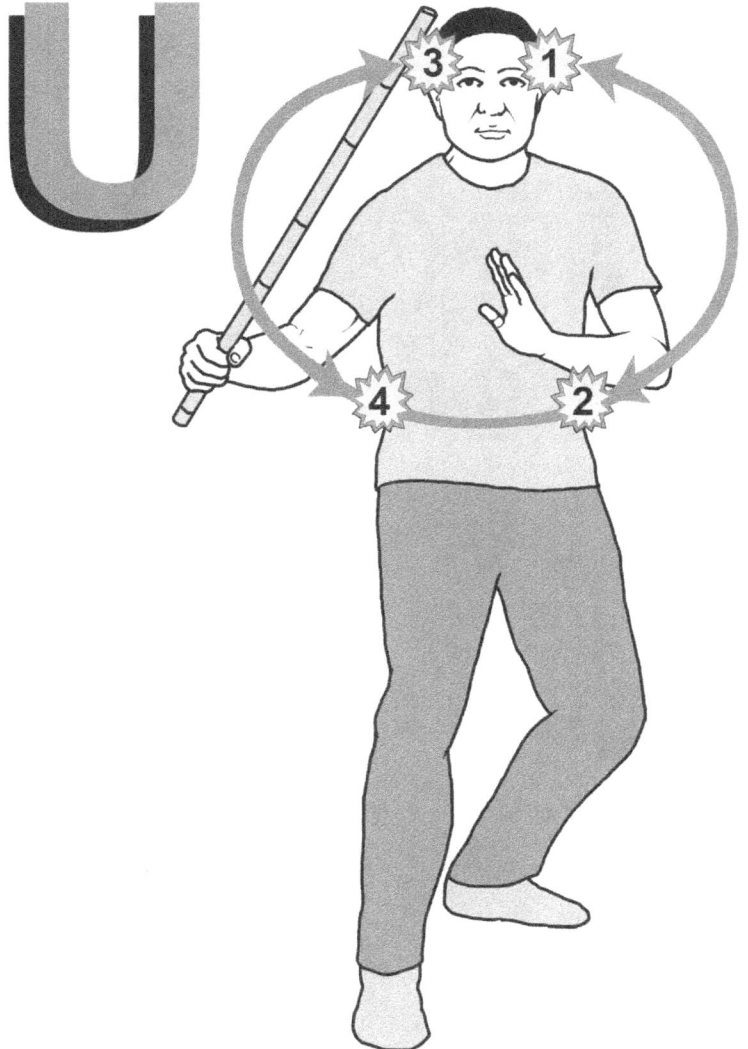

Again, you see that the targets are the temples (nervous system) and the epigastric region, specifically the diaphragm (respiratory system). The quick change of both level and angle of attack makes this a very difficult combination to defend against.

Solo Practice: Start with a high snap strike.

Flow smoothly into a number 4 right-to-left horizontal full strike.

Cut back with a high backhand snap strike to the opposite side.

Flow smoothly into another full strike, this time from left to right. Repeat the pattern, starting with another high snap strike.

LEVEL 4: MIDDLE-RANGE OFFENSE 123

With a Partner: Start with a high snap strike to the opponent's head.

Use the bounce from that strike to flow smoothly into a number 4 right-to-left horizontal full strike.

Flow into a high backhand snap strike to the other side of the opponent's head.

Again, use the recoil from the head shot to flow smoothly into another full strike, cutting across the opponent's abdomen, this time from left to right. Repeat the pattern, starting with another high snap strike.

W Pattern

The W is a subtle variation on the U pattern, but there are twice as many strikes, thus the name, *double-U*. The original W only had six strikes. Over the years, I've modified it slightly, adding two low strikes at 4 and 8.

Start with two high backhand snap strikes to the left side of your opponent's head (*1, 2*). Use the bounce from the second strike to flow smoothly into a #4 right to left horizontal full strike across the abdomen (*3*). As soon as your tip clears the opponent's torso, cut back and strike him on the other side of his body with a number 3 snap strike (*4*). Since this draws the opponent's attention down, flow into two high backhand snap strikes to the other side of the opponent's head (*5, 6*). Again, use the recoil from the second head shot to flow smoothly into another full strike, cutting across the opponent's abdomen, this time from left to right (*7*), before quickly reversing the direction of your stick to hit the opposite side of the opponent's body (*8*). Use the recoil from the impact to flow into another high backhand snap strike, beginning the pattern again (*1, 2*).

LEVEL 4: MIDDLE-RANGE OFFENSE   125

Training Equipment: Weighted Clubs

In Okinawa, karate masters traditionally practiced with heavy stones mounted on wooden handles called *chi ishi*, or strength stones. In India, wrestlers have a very long tradition of using weighted clubs called *gada* to develop good overall body strength. In Persia, they used large wooden clubs called *meels*. At the turn of the twentieth century, vaudeville strong men like Gus Hill made swinging Indian clubs very popular. Hill, who weighed only 150 pounds, would routinely challenge much larger men in the audience to match his feats with clubs weighing as much as 115 pounds! While still unconventional, weighted sticks of various sorts are popular training tools in many martial arts schools around the world, especially for stick fighters and swordsmen.

All sorts of weighted training tools are readily available online, including a variety of very nice clubs and mace bells made of wood or steel. These can get pretty heavy, but since building excessive muscle mass is not your goal for stick-fighting training, I recommend starting with very light weighted sticks. In fact, you can easily make your own! All you need is a stick, a soup can, and some quick-setting concrete. See the appendix at the end of this book for blueprints and more precise instructions on creating your own weighted sticks.

Weighted sticks provide excellent warm-up and conditioning for the fingers, wrists, arms, shoulders, and other related muscle groups. When used correctly, weighted sticks can be used to increase shoulder flexibility and mobility. You can use them singly or in pairs. Since there are many exercises one can do with them, I recommend watching some tutorial videos to help you understand how clubs are commonly and safely used. However, since your focus is on developing strength and speed for stick fighting, in practice be sure to start slowly and build up to include fighting techniques such as various figure eights, the nine basic strikes, the six-count flower, and various combinations such as the S, T, U, and W.

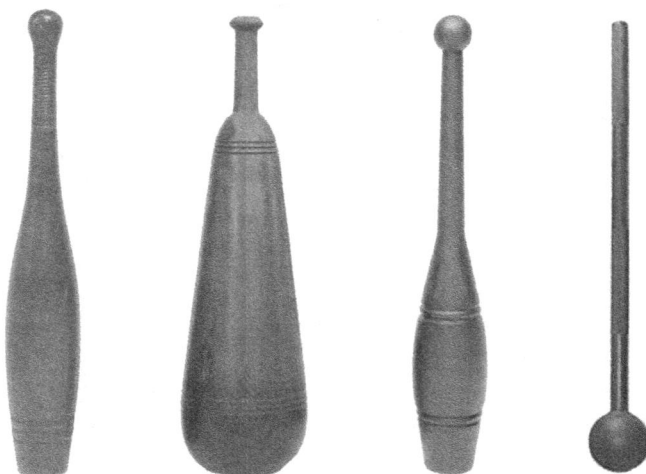

Constructing your own custom weighted sticks is simple and inexpensive. You'll need a clean, empty can and a short length of stick to act as a handle. Drive some screws or nails into one end of the handle to act as anchors, then put that end in the can. Fill the can with quick-setting concrete, making sure the handle is held straight until it sets. You might want to create a matched pair for double arm exercises. As your training progresses, you can create heavier weights by using larger cans or longer handles.

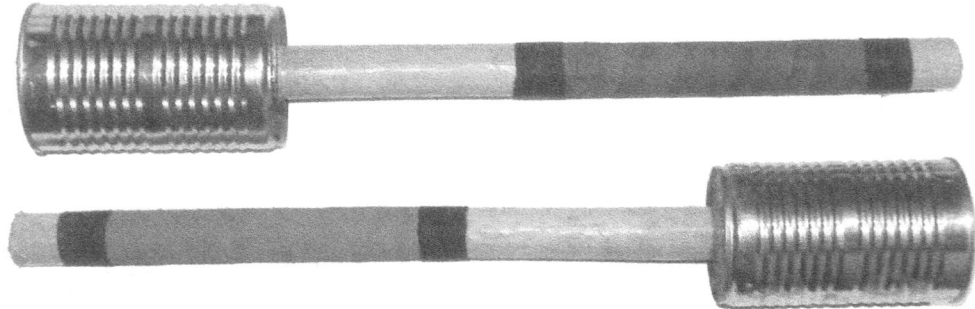

Ballistic exercise with weights creates great strain on your muscles, so always begin slowly with great care and control. Always start with light sticks and gradually work your way up to heavier ones. Since weighted sticks are heavier at the end, the farther down you grip the handle, the harder it will be to move the stick. Therefore, to make any exercise easier, simply choke up on the stick, moving your hand closer to the weighted end. As you warm up and feel ready to increase the challenge, slowly move your hand farther down the handle.

LEVEL 4: MIDDLE-RANGE OFFENSE

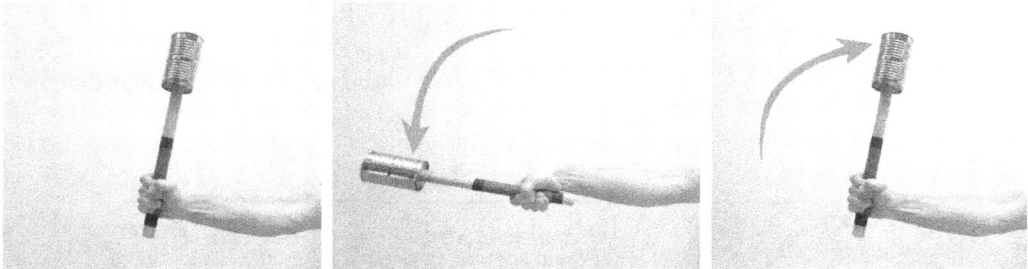

Start by simply extending and flexing your wrist.

When working with the weighted sticks, keep a stable stance with your feet about one shoulder width apart. Maintain a strong structure by bracing with your core and keeping your shoulders back and down. Keep a firm grip on the handle, but do not clench the handle too tightly. Your wrist should be relaxed but not limp. A good rule is to make sure you can do any motion well before you do it fast; perfect your form, then gradually add speed.

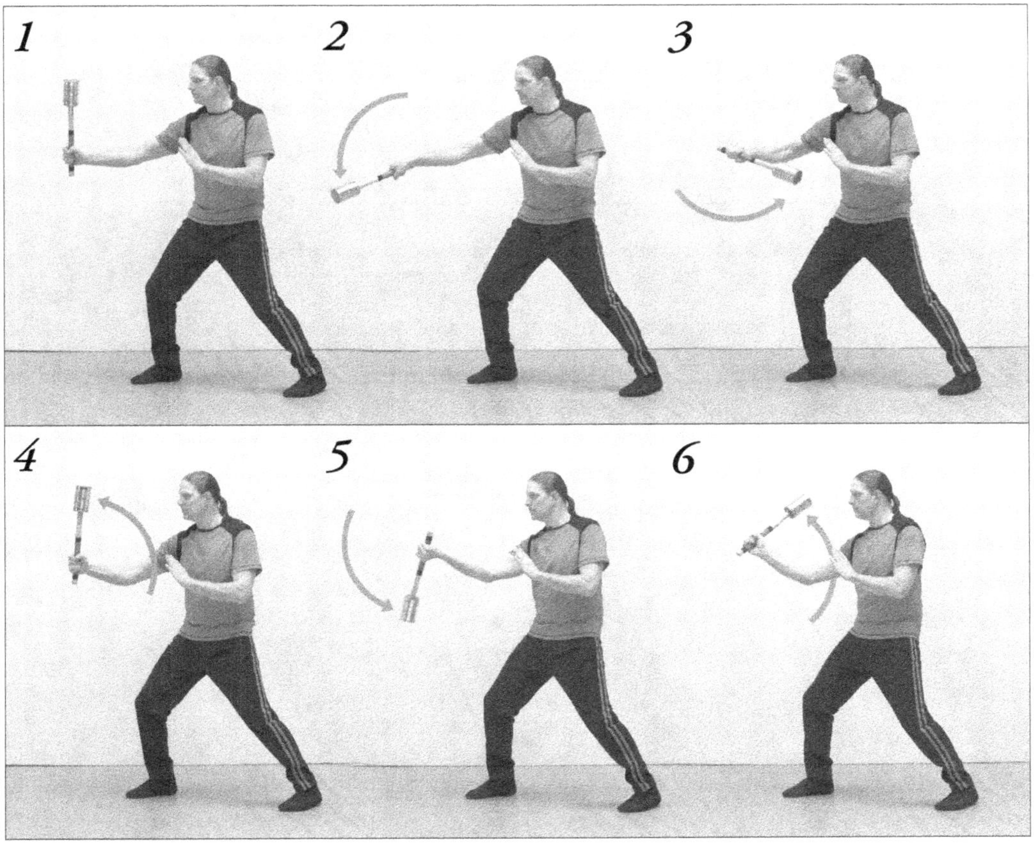

A simple figure eight performed with a weighted stick.

The Middle-Range Battle Plan

Let's look at how you can combine the various middle-range offensive and defensive strategies and tactics into an effective overall plan of attack.

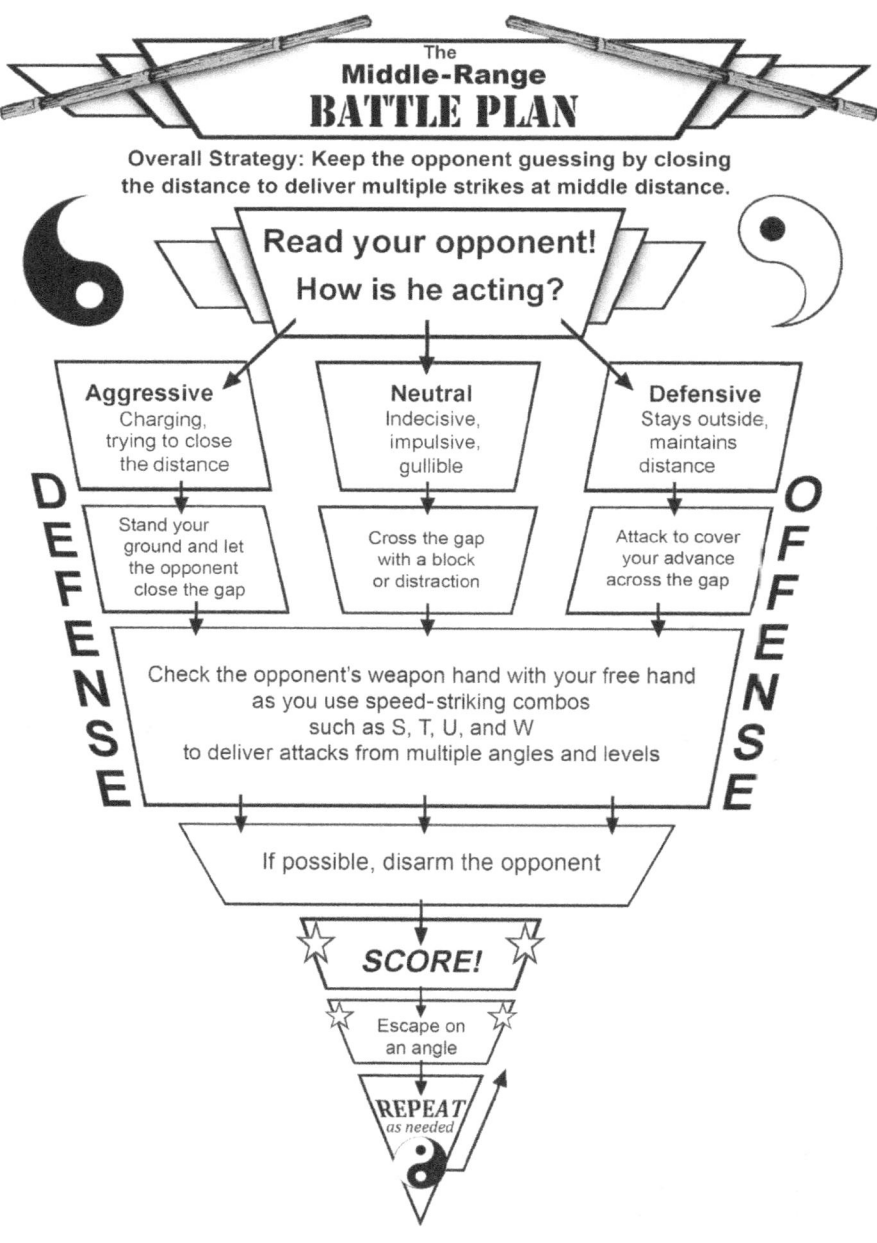

Level 4 Workout

Objective: This sixty-to-ninety-minute workout is designed to develop your middle-range offensive fighting skills.

1. Warm-Up: 15–20 Minutes. Start with some light stretching. See the guide at the beginning of this book for a sample stretching routine. Follow this with five to ten minutes of jumping rope. Do some light stretching until your heart rate returns to normal, then grab your stick and work through some basic combinations, including S, T, U, and W. Remember, you are still warming up, so work slowly and take this time to perfect your technique.

2. The Middle-Range Battle Plan: 15–25 Minutes. Stand across from your training partner, just outside his effective striking range. Practice offensively and defensively crossing the gap using different tactics. Each time you successfully enter, counter with various combinations on the inside before disarming your partner or exiting on an angle.

Again, resist the urge to start sparring. Keep things slow and controlled. Practice everything at half speed. Use this time to learn how to see, feel, and flow with the stick. Speed will come later of its own accord, and, when it does, your techniques will be fast without the appearance of being rushed. Even though you should both be moving slowly and with good control, it is recommended that you put on protective gear. At this point, gloves and a helmet should suffice.

If you don't have a partner, use your tire dummy or heavy bag as though it were an opponent and visualize his reactions as you practice.

3. Bag Work: 15–20 Minutes. You need to be able to deliver fast, debilitating combinations. Since you can't really hit your partner with full power, it is very important to regularly work the tire dummy or heavy bag. Rep all your combinations on the bag, working up to at least a minute each of S, T, U, and W. Finish with a round of freestyling where you just flow and mix all of your techniques together.

The forces generated by hitting the bag cause your stick to rub against your hand. Be on the lookout for blisters! Once you feel a blister starting to form, stop and let it heal. If you continue and it rips open, it will take much longer to heal and have a greater impact on your training.

4. Strength Training: 10–15 Minutes. Pick up your weighted sticks and work through the same basic movements you warmed up with earlier (figure eights, flowers, and combos). Begin slowly and move with careful control. Always start choked up on the stick, with your hand close to the weight. As you feel ready to increase your challenge, slowly move your hand farther down the handle to increase the resistance.

5. Cooldown: 5–10 Minutes. Take a few minutes to take your body from fight-or-flight into rest-and-digest. Now is the time to use static stretching to increase your flexibility and break up the lactic acid that has accumulated in your muscles.

Follow-Up: Don't forget to record each of your workouts in your training log. Keep pushing yourself by setting new goals. Use these goals to stay motivated and to keep your training fresh and exciting.

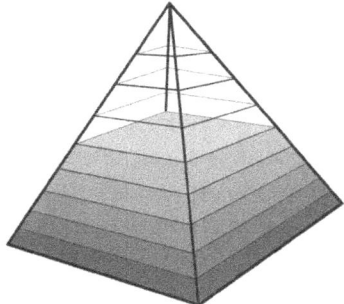

LEVEL 5
Middle-Range Defense

Checking

An important part of middle-range fighting is to monitor and manipulate the opponent's weapon hand with your free hand. This is done at the same time that your other hand is striking. Checking is very similar to chi sao, or "sticky hand," exercises common to some kung fu styles such as wing chun. The idea is to stick to the opponent's weapon hand in order to weaken or even neutralize his attacks. This is accomplished through a variety of movements that include checks, parries, holds, taps, locks, scoops, pushes, presses, pulls, and sweeps. Regardless of which action you choose to employ, they all require that you maintain some sort of cohesion with the opponent's weapon arm.

Some of the different positions encountered when practicing the sticky hand checking drill.

The sticky hand checking drill is used to practice using your off hand effectively. Square up across from a partner and lightly touch his weapon hand. As your opponent slowly moves to strike you, maintain that contact and gently but firmly check or redirect his strike. Focus on controlling your partner's weapon hand as opposed to his wrist or forearm, as this usually provides the greatest degree of control, although there will be times when you will check or manipulate farther up the arm.

Blocking and Parrying

While avoiding the opponent's strike is the best way of not getting hit by your opponent's weapon, this is not always a viable option. Blocking is a defensive maneuver that impedes or stops the forward momentum of your opponent's weapon. On the other hand, parrying is the action of redirecting the momentum of the opponent's stick in such a way that it does not hit you without bringing the opponent's weapon to a stop.

Blocking and parrying are skills that must be learned and practiced if you are ever to employ them effectively during a fight. The following progression—static blocking, jamming, and dynamic blocking—is designed to help you become comfortable with and competent in blocking the opponent's weapon.

Static Blocking

Static blocking occurs in the opponent's strike zone. When someone swings a stick at you, your body's natural reaction is to move to defend yourself. The ability to stay calm in a stick fight begins with learning to control this instinctive flinch response. While moving is usually preferable, static blocking teaches you to stand your ground and "take the shot" using minimal footwork and staying in your partner's strike zone. The idea is to become so confident in your blocking that you no longer panic when an opponent swings at you. This allows you the calmness of mind to read the opponent's intentions and respond appropriately.

Practice static blocking until you can calmly observe your opponent while he is swinging at you. Watch for telegraphing movements that first tell you what side he will be striking from, and then at what level. If the opponent starts from a closed position, you know he is chambered for a backhand strike, whereas an opponent with his arm held so that his body is open is in a position to deliver a forehand strike. Other clues, such as the level of the weapon and where the opponent's eyes are directed, can tell you what level he is intending to attack. Use this information to set up a block before he can get to the target. After you block, you can practice adding a counterattack, but always make sure the blocking maneuver takes priority.

When you can stand still and block without flinching, it is time to add proper footwork. If the attacker chambers for a forehand strike, circle into his left side with your right foot. If the opponent is chambered for a backhand strike, angle into your left with your left foot. As you angle into the opponent, keep your centerline aligned with the line of combat. This allows you to use both your weapon and your free hand to neutralize the attack. If possible, use your free hand to turn your opponent's center away from you so he won't be able to strike you again.

High-level block against a number 1 high downward diagonal forehand strike.

High-level block against a number 2 high backhand strike.

Middle-level block against a number 3 middle-level forehand strike.

Middle-level block against a number 4 middle-level backhand strike.

Low-level block against a low-level forehand strike.

Low-level block against a low-level backhand strike.

 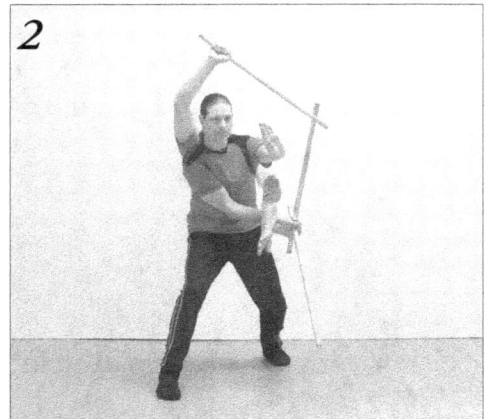

These six basic blocks can cover your whole body on both sides from head to foot.

When you first make contact with the opponent's stick, block hand to hand and stick to stick. Intercept the opponent's stick with the middle of your stick on a perpendicular angle to absorb the energy of his strike and bring his stick to a complete stop. This also maximizes your blocking surface, giving you a higher chance of success in blocking his attack. Keep your blocking movements small and economical. If your tip is facing up when the opponent strikes, keep it up as you block, and vice versa. Attempting to switch from a tip-up to a tip-down position midblock leaves you momentarily exposed and unable to block at all.

At the same time you are blocking the opponent's stick, use your empty hand to check his weapon hand. It is difficult to check the opponent's weapon with an overly tense arm. Your checking hand must be relaxed and responsive to his motions. Avoid grasping the opponent's wrist. Rather, stick to his hand, checking his weapon with soft but firm motions that prevent him from obtaining a clear line of attack.

In practice, your partner should swing at a speed that allows you to achieve an 80 percent success rate for optimal learning. When you succeed consistently less than that, you get discouraged and learning slows down. If you succeed more than that, you don't learn as much because you are not being adequately challenged. Therefore your partner should strive to attack at a rate where you get hit about one time in five. Sometimes it will be more, and sometimes less, but this would be a good proportion to encourage personal growth. Practice solo in front of a mirror to observe your movement and perfect your positioning.

You can alternate striking and blocking with your partner. Begin with high strikes and high blocks, continue with midlevel strikes and middle blocks, and finish with low strikes and low blocks before starting again from the top. One partner strikes while the other blocks and then strikes back at the same level, allowing both partners to attack and defend. Add some simple movement, stepping around in a circular pattern as you strike and block. Remember to always check the opponent's weapon hand with your guarding hand. Try different variations on this drill by changing the order of the blocks.

LEVEL 5: MIDDLE-RANGE DEFENSE 139

The Basic Blocking Drill: high (1&2), middle level (3&4), and low (5&6).

Practice the basic blocking drill until you can calmly observe the opponent's movements and quickly identify what side he will be striking from, and at what level. Once you can comfortably stand your ground and not flinch when your partner swings at you, you will begin to move with more strength and confidence. Then it is time to move on to jamming and dynamic blocking.

Jamming

Block as you did in the basic, static blocking drill, but add a step. Move in to jam the strike in the acceleration zone, before it reaches full speed. Strive to strike the opponent's hand with your block while you use your empty hand to check the opponent's arm or attack his face.

The Basic Jamming Drill: high (1&2), middle level (3&4), and low (5&6). Notice that the block is now focused on the opponent's hand rather than his stick.

Dynamic Blocking

Ideally, you want to avoid as much of the opponent's striking power as possible. Dynamic blocking uses circling footwork to avoid the opponent's attack by moving you into the deceleration zone, where his strike has begun to slow down. The free end of your stick neutralizes the incoming attack with a short but powerful "pulse strike." Establish contact between your checking hand and the opponent's weapon hand as soon as possible and maintain cohesion to control his weapon. Immediately follow up with a decisive combination of techniques.

Dynamic Blocking: As the opponent chambers to strike, prepare to move off-line.

As you move off line, block the opponent's strike, but since you are moving out of range, do not check his hand.

As the opponent's weapon clears your stick, counterattack to his head.

Dynamic blocking is much like parrying, in that the opponent's stick is not stopped but rather intercepted and redirected off its intended line of attack while the strike's momentum carries it through. The difference is that when blocking, your stick is in front of the opponent's weapon, but when parrying, your stick redirects the opponent's weapon from the side or back.

The overhead block used in crossing the gap is actually somewhere between a block and a parry. Sometimes the opponent's weapon hits nearly perpendicular to your stick. In such a case the incoming force is brought almost to a complete stop. If the opponent's stick hits your stick at a greater angle, it tends to glance off and be safely redirected to the side. Because the opponent's weapon keeps moving, the technique is a parry, not a textbook example of a block.

Parrying

A parry redirects the opponent's weapon without stopping it. Parries are exceptionally useful against thrusting attacks. However, whenever you hold the tip of your stick low, you expose your high line and will be tempted to parry your opponent's incoming thrust upward from below. This can result in the unfortunate possibility of parrying a thrust to your midsection up and into your own face. It is much safer to parry to the sides, which allows you to redirect the strike clear of your body with the smallest motion, since your body is taller than it is wide. Of the sides, it is safer to parry to your right against a right-handed opponent, because this takes away the opponent's effective use of his guarding hand.

Backhand Parry: Begin from a closed guard.

As the opponent swings, lean back slightly and move to intercept his strike.

Make cohesion at the earliest opportunity in order to redirect his strike.

Do not overcommit to your parry. Stop as soon as his strike has cleared its intended target.

LEVEL 5: MIDDLE-RANGE DEFENSE

Take advantage of the fact that he is out of position and cut back along the open line of combat.

Complete the combination with a strike to his face with the tip of your stick.

Tres-Tres

This drill makes a nice culminating activity for this section on blocking. It is a version (of which there are many) of an eskrima drill commonly referred to as tres-tres, or three-three, since there are three moves that repeat themselves on each side. The drill is said to have been adapted from a Spanish sword-fighting exercise. It teaches three blocks followed by three very effective counterattacks. There are many ways to do tres-tres; this version is adapted for middle range.

As always, your free hand should check and control your partner's weapon hand whenever possible. If you were to use your checking hand on any of your blocks to hook, grab, trap, or otherwise impede your partner's blocking motion for even a split second, he would be unable to defend against your counterattack. Therefore, although the drill consists of many blocks and strikes repeated over and over again, the application of these moves in a "real" situation would consist merely of one block and one counter, or many counters, depending on the situation.

Additionally, tres-tres helps you develop effective footwork and body movement. Stand at maximum fighting range. When you are defending, shift back into a cat stance to block before lunging forward with your counterattack. Remember to always push off with the ball of the front foot, not your heel. Strongly contract your adductors (inner thigh muscles) to pull your front foot back into a stable cat stance. The moves should flow smoothly from one into the next. With practice, your speed and timing will improve.

Perform a right-to-left low block in cat stance. Your stick is held vertically, with your thumb down and palm facing outward (toward the opponent), as though you were blocking a strike to your right leg. Simultaneously check the opponent's weapon hand with your free hand, left arm under right, thumb pointing down (figure 1 in the accompanying figure).

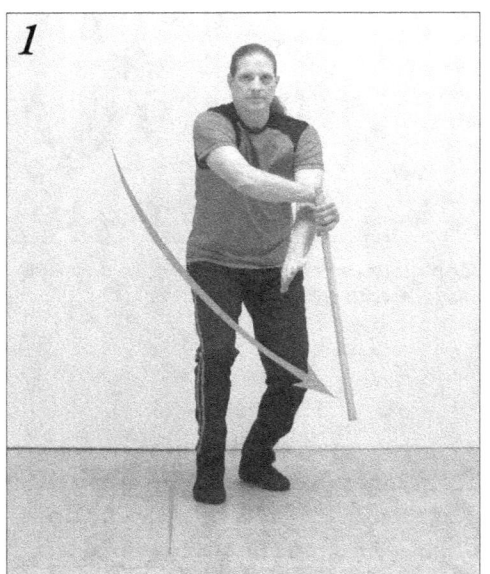

Step forward into a right lunge stance as you rotate your weapon hand in a clockwise circle, striking to the opponent's lead shoulder. It is important to move from the wrist and not from the elbow. Your free hand should be in a guarding position in the center of your chest (figure 2).

Withdraw your right foot into a right cat stance as you perform a high roof block with the stick held over your head with the tip angled downward slightly. Simultaneously check the opponent's weapon hand with your free hand (figure 3).

Step forward into a right lunge stance with a low number 1 strike from right to left, aiming for the opponent's lead knee. Do not strike through the target. Rather, stop as soon as you sense that your opponent has successfully blocked your strike. Your free hand should be in a guarding position in the center of your chest (figure 4).

Push off with the ball of the front foot and contract you adductors to withdraw your right foot into a right cat stance as you perform a middle-level wing block with the stick held over your right (lead) shoulder with the tip angled slightly downward. Simultaneously check the opponent's weapon hand with your free hand (figure 5).

Step forward into a right lunge stance with a number 7 strike vertically downward to the opponent's head. Your free hand should be in a guarding position in the center of your chest (figure 6).

You have now completed one revolution of the drill. Start over again and repeat. The pattern repeats low, middle, high and attack, defend, attack. Practicing the drill over and over again allows you to do massive repetitions of the strikes and blocks, as well as quick lunging and retreating footwork. As your skill with the drill increases, include different footwork like circling and experiment with changing the range, flowing from close through middle to long and back again. Your ultimate goal is to be able to apply these blocks and counters in a free-fighting situation.

A: Attack with a low number 1 downward diagonal strike to the inside of B's lead knee.
B: Defend low with a right-to-left inverted block, leading with the knuckles.

B: Attack middle with a vertical downward snap strike to the right shoulder.
A: Defend by withdrawing to an inverted block over your right shoulder, commonly called a wing block.

A: Attack high with a number 7 vertical downward strike to B's head.
B: Defend high with a roof block, tip over your left shoulder. Reverse roles and repeat.

B: Attack low with a number 1 downward diagonal strike to the inside of B's lead knee.
A: Defend low with a right-to-left inverted block, palm facing out.

LEVEL 5: MIDDLE-RANGE DEFENSE 147

A: Attack middle with a vertical downward snap strike to the right shoulder.
B: Defend middle by withdrawing to a right wing block.

B: Attack high with a number 7 vertical downward strike to B's head.
A: Defend high with a roof block, tip over your left shoulder. Reverse and repeat.

Middle-Range Disarms

Middle-range disarms differ from long-range disarms because you can grasp the opponent's stick with your free hand. A good opportunity to grab the opponent's stick to disarm him comes immediately following a block, before your opponent can retract his strike. Technically, to strip the weapon, all you must do is overcome the coefficient of friction between his hand and the stick, but practically, this takes good timing and a basic understanding of how to disarm your opponent.

The Lever

You can initiate a lever disarm from any checking motion that gives you cohesion with the opponent's weapon hand. From this position, grasp and twist the opponent's stick sharply down along the back of his hand. This single-handed disarm breaks the opponent's grip by forcing his stick through weakest part of his hand, the gap between his thumb and forefinger.

Strike-Assisted Lever: Use a roof block to counter your opponent's number 1 strike aimed at your head.

Quickly grab your opponent's stick and twist it so the tip points downward. For maximum control, grab it close to your opponent's hand.

The lever disarm can be assisted with a strike to the opponent's weapon hand with either the butt or the tip of your stick to encourage him to release his grip.

This helps twist his wrist and force the stick out of his hand.

LEVEL 5: MIDDLE-RANGE DEFENSE

Punch-Assisted Lever: Block an incoming number 4 horizontal strike with a tip-up block.

Grasp the opponent's stick and twist counterclockwise away from you as you place the knuckles of your weapon hand firmly against the back of your opponent's weapon hand.

Assist the lever disarm with a punch to the back of his weapon hand with your weapon hand.

This helps twist his wrist and force the stick out of his hand.

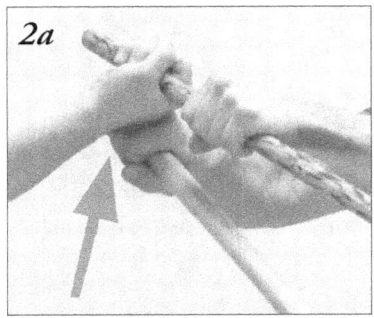
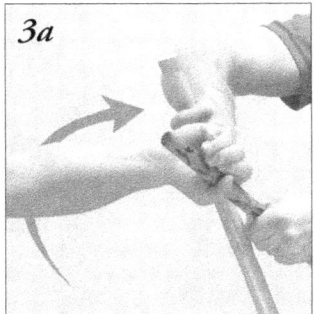
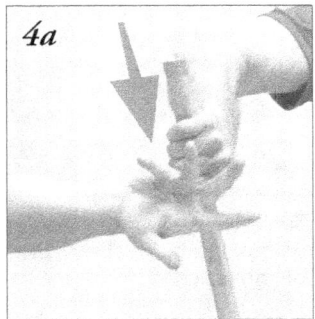

The Hook

A hooking disarm strips the opponent's weapon using the butt end of your stick to pry his stick out of his hand.

Hooking Disarm: Block and catch the opponent's stick.

Bring your hand up and hook his wrist with the butt end of your stick Full-contact application includes striking the opponent's hand with your hook, but be very careful not to hurt your partner's wrist during training. The impact helps to break his structure and overcome any muscular resistance he may use to resist your disarm attempt.

Simultaneously attack the opponent's head with a number 4 strike, hitting with the tip of your stick.

Turn your body to complete the disarm.

If your initial disarm attempt is unsuccessful but you still have his stick in your hand, don't let go! Hit him with your stick while his weapon is immobilized, or better yet, take advantage of the opportunity to quickly attempt another disarm.

The Snake

The snake, also known as the vine, is performed by wrapping your arm around your opponent's arm, then twisting sharply to break his grip on his stick.

The Snake: Begin from a checked position.

Flow your hand over the top of the opponent's weapon hand.

Continue to flow under his arm.

As you complete the entwining of his arm, his stick should be funneled into a trap under your arm. Do not trap the opponent's hand against your body; his hand must lie in the crook of your arm with the stick trapped against your body.

Twist your body sharply to the outside.

Pry the stick out of his hand.

In 2015 I was fighting in the Doce Pares World Championships in New York City when I went for a snake disarm. However, because of the bulky vests and general chaos of the fight, when I snaked around my opponent's arm, I could not tell that I had actually trapped his hand against my body. I stepped back and twisted sharply, but instead of taking my opponent's stick, I accidentally threw him headfirst all the way across the ring. To my great relief and my opponent's credit, despite being in full armor, he did a beautiful shoulder roll and bounced right back up for more. The judges, however, were less than happy with me, as takedowns were explicitly against the rules (I got a stern warning, but I'm happy to say I still won the fight).

LEVEL 5: MIDDLE-RANGE DEFENSE

The Pop

Popping is the act of using a sharp force to dislodge the opponent's stick from his grip. Secure the opponent's stick by grabbing it with your free hand, then strike his arm to dislodge the stick from his grip. Conversely, you could grasp the opponent's arm and perform the pop against the stick to knock it from his grasp.

Pop: You and the opponent are checking each other's strikes.

Grasp the opponent's stick with your free hand.

Strike upward from below with your right forearm, popping the opponent's stick from his grip.

Level 5 Workout

Objective: This sixty-to-ninety-minute workout will develop your middle-range defensive techniques, including checking, blocking, and disarming.

1. Warm-Up: 15–20 Minutes. Start with some light stretching. See the guide at the beginning of this book for a sample stretching routine. Follow this with five to ten minutes of jumping rope. Do some light stretching until your heart rate returns to normal, then grab your stick and work through some basic movements. Remember, you are still warming up, so work slowly and take this time to perfect your technique.

2. Cohesion Drills: 10–15 Minutes. Stand at middle range across from your partner, with your free hands touching each other's weapon hands. Strike slowly from all angles and levels while simultaneously checking your partner's stick, preventing him from striking you. All the while, your partner does the same to you. This is *not* a sparring drill! It is a sensitivity drill, so it is important that you both continue to move slowly with good control and little or no force behind your strikes.

3. Disarms: 10–15 Minutes. From the cohesion drill, practice disarming your partner using the lever, hook, snake, and pop.

4. Blocking and Striking: 10–15 Minutes. Use the static blocking drill, alternating striking and blocking with your partner. This will warm up your mind and body to the reality of someone swinging a stick at you.

5. Tres-Tres: 10–15 Minutes. Practice the more dynamic tres-tres drill to warm up your footwork and stances.

6. Cooldown: 5–10 Minutes. Take a few minutes to take your body from fight-or-flight into rest-and-digest. Now is the time to use static stretching to increase your flexibility and break up the lactic acid that has accumulated in your muscles.

Solo Training: If you don't happen to have a training partner, train on your own! Of course, you will have to modify the drills. Shadowbox or use a tire dummy, perhaps equipped with its own stick.

Follow-Up: Don't forget to record each of your workouts in your training log. If you still haven't started one, what are you waiting for? Include how long each training session lasts, as well as a short summary of what you did. Keep pushing yourself by setting new goals. Use these goals to stay motivated and to keep your training fresh and exciting.

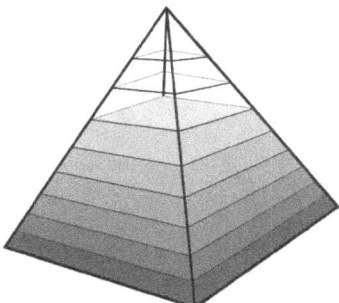

LEVEL 6
Close Range

Infighting

Long range is the distance at which you can touch your opponent with the tip of your weapon. Middle range is the distance at which you can touch the opponent's hand with your free hand. Close range is the distance at which you can touch the opponent's body with the butt end of your weapon. There are specific tactics that should be employed when you are within arm's reach of your opponent that differ from those used at other ranges.

Punching

Perhaps the most often overlooked technique at close quarters is punching with the clenched fist. Do not become preoccupied with employing your stick when you have better tools available. If you have training in any striking arts, now is the time to employ it. Momentarily disregard the weapon in your hand and punch. Close-quarters weapons also include your elbows, knees, feet, and even head.

Pass and Punch: Your opponent is checking your weapon hand.

Hook the butt of your stick inside his wrist.

Pull his hand down and back to clear the line of combat.

Punch forward with a punch such as a boxing cross or karate reverse punch.

Butt Strikes

Butt strikes are delivered with the short end of your stick and are ideal for close-range infighting, especially when the weapon is being held in only one hand. Striking with the butt of the stick is a natural motion, like hitting with a hammer but with your forearm as the handle. The result is a powerful strike that is further amplified by being concentrated into the very small striking surface on the end of the stick.

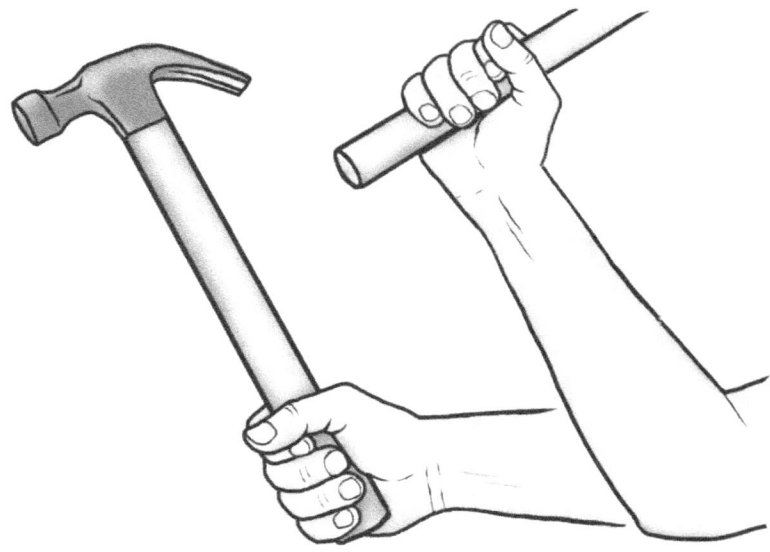

When fighting on the inside, your motions are usually restricted by limited space, making it more difficult to generate speed and power. Therefore, although you may be able to deliver full strikes with the edge of your stick, they will be relatively weak. Using a snap strike to arc the tip of your stick into the target can be a faster and more effective way to strike, but when you get too close to the opponent, it becomes harder to manipulate the stick and strike with focused accuracy. You can also thrust with the tip of your stick at close range, but you will need to draw your hand back to align the tip of the stick with the target, and when you do, you are vulnerable. Therefore, these strikes are also best delivered at middle range.

You can double your striking potential by following butt strikes with tip strikes. The initial butt strike will often result in recoil that gives you enough space to follow through with a strike with the shaft or tip of the weapon.

Butt Strike with Tip Follow-Through: The opponent is checking your weapon hand.

Hook inside and yank his checking hand sharply downward to open the line of combat.

Drive the butt of your stick forward into the opponent's neck and jaw area.

Follow up with a tip strike to the exposed pocket of the neck.

Hubud

Hubud is a versatile sensitivity drill that teaches checking and parrying for close-range fighting. The name hubud (pronounced "hoo-bud") is actually short for *hubud-lubud*, Pilipino for "tie-untie" or "tangle-untangle." The drill teaches you how to intercept and redirect an incoming attack, then stay connected to your opponent in order to control him while placing yourself in an advantageous position.

The basic drill is performed with a partner and consists of just four repetitive motions. The drill begins with one partner attacking the other with a number 3 horizontal forehand strike to the neck at close range. The defending partner makes a blocking or parrying maneuver that guides the opponent's stick past its intended target. Once his stick has crossed the centerline, control of the opponent's weapon hand is then passed to the defender's other hand. The first hand then reconnects to check the weapon arm, freeing the second hand to counterattack. This process of connecting and disconnecting continues until the drill stops, usually when one partner applies a decisive technique.

Hubud can be performed using the same concept against butt strikes coming from many different angles, including the horizontal forehand (described here), vertical, horizontal backhand, and straight punch. There are even low versions of the drill.

Hubud-Lubud: Two partners face each other.

Partner A throws a right horizontal butt strike; partner B turns in toward the technique with a left block with the elbow kept down.

LEVEL 6: CLOSE-RANGE 159

Without breaking the momentum of the initial attack, partner B's right hand parries the blow over his head as his shoulders turn square to the front.

Partner B then checks the opponent's arm as his body finishes turning to the right.

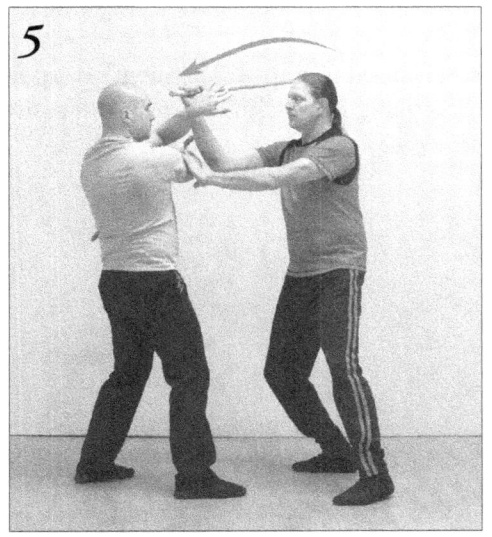

Partner B then begins the sequence again with a right horizontal butt strike of his own, and the drill repeats with partner A blocking the attack.

Partner A's right hand parries the blow over his head.

Partner A then checks the opponent's arm.   Partner A then begins the sequence again.

A-Frame Lock

The hubud drill acts as a framework for practicing all sorts of strikes, traps, locks, and disarms.

The A-frame lock is a simple technique that can be used to trap an opponent's weapon arm. Take care not to use too much force when practicing this technique, as it can easily injure your opponent's shoulder.

LEVEL 6: CLOSE-RANGE

A-Frame Lock: The A-frame is an arm lock that can be applied off the first move of hubud, a number 1 downward diagonal strike with the butt of the stick.

Block the attack with a high block.

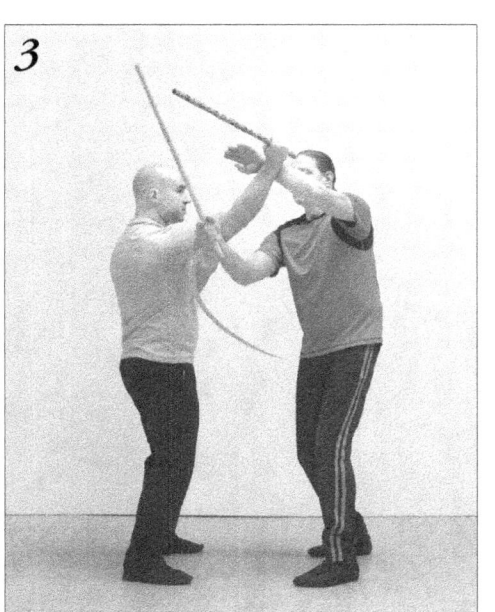

Bring your stick up and behind the opponent's arm.

Connect your weapon hand and free hand.

Lever the opponent's arm back and downward, maintaining a 90-degree angle at the opponent's elbow for maximum effect.

Strike to the opponent's face with your stick as you lever backward on his arm. Cranking hard on the opponent's arm can result in a rotator cuff injury, takedown, or both.

LEVEL 6: CLOSE-RANGE   163

Arm Press: Parry the opponent's butt strike with the first two moves of the hubud drill.

Use the butt of your stick to hook the opponent's wrist and pull it down to your right; your left hand helps by grasping the opponent's wrist.

Press your left elbow against your opponent's extended arm.

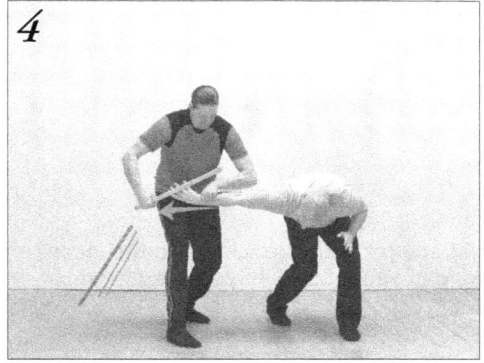

Hook the opponent's stick and yank back sharply to knock the stick from his grasp.

Arm Press

Whereas the A-frame depends on catching the opponent's swing early, the arm press locks his arm after you have parried his strike over your head. Pull on the opponent's wrist to straighten his arm, then press on the back of his elbow with your elbow.

Takedowns

Hubud also offers several opportunities to take your opponent to the ground. This could be accomplished with a foot sweep, a hip toss, or, in this case, a neck press.

Neck Press Takedown: The opponent attacks at close range.

Parry the strike with the first two moves of hubud.

As you parry the attack, grasp the loose end of your stick with your free hand.

Press down into the pocket of the opponent's neck with the middle of your stick.

The opponent's adverse, defensive reaction to this pressure should disrupt his structure enough to allow you to drive him to the ground.

Check the opponent's legs with your free hand to keep him from kicking you as you position yourself to follow up as needed.

Hooking

At close range, you can use the tail end of your stick to hook and crush an opponent's arm, or even his lower leg.

Forearm Hook: This technique requires that you walk your hand up the stick to increase the length of the butt end.

Use this extended tail to hook the opponent's arm.

As soon as you have hooked the appendage, quickly grab the bottom of your stick from underneath with your free hand and squeeze the shaft tightly against the bony ridge that runs along the edge of your right forearm, pinching the opponent's limb in between.

To protect yourself from strikes from the opponent's free hand, tuck your head and turn away from his strikes as you apply pressure to the lock.

Once you have disrupted the opponent's structure, twist to your left to take him to the ground.

Double-End Grip

At close range a double-end grip can be very effective, as it allows you to butt strike or hook with either end while also using the center section to strike. When fighting with your stick in double-end grip, grasp each end of your stick in a natural grip, wrapping your fingers firmly around the stick.

Cross-Check

In the sport of ice hockey, cross-checking is defined as "the action of using the shaft of the stick between the two hands to forcefully check an opponent," and it is illegal because of the high risk of injury. Considering hockey's reputation for gratuitous violence, that is saying quite a bit, so use caution when practicing these techniques.

Cross-Check: Hold your stick in two hands, with one on either end. Draw a strike by lowering your guard, leaving your head exposed.

When the opponent goes to strike, step forward to close the gap as you cross-check him by punching with both hands simultaneously, driving the middle of your stick forward across his high line.

LEVEL 6: CLOSE-RANGE 167

Block and Slide: Begin at middle range, baiting the opponent by exposing your head.

As he attacks with a number 7 downward vertical strike to your head, grasp the free end of your stick with your free hand and block.

If you find you are initially out of reach to strike the opponent's weapon hand directly, maintain forward pressure on his stick and slide down along the shaft of his weapon, driving the middle of your stick sharply into his weapon hand.

Follow up with a butt strike to his face.

Double-End Hooking Disarms

The double-end grip allows you to use either end of your stick to hook the opponent's stick or arm to disarm him.

Double-End Hooking Disarm: Begin at middle range, holding your stick in both hands. Draw a strike by leaving your head exposed.

When the opponent strikes, block upward and forward.

Continue checking the opponent's stick as you slip your right hand over his wrist.

Sweep your right hand down and hook the opponent's weapon hand with the butt of your stick; pull his stick toward you, pinning it against your body.

Step back and twist your body sharply into the hook to complete the disarm.

LEVEL 6: CLOSE-RANGE 169

Cross-Check and Arm Lock: You can use the cross-check to block an attack starting at middle range.

As the opponent attacks, grasp the free end of your stick with your free hand and strike sharply to his weapon hand with the intent of smashing it.

You can then follow up with a butt strike to the head.

Hook inside the opponent's elbow as you continue checking his weapon.

Keep his elbow at a right angle as you bring your right hand down to lock his arm.

Snap your right hand down and forward against the butt of his stick to disarm him.

Double Leg Reap: This technique is an excellent method of quickly taking an opponent to the ground. Starting at long range, bait the opponent by exposing your head.

Cross the gap with an overhead roof block to protect from the attack.

Parry his strike to your right with your free hand as you swing your stick behind his knees.

Duck your head toward the opponent's right hip as you snap the tip of your stick around the opponent's legs at the knees and grab the free end of your stick with your free hand. Pull back and upward as you drive your shoulder into the opponent's abdomen, knocking him to the ground.

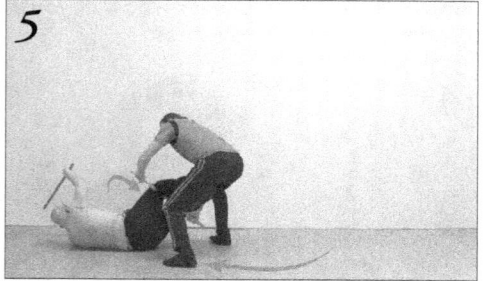

From here you can use your stick to turn the opponent over onto his stomach.

Pin him with your knees so he can't turn back toward you, allowing you to free your weapon to continue attacking if needed.

Chokes

Like disarms, chokes are usually incidental. That is, you don't start out the fight planning to apply a choke, but in the course of fighting you may find yourself in a position to apply one, so it is important to have them in your arsenal.

Be very careful using chokes. This cannot be stressed enough. Some chokes concentrate extreme pressure into the very end of your stick, while others use the shaft to squeeze an opponent's neck. Either technique is capable of crushing an opponent's windpipe, and, as if the initial injury were not severe enough, swelling of the throat could further inhibit breathing, leading to serious injury or death.

Fang Choke

At close range it is generally easier to manipulate the shorter end of your stick into position for a choke than the long end, which is more easily grabbed by the opponent. Choking with the butt of your stick is commonly referred to as a fang choke.

Fang Choke: Leave an opening to draw an attack.

The opponent throws a right strike.

Use the first two moves of hubud to parry the blow over your head.

Assist his momentum by pushing with your left hand against his right shoulder to turn him to his left as you move the butt of your stick toward his neck.

As you move behind the opponent, turn your weapon hand palm up and drive the butt of your stick into his throat.

Use your left hand to assist the choke. Pin the opponent between your body and your stick as you pull back firmly with both hands.

Cross Choke

The cross choke is like the fang choke, but instead of pressing the butt end of the stick into the opponent's throat, you are instead using the shaft to compress the neck.

It should be noted that it is difficult to apply rear chokes on someone who is much taller than you. But fear not, a sharp stomp to the back of the knee can quickly bring a taller opponent down to size.

Fang Choke to Cross Choke: The opponent counters by pushing your hand to relieve the pressure on his throat.

Release your left hand and grasp the free end of your stick.

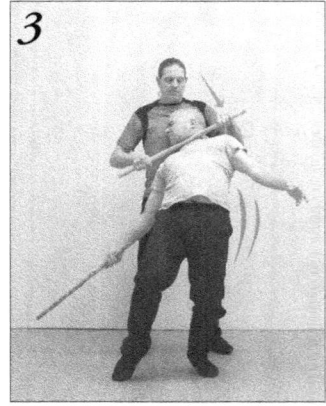

Withdraw your hand to your left shoulder to place the shaft across the opponent's throat as you pull back firmly with both hands.

Neck Hook

The neck hook is a devastatingly effective choke that is so painful it can bring even the strongest opponent to his knees. Applied to the sides of your opponent's neck, it is a vascular choke that pinches closed the carotid arteries, which supply blood to the brain, in order to render him unconscious. This choke hurts a *lot*, so be very careful applying it on your partner during training. Be especially careful to only target the sides of the neck, as pressure to the front could crush a windpipe.

Neck Hook: Walk your hand up the stick a considerable length to increase the length of the butt end until you have enough tail extended to hook around the opponent's neck.

Block the opponent's attack with an overhead roof block and check his weapon hand with your free hand.

As you do so, drive your right forearm into the side of his neck.

Quickly grab the bottom of your stick from underneath with your free hand and squeeze the shaft tightly against the bony ridge that runs along the edge of your right forearm, pinching the opponent's neck in between.

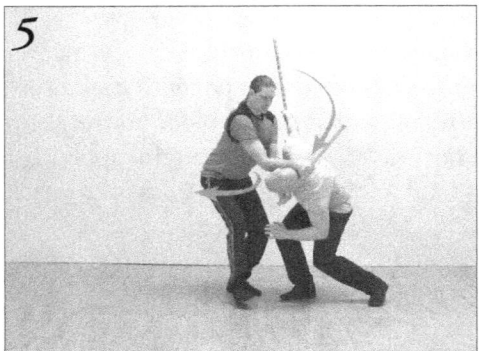

Twist your body to the right to take your opponent to the ground.

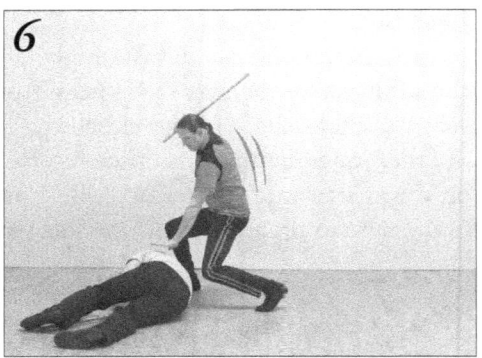

Check the opponent and position yourself to counterattack if needed.

Training Equipment: Compression Dummies

The forearm hook, neck hook, and other compression techniques are too painful to apply with much force on a partner. To develop your power in these techniques, you will need an appropriately sized object with the right compression qualities to mimic a neck or limb.

To practice the forearm lock, you can tape two padded sticks together to mimic the two bones of the forearm. Have your partner swing them to mimic an arm. Hook the arm compression dummy with the extended tail of your stick and compress the sticks. Feel free to apply maximum pressure. Rotate your body to wrench the dummy from your opponent's grip. Imagine the effects on an actual opponent if you were to apply the same force to his arm. Plans for the arm compression dummy appear in the appendix at the end of this book.

The arm compression dummy.

LEVEL 6: CLOSE-RANGE 175

Forearm Hook: Have a partner swing an arm compression dummy at you.

Hook the incoming strike and squeeze. Since it is a dummy, you can apply maximum pressure.

Rotate your body to wrench the dummy from your partner's grip.

To practice chokes, you can make a dummy that more accurately represents the architecture of the head and neck area. A rolled-up piece of foam rubber or old carpet works well for the neck. Wrap an additional piece around the top to represent the head, and then wrap the entire apparatus in duct tape. Plans for the neck compression dummy also appear in the appendix at the end of this book.

Three different chokes demonstrated on a choke dummy (*left to right*): cross choke, neck hook, and fang choke.

Level 6 Workout

Objective: This sixty-to-ninety-minute workout will help you train the skills required for effective close-range fighting.

1. Warm-Up: 15–20 Minutes. Start with some light stretching. See the guide at the beginning of this book for a sample stretching routine. Follow this with five to ten minutes of jumping rope. Do some more light stretching until your heart rate returns to normal, then grab your stick and work through some basic movements. Remember, you are still warming up, so work slowly and take this time to perfect your technique.

2. Hubud: 15–20 Minutes. One of the best ways to train cohesion in close-range fighting is to practice hubud with a partner. Keep in mind that hubud itself is just the pattern. The functionality of the drill lies in the techniques that you interweave into the sequence. Practice all the techniques presented in this level. You can even practice the fang choke and combination fang choke to cross choke.

Remember that this is *not* sparring, it is a cooperative sensitivity drill, so it is important that both partners move slowly with good control and little force behind their strikes. Maximize your repetitions by keeping the drill moving, flowing straight from a lock or choke back into the drill.

3. Double-End Grip: 15–20 Minutes. Practice using the double-end grip. Start with the basic cross-check to the head. Then move on to cross-check block and disarm, block slide and strike, neck press takedown, forearm press, double leg reap, and double-end hooking disarm.

4. Chokes: 10–20 Minutes. Carefully practice the fang choke, cross choke, combination fang choke to cross choke, and neck hook with a partner. Be very careful, as any injury to the neck could inhibit breathing, leading to serious injury or death. Develop your power on a neck compression dummy.

5. Cooldown: 5–10 Minutes. Take a few minutes to take your body from fight-or-flight into rest-and-digest. Now is the time to use static stretching to increase your flexibility and break up the lactic acid that has accumulated in your muscles.

Follow-Up: Don't forget to continue recording each of your workouts in your training log. Keep pushing yourself by setting new goals. Use these goals to stay motivated and to keep your training fresh and exciting.

LEVEL 7
Single-Stick Sparring

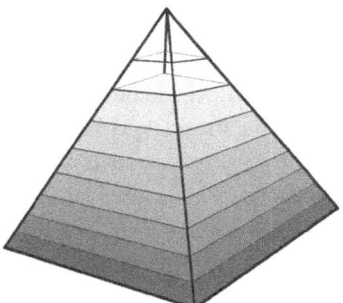

The Moment of Truth: En Garde!

Hopefully you've trained hard and learned well the lessons from levels 1–6, because now it is time to see how well your knowledge fares against an actual opponent. Level 7 focuses on putting together everything you've learned in order to develop your own personal stick-fighting method and test it against a noncompliant opponent.

It is not unusual for sparring with the stick to feel awkward at first. After all, there is a big difference between doing training drills with a partner and experiencing the chaos of fighting against an opponent who is trying his best not only to avoid getting hit but also to hit you in return. Stick with it (no pun intended). Your techniques may not seem to work well at first. You will get hit. You may get hit often. Sometimes it will hurt. Deal with it. Open yourself to the thrill that comes with training in fighting arts, the satisfaction of overcoming hardships, and the confidence that comes with knowing that your techniques will actually work for you should you need them.

When sparring, you should use special equipment, including specially padded sticks and protective gear. All the same, keep in mind that this is just *mock* combat, and that no amount of padding or protective gear can make up for a good temperament, good technique, and good control. The fact is that injuries can occur whenever you are engaging in activities that involve physical contact, so remember that you are not out to actually hurt your partner (at least I should hope you are not!). Discuss how hard of a hit you are each comfortable with, as well as other rules such as "no kicking" or "only controlled takedowns." Once you are confortable with the ground rules, start out fighting slowly and with little power. Such fighting is good as both a mental and physical warm-up and an opportunity to feel out your opponent. After a few moments you can gradually step it up a little, until you are fighting at an intensity level that is agreeable to both combatants.

When sparring, always keep your head and never lose your cool. It is common to talk a good game, thinking you'll do one thing, only to find that you respond differently when under pressure. Stick to your game plan. Do some deep, full-cycle breaths, breathing in through your nose, filling your lungs, and exhaling through your mouth. This will help you stay calm and focused. Training with such a mind-set will improve your weapons skills much more quickly than a simple "hit them more than they hit me" attitude.

179

Although it can be fun, take sparring seriously, always keeping in mind that if these were real weapons, a single blow, even just a shot to the hand, could decide everything. Remember that a good defense is essential. Try to anticipate where your opponent will strike you, and then block or move out of range, but remember that defense alone will not win a fight. As for specific fighting tactics, remember to stay flexible and continually adapt to the ever-changing circumstances of the fight. Most importantly, train hard, but train safe and have fun!

> **Attack when your partner changes position or is retracting his weapon.**
> —Bruce Lee, *Tao of Jeet Kune Do*

Safety Equipment

There are several different methods by which you can safely hone your weapons skills against an actual opponent without holding back very much, if at all. The secret lies in the proper combination of two key components: good protective gear and properly padded weapons. Over the past decades, I have created and experimented with many different types of armor and weapons, testing them all in hours of full-contact sparring. Some work better than others. I will go over padded weapons first, since they are safest and require a minimal amount of equipment. Then we will take a look at the best available armor, so you can eventually work up to full-contact sparring with unpadded rattan sticks.

Training Equipment: Padded Sticks

When it comes to padded sticks, you have to be discerning. Some commercially sold padded sticks are not suitable for sparring. Anything described as foam over a rigid PVC inner core should probably be avoided. In my experience, although inexpensive, these sticks are usually unsuitable for even moderate sparring. The foam is often thin and can be easily ripped. The cores themselves are sometimes brittle and easily broken, and when they do break, the PVC is often sharp.

I have had better results making my own PVC sparring sticks at home. You can build durable, inexpensive padded sticks from easily obtained materials. The design that appears in the appendix of this book features a PVC core covered completely with closed-cell pipe insulation, with thick foam striking caps on each end. The entire stick is then covered in a smooth layer of duct tape.

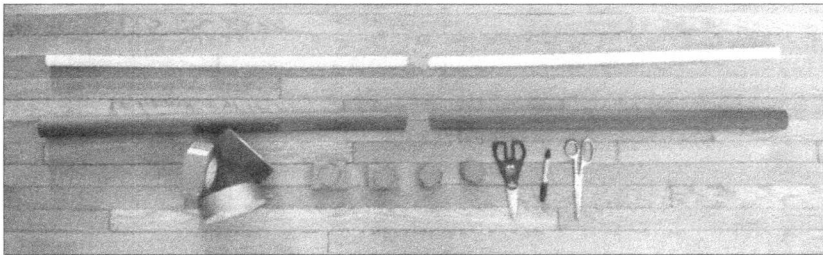

All the materials you will need to make your own padded sticks.

When constructing padded weapons, it is important to know a little about PVC. Polyvinyl chloride is a readily available and relatively inexpensive product that comes in two general forms. One is called rigid PVC (RPVC) or unplasticized PVC (uPVC). This type of PVC tends to be brittle and thus unsuitable for padded weapons construction. On the other hand, regular PVC is softer and more flexible than uPVC because of the addition of plasticizers. Flexible PVC is used in construction and so is commonly available at most hardware stores.

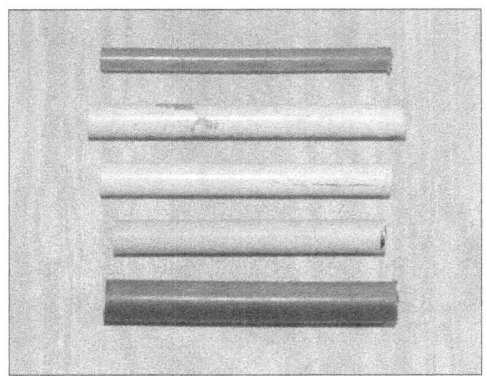 

Different types of PVC and plastic pipe (*left*). Always submit a sample to the crush test to see if it is suitable for padded weapons construction (*right*).

To test whether the PVC you are working with is suitable for padded weapons construction, take a short length and apply the crush test. Put your sample into a vice or onto a hard surface and strike it with a heavy hammer. Plasticized PVC will fold and compress, while brittle PVC will shatter (so wear eye protection). You might want to wrap the end of your test piece with a paper towel to keep shards from flying, and for easy clean up. Only use impact-resistant PVC in your padded weapons construction! Plans to make your own padded sticks appear in the appendix at the back of this book.

Examples of commercially produced padded sticks.

While you can make your own PVC sparring sticks, the best padded sparring sticks are commercially produced and can usually be distinguished from cheaper foam-covered PVC sticks by their cloth coverings. These quality padded sticks are lightweight, rigid, and durable. Companies that produce quality padded weaponry include ActionFlex, Bunal Brand, and STIX Arnis Gear. New products are being made available every day, so I suggest you search the internet to see what is available.

Armor

When sparring with padded sticks, you can often get away with wearing a minimum of protective gear. Usually all you need is a fencing or eskrima mask to protect your head and neck, a pair of padded gloves to protect your hands, and a cup to protect you from groin strikes. However, if you wish to fight with nonpadded sticks, you will probably want to wear body armor, as well as protection for your elbows and knees. In the end it is important that you experiment with different types of protective gear, pads, and armor (forearms, elbows, knees, body, etc.) until *you* feel adequately safe and protected. Oh yeah, gentlemen, I'll say it again: wear a cup!

Padded weapons gear compared with the equipment required for live stick fighting.

Gloves

The foam hand gear used in karate protects the hand and knuckles well, but since it was not designed for holding a weapon, it can leave your thumb exposed and vulnerable to injury. Motorcycle gloves with plastic finger and knuckle protection work well and look pretty cool. ActionFlex also offers a padded gauntlet that is suitable for padded stick fighting. Welders' gloves, available at most hardware stores, are usually heavy enough to ward off the sting of most blows, making them suitable for light-contact sparring.

When it comes to using unpadded sticks, lacrosse and hockey gloves offer excellent hand protection, but even these can sometimes leave your fingers open to hard strikes. Goalie gloves are specially designed with more padding, especially on the vulnerable thumb.

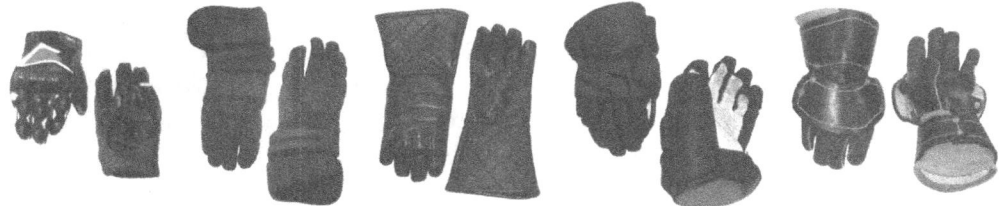

From left to right: motorcycle gloves, ActionFlex padded gloves, leather fencing gloves, lacrosse gloves, and leather half gauntlets.

Helmets

Your head contains your brain, and so it needs to be protected. Furthermore, face shots are painful and can lead to expensive hospital visits (as me how I know). One good neck shot can render you unconscious, or worse. Therefore, it is wise to invest in a good helmet to protect your head and neck. Open-faced foam karate sparring headgear is useless against any blows to the face and should be avoided.

Fencing masks work well and offer superior face protection, but they don't protect the sides of the neck or back of the head. HEMA (historical European martial arts) masks tend to be a little sturdier and have an additional cover for more protection.

For padded weapons sparring, I prefer the Proforce Thunder padded combat head guard with a face cage. The design offers good all-around protection. The holes in the mask are large, making it easy to breathe and see, but would be too large to protect against thrusts with unpadded rattan sticks. Therefore, when I fight full contact with unpadded sticks, I wear a heavier-duty eskrima helmet with closer bars on the face cage. Eskrima headgear is padded all the way around and has a large bib to protect your neck from the sides as well as the front.

Whatever headgear you choose to use, be sure that the weapons you are using cannot poke through the holes in your facemask.

   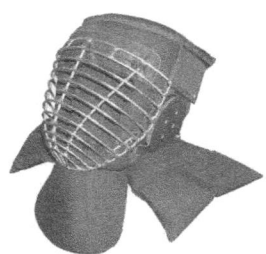

From left to right: fencing mask, HEMA mask, padded head guard, eskrima helmet.

Body Armor

The best body armor is probably an eskrima jacket. Made especially for stick fighting, this is usually a long, smock-like shirt that closes in the back. Rubber or plastic plates are sewn into the jacket to absorb the impact of stick strikes, which they do very well. However, the jacket does not offer protection to the arms and legs. Most eskrima jackets tend to be bulky and loose fitting; however, some companies are developing sleeker-looking armor, notably STIX Arnis Gear. I suggest you search the internet to see what is available.

SWAT gear or riot gear is another option. It offers excellent protection and is very mobile. A full suit will cover your arms, legs, and even feet. On the downside, riot gear tends to be expensive and has to fit you pretty well.

Other choices include sports gear such as hockey, lacrosse, motocross, BMX, or tae kwon do gear. Since each type is made to offer specific protection under a different circumstance, none of which are stick fighting, they tend to leave areas exposed that you would probably rather have protected. All the same, some protection is better than no protection.

Practitioners of HEMA are probably already familiar with the padded gambeson, a quilted shirt that offers enough protection for light to medium contact. A heavy fencing jacket could also work, especially for padded weapons fighting. Full contact with unpadded weapons would require the addition of heavier armor, usually leather, chain mail, or some combination of the two. For maximum protection, nothing matches boiled leather or, better yet, steel plate, but that's probably a little excessive for stick fighting.

From left to right: fencing jacket, eskrima vest, STIX Body Armor, motorcycle armor.

Types of Matches

When you finally square off with your partner, you should each have a good idea of what the rules are. This often depends on what type of match you are fighting.

Point Fighting

In a fight, the first hit can have a great impact on how the rest of the fight progresses. Point fighting is much like what you see at most karate tournaments today, only with a weapon. In these matches, the first contestant to score a solid blow is awarded a point. Sometimes different points are awarded for different targets according to their difficulty. For example, a hand or arm shot may be worth one point, whereas a headshot may be worth two. These matches usually take place at long range, and only occasionally go to middle range. At tournaments, matches are run with judges and referees to call the points, but this is not always feasible or desirable. It is usually a simple affair for you and your partner to call your own points. If there is a dispute as to whether a point was scored, let it go and move on. The point is to fight, not to argue.

Continuous Fighting

Inspired by Western boxing, continuous fighting is just that: the participants do not stop fighting until the round ends. Traditional Filipino stick sparring is usually performed for three one-minute rounds. The final score is also awarded as in boxing, with the ten-point must system, where judges score on a ten-point scale. If the fighters are both skilled, most rounds will end ten to nine, with the more dominant fighter receiving ten points, the other receiving nine. If an opponent is disarmed, the referee deducts an additional point from that fighter's score before the fighters are rearmed and the fight continues. This type of sparring usually emphasizes long- and middle-range fighting and has strict rules against butt strikes, grappling, takedowns, striking with the middle of the stick in a two-handed grip, and other infighting techniques that are deemed too dangerous for competition.

House Rules

While it is possible that a fight could be ended with a single, well-placed strike to a vulnerable target, the truth is that the human body is very resilient and fights are rarely ended by the first shot. For a more realistic fighting or sparring experience, let each exchange run its course, then break and reset. You may decide that the initial strike was actually enough to stop the fight and reset the match right there, or you may judge that a strike did not have sufficient stopping power and continue, usually until one participant gives in and admits defeat. This is my preferred format, as it is perhaps the most realistic method of testing your stick-fighting skills for self-defense. Our house rules are generally "No harm, no foul" and "It's not over until it's over." Otherwise, just about anything goes. So long as you have sufficient skill and use good control, you can kick, punch, butt strike, takedown, and even grapple with the stick. Disarmed? Keep fighting until you feel you could no longer go on.

Controlling the Fight

My first karate sensei was fond of saying, "Old age and treachery beats youth and skill every time." Then, since I was her senior student at the time, she'd usually do something painful to me to demonstrate her point to the class. Since she knew so much more than me, she had no problem predicting my movements and controlling the action. Now, over thirty years later, I am happy to say that I have accumulated a good deal of treachery of my own. The sad fact is that this takes considerable time to learn. You need a lot of experience, and there is no substitute for practice. That being said, I am happy to share what I have learned. Let's take a peek behind the curtain.

Know Yourself

In his classic *The Art of War*, Sun Tzu quotes a famous Chinese proverb, "If you know your enemies and know yourself, you will not be imperiled in a hundred battles." Sounds simple enough at first, but what does it actually mean to know yourself? What do you need to know about your opponent, and how can you go about learning it? In a stick fight, these are the types of questions that separate the winners from the losers, so they are well worth considering. Let's start with a little self-examination. What do you know about yourself?

Know your physical resources and abilities. What is your body type? Are you long and lean, or short and stocky? Do you have the cardio to maintain an energetic pace for the duration of the fight, or will you need to conserve your energy? Do you have an aggressive personality and like to make things happen, or do you naturally adopt a more defensive, reactionary mentality?

What are your strengths? Well, you have a stick, so let's start there! What type of stick do you have? What is your effective range? Is it short or long? Is it better for long range or close-range infighting? Is it heavy or light? Once you have accumulated this information, you must intuitively know how to put this particular weapon to best use. The more you practice with different weapons, the easier this will be.

Know which techniques work best for you in a given situation. What is your favored approach to an aggressive opponent? How about a defensive opponent? What is your preferred method of crossing the gap? What is your favorite method for drawing an attack?

What are your weaknesses? By identifying them now, you can train to compensate for them later. What techniques score on you most often? Do you leave your head exposed, or perhaps expose your front leg by leading with it too far forward? Are you often too aggressive, hurried, or overconfident? Or are you overly defensive, nervous, or easily baited?

In addition to knowing yourself, it is imperative that you know your environment! Where are you? Who is your opponent? What kind of fight you are in? Is this a sports competition? If so, is it a point match, continuous fighting, or house rules? Is it a self-defense situation? Are you facing a drunk at a bar, or a predator who wants to rob you, or worse? Are there witnesses present? Can you avoid the confrontation, maybe run away? Each situation is different and requires a different approach.

Know Your Opponent

While you learn to know yourself through introspective training before a fight, you usually don't get to know your opponent until you cross sticks with him. Therefore, in order to know your opponent, it is important to learn how to read his movements. If you can predict what your opponent is going to do and when he is going to do it, you will have a tremendous advantage over him.

The key to reading your opponent is learning how to look. This entails not simply seeing but also knowing what to look for. Watch for those subtle clues, or tells, that give away your opponent's capabilities and intentions; these come in many forms. Use the first moments of the fight to make some observations about your opponent that will help you choose the best strategy and tactics to defeat him.

First, note your opponent's physical traits. Is he taller or shorter than you? If he is taller, he will likely have greater reach and longer steps, whereas the opposite is usually true of a shorter opponent. Is he lean or stocky? A fit opponent is usually faster and more mobile than one who is more muscle bound or heavier set.

Reading Your Opponent: What sort of guard has he assumed? Where he holds his stick can tell you where his strike may come from. A high open guard is an obvious tell for a number 1 strike.

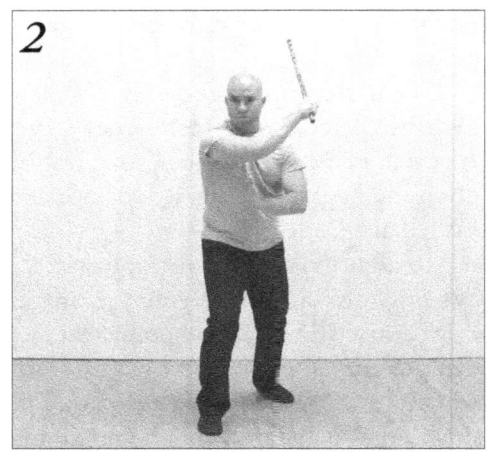

Chambering on the other hand readies him for a number 2 strike.

A low open or closed guard is an invitation for you to strike him in the head, and if you take the bait, he is likely to target your weapon hand (*3 and 4*). Remember that these are guidelines only; it is possible to deliver a strike of almost any angle from any given guard.

If he leads with his weapon hand like he is fencing, he has effectively removed his free hand from the game and may be gearing up for a long-range fight. On the other hand, an opponent who squares up on you may be looking for an opportunity to block and counterattack.

Is the opponent timid or aggressive? Observe where his tension is located. Is it in his weapon arm? If so, he is probably thinking of striking, so be ready for a quick attack. Is he loaded for a forehand or a backhand strike? If he holds his stick extended in front of him like a fencing sword, he is chambered for neither and will have to make a telegraphing movement before he can strike. Where he is looking can give you a good idea of what level he is thinking of attacking.

Look for patterns in your opponent's movements. When you move forward, does he step straight back or does he circle? What techniques does he favor? Does the opponent make short snap strikes or attack with big, full swings? If he is using snap strikes, he is likely more defensive and protecting his centerline. A wide swinger who is not controlling his own centerline will have trouble controlling the line of combat and hence the fight in general. You might have to get hit a few times to learn this, but each time he attacks, you should be collecting data to be used against him presently.

When the opponent strikes, does he make a telegraphing movement, such as pulling his striking arm back to load up for his swing? Watch for any change in his posture or guard that gives you advance warning of what he intends to do as soon as, or even before, he moves to do it.

Where is the tension in his lower body? If one leg is loaded or flexing, it can tell you a lot about his intentions. Is it his front leg? Is his back leg extended? If so, you can assume that he is adopting a defensive strategy. Keep in mind that he may be baiting you; his front leg may be ready to push him back so he can lean just out of range to avoid your strike, then counterattack as your stick goes harmlessly by.

Defensive Posture: Your opponent is leaning back.

This tells you he is prepared for a quick retreat.

Is he leaning back? If so, he may be ready to retreat. You can try leaning or stepping in for a deeper strike, but he is likely to simply step or jump back out of range. However, if the distance is greater than a step or two, you will be able to travel faster moving forward than he can moving backward. Therefore, charging in with an overhead block might be just what the doctor ordered.

Offensive Posture: The opponent is leaning forward, with tension in his back leg.

This tells you he is loaded and ready to spring forward.

Or is he leaning forward, with springlike tension in his back leg? If so, be wary. This is a more aggressive stance because he is loaded and ready to spring forward. Be ready to adopt defensive tactics such as circling out in case he charges. Better yet, bait him in order to draw a charge just so you can sidestep it and hit him as he goes by. This is an example of controlling the fight by getting the opponent to do what you want him to do.

See how the opponent reacts to an obvious attack. For example, if you make a downward vertical strike to his head, does he back up or answer with an overhead block? Whatever his reaction, the chances are good that you could make him do it again. All you need to do is figure out how you can take advantage of the momentary opportunity that will present itself when he does. Feint your initial movement to draw the response, then smoothly switch to another strike aimed at an undefended target before he can respond.

Keep in mind that a smart opponent will also be keeping a sharp eye out for any clues you might be giving off in an attempt to read you. Stay relaxed and unpredictable, being very careful not to telegraph your intentions. Keep the initiative and stay one step ahead of your opponent by controlling the pace and range of the fight. Do you know what he expects you to do? Take advantage of the fact that he is reading you by establishing a rhythm or pattern, only to break it midstride as soon as he picks up on it.

The Three-Step Rule

Drawing is tactic common in Western boxing in which you purposely leave an opening in an attempt to get your opponent to attack you. While this may seem counterintuitive, it can be useful to create an opening for you to counterattack, and, since you are expecting the attack, you will be prepared to evade or defend against it. The Three-Step Rule can help you create effective drawing skills by developing a variety of effective tactics based on sound strategy.

The Three-Step Rule is as follows:

(1) Leave an opening your opponent cannot resist.

(2) Wait until he is committed to his attack.

(3) Counter where you know he will be open.

There are many different ways you could apply the Three-Step Rule. For example, since a right-to-left diagonal strike is one of the habitual methods of attack, there is a very good chance that you can draw that strike by leaving your head exposed. The opponent will strike fast and hard when he takes the bait, and he may take it the instant it is offered, so don't get caught sleeping! Be prepared to put up a block the instant your opponent moves to strike. Immediately counterattack and continue striking until the attacker is completely neutralized.

In another example, you might overextend your lead leg. Watch for the opponent to lunge into range and attempt to strike you in the knee. When he does, withdraw your front leg as you strike down on his exposed arm.

Learn to use the Three-Step Rule to subtly set up your opponents. The key is hours of slow practice with a partner. Leave openings and have your partner attack as he would in free fighting, but at half speed. React and counterattack at half speed as well. Moving slowly allows you to concentrate on refining your techniques, as opposed to moving quickly and instinctively, which does not allow for analysis and evaluation during the execution, the time when the most progress and improvement takes place. Use this time to learn how to see, feel, and flow. Speed will come later of its own accord, and, when it does, your techniques will flow quickly without the appearance of being rushed.

> From one thing, know ten thousand things.
> —Miyamoto Musashi, *A Book of Five Rings*

The Grand Overall Strategy

When confronting an opponent, it is advisable to begin with a sound overall strategy that has been tested and proved effective in combat. While I encourage you to develop your own overall strategy (actually a set of different strategies with corresponding tactics) based on what works best for you, I have found that the following overall strategy, when applied aggressively, works well against most opponents.

The Grand Overall Strategy is best learned in full-speed, full-contact matches, where either the participants are armored or the weapons are padded, or both. The strategy is a simple (easy-to-remember) and general (easy-to-apply) two-phase road map to victory.

Begin the opening phase of the fight playing the outside game. Stay out of range of your opponent's strikes while feeling him out by continually striking to the closest available targets (usually the hands and front knee or ankle) the instant they cross into your range (the circle of death). Remember that you should avoid taking any hits and that this feeling-out period will probably not last very long. You must be ready to jump into phase 2 at any moment.

Phase 2 begins when your opponent realizes that he is taking damage while not delivering any. The wittier your opponent is, the quicker he will realize the secret to your success, the outside game. Usually the opponent will then try to adopt the long-range strategy himself to level the playing field. However, victory comes easiest on an uneven field, so, while you may engage in long-range fighting for a few more moves, at the earliest opportunity you should cross the gap with an overhead block or parry. Once inside, shift to fighting with middle-range tactics, checking his weapon with your open hand while speed-striking with your stick. Since your strikes will be hitting quickly from both sides, the opponent will be momentarily overcome while he struggles to block or counter. This is an excellent opportunity to attempt a disarm.

As soon as the opponent mounts a solid defense, you should immediately disengage, retreating on an angle as you shift back to long range. Don't drop straight back, or you may become the victim of a countercharge by your opponent. It is important that you cover your retreat by dropping some long, sharp strikes on the opponent to prevent him from locking back on you, all the while looking for the best angle and target for your next attack.

Take care to not let your opponent do to you what you did to him. Control the fight by keeping your opponent at long range until you see the need to wade into middle range again, usually just after the opponent has had the bright idea that he might do better fighting the outside game. In this manner, it is possible to stay one step ahead of the opponent. As long as he keeps chasing your lead, you should be able to dominate the fight, as he will be caught in a loop of trying to reorient himself and, therefore, rendered unable to mount an effective strategy of his own.

Remember that the Grand Overall Strategy is used in conjunction with everything you have already learned and includes feints, combinations, programming, and every other technique in your arsenal as you switch between ranges and grips to outwit and ultimately defeat your opponent. Your ultimate goal must be the seamless integration of all the various techniques at your disposal, applied in such a way that your opponent gets hit while you do not.

More Tips and Tricks

There are many ways to control the fight. Here are some more tips and tricks that you can use to become a better tactician and fighter.

Number one is to remember to breathe! A fight can be a scary thing, even if it is only a competition, causing your body to switch into fight-or-flight mode. Once your sympathetic system has kicked in, your mouth will become dry, your breathing will become shallow, your heart will race, and your tummy will tumble. Taking a few deep, calming breaths will reduce these effects, allowing you to regain control of your body and focus on the task at hand. Continue to breathe calmly throughout your match, providing your body with the oxygen it needs for the intense physical activity of stick fighting.

Second, hide your intentions (offensive or defensive) by starting all your motions from your center and moving from your core. This keeps you from reacting too soon or over-committing to a course of action. Moving from your center also serves to disguise your intentions until the last moment, giving your opponent minimal time to react.

If the opponent makes full swings or does not hold center well, you can strike into the gaps between his attacks. As with most things in stick fighting, it is always better to know what technique your opponent is going to use, so start by drawing a strike. When it comes, lean just out of range to let the strike pass by, then immediately strike him while he is out of position.

Many times you can draw a particular attack by first making the same attack yourself. The opponent will often unconsciously mimic you and answer with the same attack a moment later. All you need to do is be prepared to counter the same technique, then wait for it to come. You can also draw a strike with a feint, tensing as though you were going to move or launch an attack, only to pause as soon as the opponent responds. Let his stick pass by, then strike him when he is out of position and open between strikes.

It is important that you control the pace of the fight. Psychologically manipulate your opponent through your movements. If he is aggressive, feign weakness or timidity so he will become overconfident and make a bold attack, which you will be ready to counter. If he is defensive, you may be able to intimidate him with powerful, confident attacks. Keep in mind that a smart opponent will attempt to deceive you, too, so be wary of walking into a trap.

Practice often, preferably against a wide variety of opponents. See every match as a new opportunity to learn and gather experience. Realize that every opponent has something new to teach you, if you are only receptive to the lessons. Reviewing a video of your fights will give you invaluable opportunities for calm analysis outside the chaos of competition.

Intensity

The most distinguishing factor in any effective performance, be it music, writing, dancing, drawing, fighting, or any other form of expression, is intensity. Without spirit and intensity, stick fighting is reduced to mere exercises with little meaning or practical, effective application.

So what exactly makes a performance "intense"? It begins with the eyes. Cultivate a look of determination, intention, and absolute seriousness. This feeling should permeate your entire body. Focus your mind, concentrating every fiber of your being on the task at hand. You should not be overly tense, as tension will slow your reaction time. Seek a state of ready relaxation, a simultaneous clearing of the mind and visualization of success.

I call this shift "flipping the switch," because that is how it feels to me. Before the match, I can be lighthearted and laughing, but when it comes time to compete, my whole demeanor changes and my intent focuses. This intent can be seen through my eyes; it is where I begin to dominate my opponent, as though I were going to overcome him solely with my will.

When your mind is completely focused, the intensity shows physically through the body in your performance. Moves become quicker and stronger, reflecting your intent. Strive to be completely aware and in the present moment.

There are added benefits to developing this intensity. It can be applied to all aspects of your life. Learn to *live* as intensely as you practice, increasing the quality of your life experience and enriching the lives and experiences of others. It's this quality that makes stick fighting a unique vehicle for personal growth and continued evolution.

The Seven Principal Rules

The Schoole of the Noble and Worthy Science of Defence was written in 1617 by English fencing master Joseph Swetnam. In it, he lays out his "seven principal rules where on true defence is grounded." Even in modern times, these rules still make up the foundation of almost every martial art. You would do well to learn them.

1. **A Good Guard:** When thou hast thy guard it is not enough to know it, but to keep it so long as thou art within reach or danger of thy enemie.
2. **True Observing of Distance:** Thou shouldest stand so far off from thine enemy, as thou canst, but reach him when thou dost step forth with thy blow or thrust.
3. **To Know the Place:** Thou must marke which is the nearest part of thine enemy towards thee, and which lieth most unregarded, whether it be his . . . hand, his knee, or his leg, or where thous maist best hurt him at a large distance without danger to thy selfe.
4. **To Take Time:** When opportunity is proffered thee, . . . then make a quicke answer . . . quicker than I can speake it.
5. **To Keep Space:** If thou charge thy enemy . . . recover thy weapons into their place, and draw thy selfe into thy guard againe, and so preparing thy selfe for to defend, and likewise to make a fresh assault with discretion.
6. **Patience:** [Patience] is one of the greatest virtues that can be in a man: the Wise man saith, he is a foole which cannot governe himself.
7. **Often Practice:** Without practice the Proverbe sayes, a man may forget his Pater noster.* . . . For skill to everie reasonable man is a friend . . . by which meanes such have great advantage of the ignorant and unskillful.

Pater noster is Latin for "Our Father," a prayer so prevalent in Swetnam's society that it was unthinkable that anyone could ever forget it.

Level 7 Workout

Objective: This sixty-to-ninety-minute workout will help you learn to safely and effectively apply your stick-fighting skills in free sparring, preferably against a wide variety of opponents.

1. Warm-Up: 15–20 Minutes. Start with some light stretching. See the guide at the beginning of this book for a sample stretching routine. Follow this with five to ten minutes of jumping rope. Do some light stretching until your heart rate returns to normal, then grab your stick and do some slow shadow sparring against an imaginary opponent. Move slowly at first, picturing your opponent, visualizing his movements as you react, attacking and defending. As your mind and body warm up, gradually increase your speed, but do not go so hard that you get tired or out of breath. Remember, you are still warming up, so work slowly and take this time to perfect your technique.

2. Distancing and Control: 15–20 Minutes. Do a few rounds of no-contact sparring with a partner. Even though this is a control drill, it is recommended that you wear protective gear on your head and hands. Use light rattan or even padded sticks. Begin by facing your opponent and *slowly* moving around just outside your opponent's striking range. Observe your opponent's stance and movements. When you see an opening and sense the opportunity to attack, do so, but do it slowly. Switch to middle range by crossing the gap, using speed-striking combinations on the inside, but strike slowly to your targets and *do not* make contact. Stop the action, reset, and repeat. This drill should be performed at half speed, gradually increasing in tempo only after both practitioners have become proficient at controlling their strikes.

3. Accuracy and Timing: 15–20 Minutes. As just mentioned, after a while, both partners will begin speeding up, making it harder and harder to control your strikes. This is the natural evolution of the drill, but it should be postponed as long as possible. When you do start inadvertently hitting each other, it is time to switch to the next phase. Armor up fully and begin fighting at 75 percent speed. Maintain a sense of control and do not strike with full force. Let each exchange run its course, then break and reset. Concentrate on fast, accurate shots that score while not allowing your opponent to hit you in return. Be mindful and move with purpose. The time for drills is over. Your mission now is to methodically test each technique in your arsenal at full speed to figure out what works when, and why.

4. Speed and Power: 10–20 Minutes. It is important that you end your workout with a few rounds of full-speed and full-power sparring. The idea is to push yourself and your partner slightly out of your comfort zones. Push yourself to be courageous and confident. Swing hard, but do not intentionally injure your partner. He will be trying his hardest to defeat you as well, so remember the danger and fight smart.

5. Cooldown: 5–10 Minutes. Take a few minutes to review your techniques slowly alone, perhaps in front of a mirror. Working alone after sparring allows you the opportunity to physically review, and mentally catalog, the techniques that worked for you so they will be retained in your mind and muscles for future reference and use. Follow this with some light stretching to help your muscles stay loose and recover faster. Faster recovery time means you will feel better and can get back to training that much sooner.

Follow-Up: Don't forget to continue recording each of your workouts in your training log. Keep pushing yourself by setting new goals. Use these goals to stay motivated and to keep your training fresh and exciting.

Key phrase for this workout: Don't fight hard, fight smart.

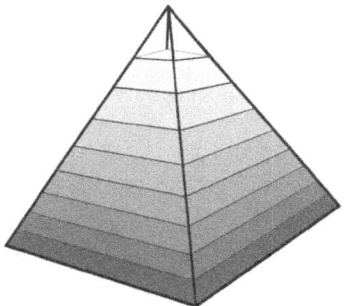

LEVEL 8
Short Stick versus Other Weapons

Mismatched weapons

Should you ever find yourself in a self-defense situation in which you have a stick, it is unlikely that your opponent will be similarly armed. What if the opponent has a short weapon like a screwdriver or a sharp knife? What if he has a long weapon like a staff or a shovel? The biggest difference between weapons is usually their effective range, and there are certain strategies that can help you to cope effectively when faced with a shorter- or longer-range weapon.

Stick versus Knife

An opponent with a blade should never be underestimated. Any encounter with a knife-wielding attacker is about as serious and life threatening as a self-defense situation gets. Since the knife is a potentially lethal weapon, any situation involving a knife-wielding opponent should be avoided whenever possible.

Defang the Snake

A snake without fangs is not as dangerous. The same can be said of a knife-wielding attacker. If you did have to defend yourself against a knife, a stick could provide a very effective defense. Use long-range skills, targeting the opponent's weapon hand with precise strikes using the tip of your stick at maximum range.

Defang from Above: Maintain distance and wait for the opponent to enter your range, but stay out of his circle of death.

Use keen footwork to keep the opponent at that range and do not let him close the gap between you.

You should be able to effect a disarm with a single solid strike, but keep your strikes short and hold your centerline in the event that you miss your initial target, allowing you to quickly strike again

Defang from Below: The attacker approaches while you are holding your stick low.

Initiate your retreating step by pressing off the ball of your front foot.

Take a full step backward as you bring your stick up.

Strike the opponent's hand from underneath.

LEVEL 8: SHORT STICK VERSUS OTHER WEAPONS

Keep the following principles in mind when training in knife self-defense with the stick:

1. Keep your vital areas out of reach of the knife.
2. Keep mobile; knees bent, with your weight on the balls of your feet.
3. Keep your mind sharp; read and respond to the opponent's intentions.

Forearm Hook

If you can immobilize the knife, the opponent will not be able to cut you. Hooking his forearm with the tail of your stick is one way of catching and controlling his knife hand. This is a difficult technique that requires you to control the fight by controlling the distance and the opponent. You control the opponent by using the Three-Step Rule, which you learned in the previous level.

Forearm Hook: You can use a hook to trap the opponent's weapon arm. This technique requires that you walk your hand up the stick to increase the length of the butt end.

Expose your chest to draw a stab.

As the opponent thrusts, turn your body to avoid his strike and use this extended tail to hook his arm.

As soon as you have hooked the appendage, quickly grab the bottom of your stick from underneath with your free hand and squeeze the shaft of the stick against the bony ridge that runs along the edge of your right forearm, pinching the opponent's limb in between.

To protect yourself from strikes from the opponent's free hand, tuck your head and turn away from his strikes as you apply pressure to the lock.

Once you have taken him to the ground, squeeze and pull sharply to get him to release the knife.

Arm Lock

Disarming an armed opponent is a difficult and dangerous task. Therefore, in order to be successful, any technique will require perfect timing, precise technique, and perhaps a little bit of luck. Even then, there is a good chance you will still get cut. If the opponent rushes in, your stick may become ineffective, turning from an asset into a liability. If this becomes the case, do not hesitate to drop your stick in order to use both hands to control the knife and take down the opponent.

Arm Lock: The attacker has closed the gap, has checked your weapon, and is thrusting his knife at your midsection.

Check the knife-wielding hand with a low chop block.

LEVEL 8: SHORT STICK VERSUS OTHER WEAPONS   203

Maintain forward pressure with your left hand and let go of your stick to check his upper arm.

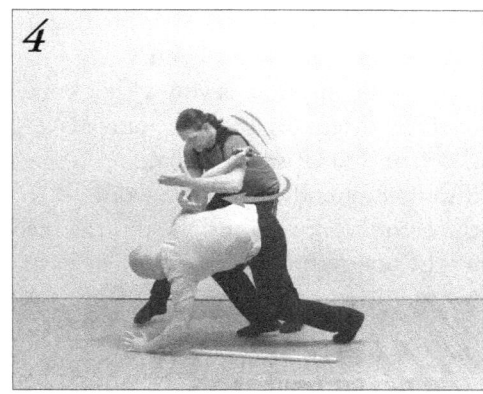

Your left hand then snakes clockwise under the attacker's elbow as you rotate your hips to bring his arm behind his back, taking him off balance.

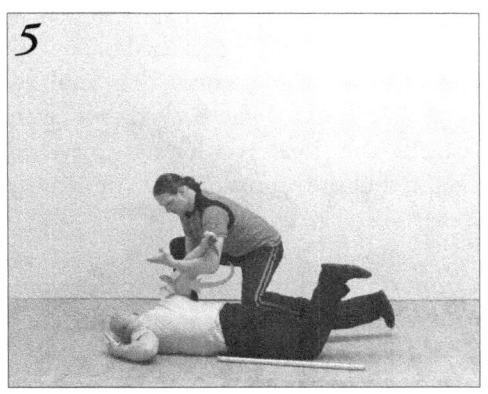

Take the opponent to the ground.

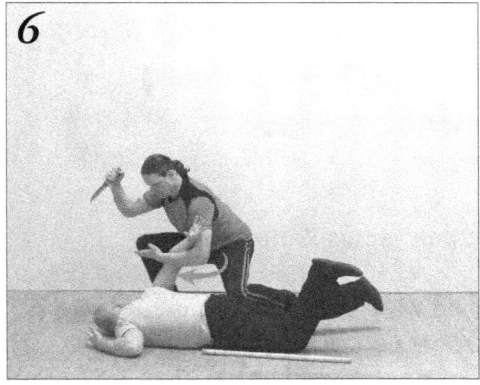

Maintain the pin by pressing his right shoulder to the floor while you strip the weapon from his hand.

Reality Check

While you can train for this scenario, there are some very sobering realities that you must keep in mind. The first is that actual knife attacks are not duels. They are usually extremely violent ambushes in which attackers stab repeatedly with quick, short thrusts at different angles. Any technique that rests on the assumption of a single, straight thrust or a wide, sweeping slash has very little chance to work. In fact, attackers rarely brandish the knife at all before they attack. Instead, they keep it concealed until the very last moment.

Studies have shown that over 70 percent of knife attacks are launched within three feet of the victim. This means you will likely have very little time and space to counterattack before being stabbed a couple of times. To further complicate things, a knife-wielding attacker will often lead with his free hand, effectively shielding the knife and allowing him to grab and control you.

If someone attacks you with a knife, you can expect to be cut and stabbed a number of times. Mentally prepare yourself. If you are cut, you must not stop and give in to the shock and surprise of the pain. You must keep your focus on your attacker and deal with him before tending to your wounds. If a cut does occur, apply pressure to the wound at the earliest opportunity to stop the bleeding and seek medical attention. Strangely, you might not even realize that you've been injured, so you should always check yourself for wounds after any physical confrontation.

Moving into the attack is critical to stop the stabbing (by reducing space and movement) and to prevent counterattacks (e.g., punch with free hand, head-butt, etc.). Don't be married to your weapon, either. If your stick becomes a liability rather than an asset, drop it so you can use your hands to control the knife. You may still get stabbed or cut, but it is better to get stabbed once than multiple times, as you would if you backed away from the attack. Therefore, you have to meet the attack and shut the aggressor down right away.

Stick versus Knife Sparring

A real knife attack is fast and furious, so it is important to know what actually works and what doesn't. To that end, I always recommend testing your skills against a noncompliant opponent. Put on the sparring gear and take turns being the knife-wielding attacker. Take care not to hurt each other, but otherwise, the sky is the limit.

Keep in mind that the knife (or stick) can be thrown. While this can keep things unpredictable, the thrower is basically self-disarming himself, so if his throw does not score, he puts himself at a considerable disadvantage for what comes next.

Training Equipment: Padded Knife

The best sparring knives I've ever used were ones I made myself from quality foam swords such as those made by Nerf.

Cut the sword down to length with a hacksaw. The tip makes the best knife because the tip is preformed. All you need to do is tape up the handle and you are ready to go.

You can use the handle to make a nice knife as well. Cut the plastic core an inch or two below the outer foam and place few small disks made from closed-cell foam (such as that used in pipe insulation) on the end to make a soft stabbing tip. Cover the end with duct tape or electrical tape to keep any sharp edges from ripping through. Finally, carefully glue the foam back into place, forming a new knife tip. Construction plans are included in the appendix at the end of this book.

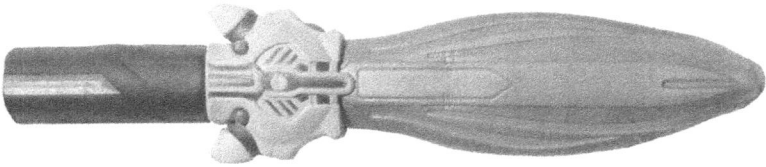

Stick versus Staff

When confronted with a longer weapon, it is natural to feel that you are at a disadvantage. However, the short stick can still be used effectively against longer weapons such as the staff.

The key to success against the staff is to close the gap using keen footwork and superior strategy. Stay out of range until you sense the right moment to attack, but don't wait too long! You must move instinctively and with good timing to avoid getting hit.

As most fighters are right-hand dominant, use your short stick to check the right side of your opponent's weapon as you enter (remember, this is a guideline only; he may use another technique, so be ready). Once you have made contact with his staff, maintain cohesion with his weapon, sliding up the shaft until you can grab it with your free hand. Once you have control of the staff, you can rain strikes down on his hands, arms, and head to disarm and neutralize him.

A high block in response to a downward strike.

A side block in response to a horizontal strike.

Stick versus Staff Disarms

Draw a strike, then use a static block to make cohesion with the opponent's weapon. Once you have one hand grasping his weapon, you can use your stick to disarm him. There are many ways to do this, but they basically settle into three categories: levers, hooks, and pops.

Lever

Levering is the action of using the opponent's staff as a fulcrum to pry his hand from his weapon. You can lever his left hand or right hand, from the inside or the outside, and from the top or the bottom, resulting in eight basic ways to apply the lever. Again, the point is that you need to understand and be able to apply the principle quickly in a variety of circumstances.

LEVEL 8: SHORT STICK VERSUS OTHER WEAPONS

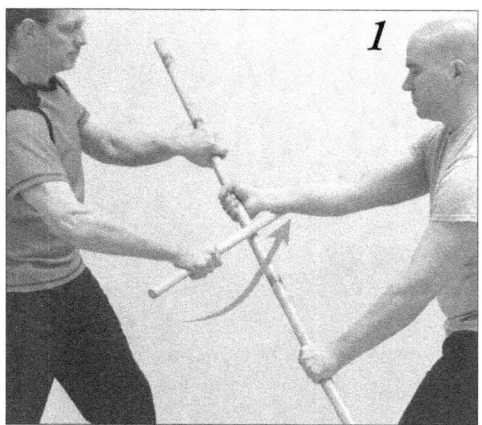

Inside Top Lever: Insert your stick into the space between his staff and forearm.

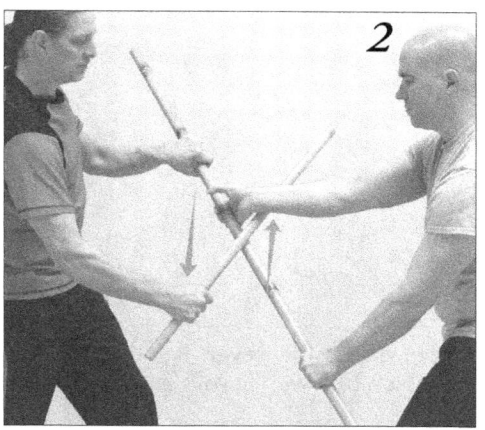

Hold his weapon firmly as you press your stick downward and perpendicular to his staff.

Forcing his hand from the weapon.

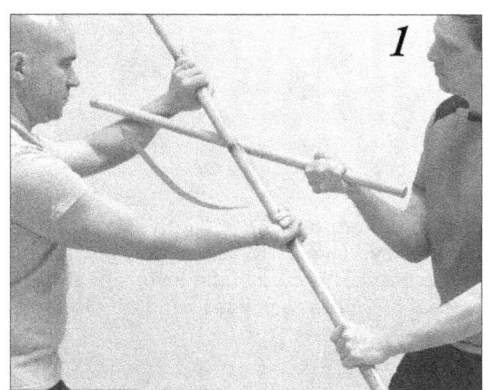

Bottom Inside Lever: Insert your stick into the space between his staff and forearm.

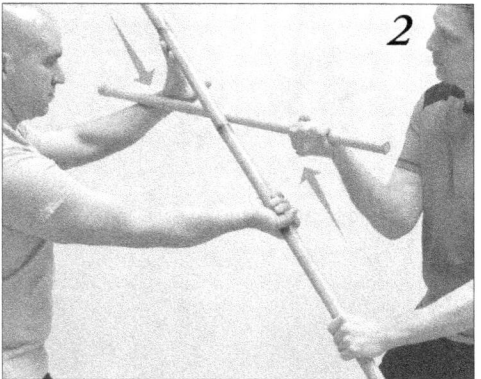

Push your stick upward, forcing his hand down and off his weapon.

Bottom Outside Lever: Bait the opponent by lowering your guard slightly.

When the opponent launches his attack, step forward to jam his strike.

Block his staff with your stick and his weapon hand with your free hand.

Withdraw your stick as you maintain the check.

Strike the opponent's lead forearm with a snap strike.

Grasp the opponent's weapon and pull it down as you insert the tip of your stick into the crook of his elbow and lever upward with the handle to pry his hand off his stick.

Hook

Hooking is the action of stripping the opponent's hand from his weapon using the butt of your stick. As in the lever, you can hook the opponent's left hand or right hand, from the inside or the outside, and from the top or the bottom, totaling eight different possible hooking disarms. While you should practice all eight, it is not important that you memorize them. It is more important that you understand the principle of the hooking disarm and be able to apply it quickly from any position.

Bottom Outside Hook: Intercept your opponent's strike with a perpendicular block; check his weapon hand with your free hand.

Use the tail end of your stick to hook over the opponent's wrist from the outside.

Pull down with your stick as you push up with your free hand to pull the staff from his hand.

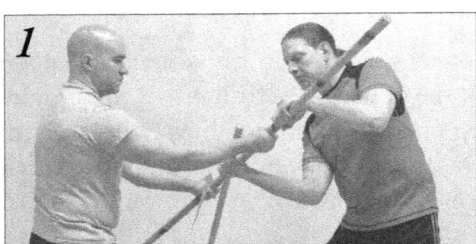

Bottom Inside Hook: After blocking and grasping the opponent's staff, thread the butt of your stick under his staff and over his lead wrist.

Rotate your stick, bringing it parallel with the staff.

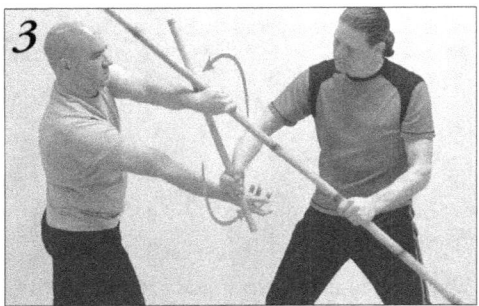

Continue the rotation to strip his right hand from the weapon.

Apply pressure with your stick against his hand as you pull the staff from his grasp.

LEVEL 8: SHORT STICK VERSUS OTHER WEAPONS

Double Hook: Control the fight by lowering your guard, baiting your opponent into making a number 1 strike with the staff.

When the opponent attacks, enter and block your high line.

Block his staff with your stick before you grasp it with your free hand.

Grasp the opponent's staff and pull it toward you as you move to strip his weapon.

Step forward and drive your right forearm downward to strip his hands from the staff.

Complete the motion by pulling the staff out of his hands. Those who have studied karate may see the similarity to a lower block.

Pop

Popping is the action of using a sharp force to dislodge the opponent's staff from his grip. To pop the staff, you must first secure the opponent's arm, then strike the staff in a direction that will knock the weapon from his hand, usually against the gap between the thumb and forefinger. It is also possible to secure the opponent's staff by grabbing it with your free hand, then striking the opponent's arm to get the same result.

Downward Forearm Pop: Block the opponent's strike stick to stick and hand to hand.

Pass your weapon hand to a high position as you grasp his staff with your free hand.

Pull up on the staff as you drive your forearm down against the opponent's arm, popping the staff through the gap between his thumb and forefinger.

LEVEL 8: SHORT STICK VERSUS OTHER WEAPONS 213

Pop and Hook: Control the fight by lowering your guard, baiting your opponent into making a number 1 strike with the staff.

When the opponent attacks, step in and block your high line.

Grab his staff with your free hand.

Pull it toward you as you drive your forearm downward against his arm to strip his hand from the weapon.

Flow into a hook with the butt end of your stick to strip his left hand from the staff.

Complete the motion by striking the opponent's neck as you pull the staff out of his hands.

Smack Down: The opponent squares off with his staff held in extended grip; draw him in by exposing your head.

As he initiates his attack, begin to shift forward and move to protect your high line with your stick.

Cross the gap quickly, using a natural, full walking step, and block his staff with your stick.

Rather than checking his weapon hand, use your free hand to deliver a palm strike to the opponent's face instead, pushing his head backward and breaking his structure.

Immediately grasp his staff and strike his neck with the butt end of your stick.

Step back and pull the staff out of his hands.

Throwing Range

The stick is a tool, and your job is to use that tool to its greatest effect. Your longest range with the stick is actually throwing range. Sometimes, it is best to use your stick as a projectile. Throwing your weapon can come as a big surprise to your opponent, giving you the opportunity to close the gap between you and neutralize him before he can recover. It can be a good strategy against a long weapon such as the staff, especially when you have an extra weapon and can afford to lose one.

Throw and Disarm: The opponent is trying to get you in range for a strike.

Throw your stick vertically to maximize your chances of hitting the attacker.

Close the gap immediately, rushing in behind your stick.

Grasp the opponent's weapon.

Twist your body to your left to break his structure.

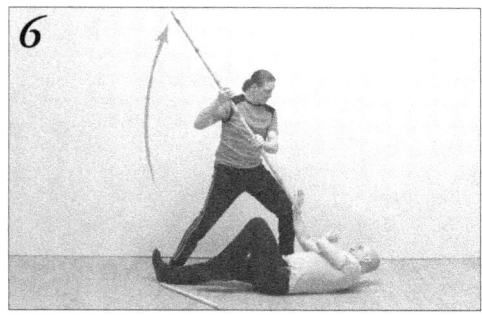

Twist the staff from his grip as you complete the takedown.

Stick versus Staff Sparring

As with all the techniques in your arsenal, you should test your stick-versus-staff techniques in full-contact sparring. This can be done with unpadded rattan and heavy armor or padded sticks and minimal body protection. Construction plans for a padded staff appear in the appendix at the end of this book.

Block and T Combo: Reading the opponent shows that he is loaded for a number 1 strike.

Rush in and cover your advance, blocking hand to hand and stick to stick.

Grasp his staff and pull it down to expose his high line as you deliver the first strike in a T combo, as described in Level 4.

Keep your control of his staff as you pivot at the wrist and strike him on the other side of his head.

LEVEL 8: SHORT STICK VERSUS OTHER WEAPONS 217

Since he is still struggling to free his weapon, you can afford an extra millisecond to jump as you chamber for the final strike in the T combo.

Drop a powerful downward vertical strike square on the crown of his head.

Training Equipment: Padded Staff

Start with a six-foot length of three-quarter-inch PVC pipe. Remember to crush test it, as mentioned in Level 7 under "Training Equipment: Padded Sticks." Tape or glue a light-duty rubber cap to each end. Heavy end caps like those used for a cane or walking stick hurt more, so don't use them. Next, carefully cover the entire length of the staff with closed-cell pipe insulation.

Cut this layer even with the ends of the weapon, and then cut several foam disks the same diameter as the end of the padded weapon. Affix at least three of these disks to each end with strips of duct tape to create a padded thrusting tip that does not allow the rubber stopper on the end of the PVC to make contact with a target.

Next, wrap an additional layer of larger-diameter closed-cell pipe insulation or other foam around the top and bottom thirds of the weapon, leaving the middle third with only a single layer of foam to make for an easier grip.

Carefully wrap the entire length with duct tape, making sure not to compress the foam more than necessary. A tightly wrapped stick does not allow the foam to absorb the impact of a strike, and it will hurt more than a stick that's been loosely wrapped.

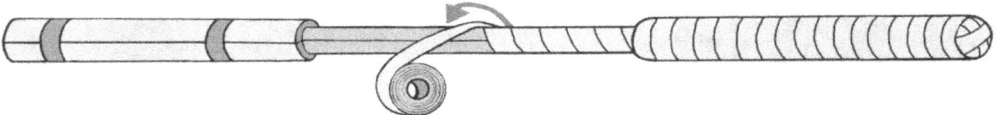

Inspect the weapon carefully to be sure that the entire length is adequately padded and that it has no rough edges that might cause abrasions.

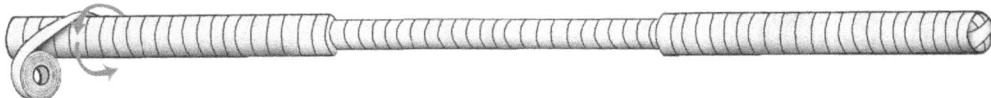

Finally, test it with your partner. Hit softly at first and gradually work up to harder and harder blows so you and your sparring partner can both get a feel for how hard you can fight safely with your particular weapons.

Stick versus Unarmed Opponent

What if the opponent is unarmed? Your first question might be, who is dumb enough to attack you if you have a weapon? Well, you may be surprised at the answer.

In a match, you may be stick fighting and get disarmed. Usually the action would stop and reset, but under house rules, you are encouraged to keep fighting until you feel you could no longer do so. An opponent may think the fight is over and let his guard down as soon as he disarms you. Train to take advantage of this opportunity, quickly closing the gap and reengaging at close range (empty hand techniques against the stick are discussed in Level 9).

In self-defense, what if an unarmed assailant approached you while you had a walking stick, umbrella, or other improvised weapon in your possession? It would be silly to toss your weapon away just because he did not seem to have one. After all, he may have a knife or other concealed weapon.

What if the opponent had a size advantage? What if there were multiple opponents? These conditions could meet the legal justification for using a stick or other weapon against an unarmed attacker in self defense. In this case, the long-range game would probably be safest. Stay outside the opponent's range while striking whatever targets come into your circle of death.

However, striking an unarmed attacker with a stick might cause more legal trouble than it's worth. So how can you use the stick to protect yourself without inflicting serious injury?

In a self-defense situation, any physical contact with the opponent could have dire consequences, physically and legally. Therefore, it is usually best to avoid physical contact all together. In the moments leading up to a confrontation, use every tactic available to defuse the situation before things get physical. Gripping the stick in clenched fists could come across as an aggressive posture. In some cases, this might work to intimidate and dissuade a would-be attacker, but in others it may serve to challenge and antagonize an angry assailant. A tight grip also gives away your intention to use the stick to defend yourself.

A good defensive posture with the stick.

On the other hand, keeping an open-handed grip looks less aggressive. Your body language says, "Stop, stay away!" as opposed to "I'm going to kick your ass!" Feigning weakness while showing strength may actually help your opponent to disengage. By not challenging the attacker, you allow him to leave the situation with his dignity intact. Legally, should any physical encounter occur and a video arise, the distinction between an aggressive posture and a defensive posture before the fight starts could mean the difference between walking away and going to jail.

The Dissuader

In 2018 I was teaching at a martial arts training camp in California when a student told me an interesting story about a recent camping trip with his family. They were cooking dinner when his wife came out of their tent only to see a bear approaching where her kids were sitting. He told me she grabbed a pan and a cup and started banging them together, screaming and yelling as she rushed the animal, which turned and ran back into the forest. She got lucky, to be sure, but her show of force was enough to dissuade the bear from coming closer.

When faced with an unarmed attacker, words alone may not be enough to deescalate the situation. Sometimes, a show of force is an effective deterrent. Persuade the assailant that attacking you would not be in his best interest—in fact, quite the contrary. Put on an intimidating show of force by swinging your weapon and shouting in an intimidating fashion. Make full-speed strikes that cut loudly through the air. The sound will hopefully make your attacker think twice about trying to attack you. Be careful not to swing too wide and inadvertently leave an opening that your opponent can take advantage of.

Hopefully your display will disrupt the opponent's attacking mind by causing him to hesitate and reconsider. Just to be sure, tell him what to do. Shout, "Leave me alone! Get out of here before you get hurt! Just leave!" This sort of suggestion can help the attacker make the choice you want him to make.

Dissuader: Swing hard and fast enough to make your opponent think twice about attempting to enter your circle of death.

Hopefully, the attacker will reconsider and leave.

Opponent Grabs Your Stick

When applying the double-end guard, be wary that the opponent may try to snatch the stick out of your hands. As soon as he moves to grab your stick, close your hands and grasp each end firmly and move out of range. If he manages to grab your stick, he will likely do one of three things: try to wrestle it away from you, push it toward you, or pull it away. Here are simple and effective counters to each.

Opponent Grabs and Pushes: Hold your stick in front of you as you are attempting to defuse the situation.

The opponent suddenly lunges in and grabs your stick, pushing it toward you.

By holding on to your stick with both hands, he has opened his low line to a kick.

Push forward with your left hand and pull back with your right, twisting the stick into a vertical position.

LEVEL 8: SHORT STICK VERSUS OTHER WEAPONS 221

As you land forward, use your momentum to press the stick downward into the opponent.

Pressing him backward as though forcing him to sit in a chair that isn't there.

Opponent Grabs and Pulls: Hold your stick in front of you as you are attempting to defuse the situation.

The opponent suddenly lunges in and grabs your stick, attempting to pull it from your hands.

Go with his pull. By holding on to your stick with both hands, he has opened his high line to a tiger claw strike to the eyes.

Drive forward with your right hand, digging your fingers into his eyes and raking his face as you pull back with your left hand and wrench the stick from his grip.

Opponent Grabs and Wrestles: The opponent has grabbed your stick and attempts to wrestle it away from you.

Push one end and pull the other to turn his body and break his structure.

Raise your foot high and aim for his lead knee.

Stomp on the side of his knee as you shove him down and away from you.

Stick Wrestling

These are only a few of the techniques you can apply should an opponent grab your stick. However, you may end up wrestling for control of the weapon. There are many ways to push, pull, twist, press, scoop, and otherwise manipulate the stick to wrench it free from your opponent's grasp. Stick wrestling can teach you how to do this. You and a partner grasp a single stick between you. Each of you then attempts to gain control of the weapon, taking it completely away from the other.

Be very careful, since large amounts of potential energy can build up, which, if suddenly released, could cause an accidental injury. Start slow and simple, without resisting your partner too much. Set rules such as "no butt strikes" or "no striking with the center section of the stick" until you are ready to add them to your exercise. Just to be safe, it is recommended that you wear helmets during this exercise.

Defense against a Punch

Your attacker might be so intent on hurting you that he attempts to punch you. Naturally, you can lunge away and simply strike his hand.

If the opponent attempts to punch you, keep away as you strike his hands and arms.

This may be enough to dissuade him from launching further attacks. However, a determined attacker may shrug off your strikes and keep coming at you. To control an unarmed attacker without striking him, hook and lock a limb. This technique requires that you walk your hand up the stick to increase the length of the butt end.

Forehand Hook: Read the opponent's intentions and be ready for his punch when he throws it.

Block it with your right forearm.

Use the extended tail of your stick to hook the opponent's arm. Quickly grab the bottom of your stick from underneath with your free hand and squeeze the shaft tightly against the bony ridge that runs along the edge of your right forearm, pinching the opponent's limb in between.

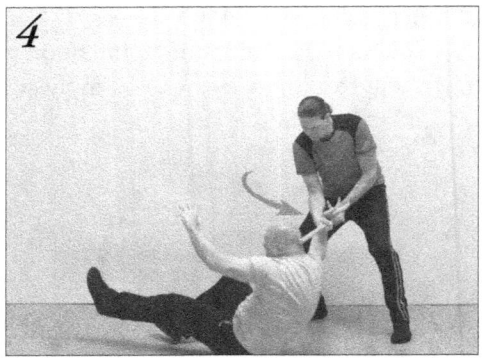

To protect yourself from strikes from the opponent's free hand, tuck your head and twist to your left to take him to the ground.

Backhand Hook: Read the opponent's intentions and be ready for his punch when he throws it.

Block it with your right forearm.

LEVEL 8: SHORT STICK VERSUS OTHER WEAPONS 225

Use the extended tail of your stick to hook the opponent's arm.

Quickly grab the bottom of your stick from underneath with your free hand and squeeze tightly.

To protect yourself from strikes from the opponent's free hand, step behind him as you twist to your right.

Finish by taking the opponent to the ground.

Defense against a Kick

If you are guarding your high line or staying out of punching range, the opponent may get frustrated and attempt to kick you.

Double-Handed Block: Maintain distance and keep your stick between you as you attempt to defuse the situation.

When he kicks, block it with a sharp downward strike at his shin.

Single-Handed Block: Maintain distance and keep your stick between you as you attempt to defuse the situation.

When he kicks, pull back out of range and strike his leg sharply.

Level 8 Workout

Objective: With this forty-five-to-seventy-minute workout, learn to safely and effectively apply your stick-fighting skills against the knife, staff, and empty hand in sparring, as well as defense.

1. Warm-Up: 5–10 Minutes. Start with some light stretching. See the guide at the beginning of this book for a sample stretching routine. Follow this with five minutes of jumping rope. Do some light stretching until your heart rate returns to normal, then grab your stick and do some slow shadow sparring against an imaginary opponent. Move slowly at first, picturing your opponent and visualizing his movements as you react, attacking and defending. As your mind and body warm up, gradually increase your speed, but do not go so hard that you get tired or out of breath. Remember, you are still warming up, so work slowly and take this time to perfect your technique.

2. Distancing and Control: 10–15 Minutes. Do a few rounds of no-contact sparring with a partner using your stick versus a knife, staff, and empty hand. Even though this is a control drill, it is recommended that you wear protective gear on your head and hands. Use light rattan or padded weapons. When you see an opening and sense the opportunity to attack, do so, but do it slowly, taking care to *not* make contact. If the partner with the staff or knife is disarmed, he may continue attacking with no weapon using the techniques described in this level. Stop the action, reset, and repeat. This drill should be performed at half speed, gradually increasing in tempo only after both practitioners have become proficient at controlling their strikes.

3. Accuracy and Timing: 15–20 Minutes. As just mentioned, after a while, both partners will begin speeding up, making it harder and harder to control your strikes. This is the natural evolution of the drill, but it should be postponed as long as possible. When you do start inadvertently hitting each other, it is time to switch to the next phase. Armor up fully and begin fighting at 75 percent speed. Maintain a sense of control and do not strike with full force. Let each exchange run its course, then break and reset. Concentrate on fast, accurate shots that score while not allowing your opponent to hit you in return. Be mindful and move with purpose. The time for drills is over. Your mission now is to methodically test each technique in your arsenal at full speed to figure out what works when, and why.

4. Speed and Power: 10–15 Minutes. In order to test the validity of your techniques and understand how they are applied against a noncompliant opponent, it is important that you end your workout with a few rounds of full-speed, and full-power, sparring. The idea is to push yourself and your partner slightly out of your comfort zones. Push yourself to be courageous and confident. Swing hard, but do not intentionally injure your partner. He will be trying his hardest to defeat you as well, so remember the danger and fight smart.

5. Cooldown: 5–10 Minutes. Take a few minutes to review your techniques slowly alone, perhaps in front of a mirror. Working alone allows you the opportunity after sparring to physically review and mentally catalog the techniques that worked for you so they will be retained in your mind and muscles for future reference and use. Follow this with some light stretching to help your muscles stay loose and recover more quickly. Faster recovery time means you will feel better and can get back to training again that much sooner.

Follow-Up: Don't forget to continue recording each of your workouts in your training log. Keep pushing yourself by setting new goals. Use these goals to stay motivated and to keep your training fresh and exciting.

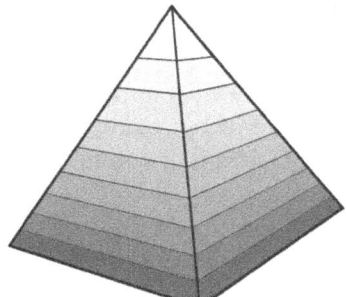

LEVEL 9
Empty-Hand Defense against the Stick

Unarmed Defense

In December 2017 I received this message from one of my black-belt students, Sensei Nick Lolli, who had moved away from Pennsylvania several years earlier:

Dear Master Joe,
    I'd just like to tell you about a situation when everything came together. I was walking home from some bars in Greenville, SC, tonight when I saw a man aggressively swinging a belt at two other men in the middle of the street. These two cab drivers had their hands up and clearly wanted no part of the altercation, so I decided to distract the man with the belt by engaging him and talking him down. I told him that he'd won the fight and that it was all over, and after a few minutes he walked over to me on the sidewalk and shook my hand. Despite this, all of a sudden he swung his belt at my head. I suppose it's due to years of being swung at by you and everyone else, but I was able to duck the belt and quickly close the gap to take him down with an osoto gari. I was able to pin him down, despite his kicks and punches, with the help of my friend who jumped on his legs after I took him down. I held him down until the police came. I'd like to thank you for not only making sure that I didn't get hit tonight, but also that I had the courage to help the two men who were clearly frightened by the man who was very obviously violent and drunk.

When confronted by any opponent with a weapon, your first course of action should be to flee the scene. However, sometimes circumstances may force you to confront an armed adversary, so it is important that you know how to defend against a weapon with your bare hands. While you mostly train with a stick, keep in mind that the stick can represent a variety of single-handed blunt trauma weapons such as a piece of wood, a pipe, a tire iron, a hammer, a baseball bat, or the belt mentioned in the foregoing story.

Let me be very clear: disarming any armed assailant is a difficult and dangerous task. Therefore, in order to be successful, any technique will require perfect timing, precise technique, and perhaps a little bit of luck. Even then, there is a good chance the opponent will get a swing in on you as you cross the gap, so you'll need to cover your advance.

Naturally, you'll want to avoid getting hit at all. However, if you can't avoid getting hit, avoid getting hit hard. If can't avoid getting hit hard, at least avoid getting hit hard in the head. With this goal in mind, here are some strategies and tactics that will help you try to make the best of a bad situation.

You learned in Level 2 that a strike can be dissected into three main parts: the initial phase, when the swing is gaining momentum, called the *acceleration zone*; the area of focused concentration, called the *strike zone*; and the *deceleration zone*, when the stick starts slowing down. Needless to say, you do not want to get caught in the impact zone! This basically leaves you with two options: enter early, before the opponent's strike has gained sufficient power, or avoid the strike and enter later, after the strike has passed by. Either way, you'll have to close the gap to close range in order to neutralize the attacker.

Practice a wide range of techniques so you will be versatile and able to respond effectively, taking full advantage of every opportunity that presents itself.

Crossing the Gap

In this scenario, because your opponent is armed and you are not, he has the obvious advantage. Therefore, to maximize your chances of success, you'll need to gain control of the fight as early as possible. To accomplish this, hover just outside the opponent's effective striking range, taking care to monitor his position and stay ready to back or circle away if he tries to close in on you.

The attacker's weakness lies in his strategy, which is usually to incapacitate you with a few hard hits. Read his movements and be prepared to act the moment you see him move to chamber for a strike. Better yet, draw a strike by feinting a quick motion as though you were moving to enter, but suddenly pause to see his reaction. Watch for the moment that the opponent begins to chamber for a strike. When he does, you'll need to either quickly charge directly in or lean just out of range to avoid the strike before suddenly entering.

The opponent's reaction to your feint may be that he begins to strike but quickly senses that you do not actually intend to enter and checks his attack. This will often be followed by a very brief moment of relaxation, which is a good time to quickly cross the gap. You must move quickly on a 1–1.2 count, exploding forward while the opponent is still in the process of mentally and physically resetting. This is difficult and therefore requires much practice, but once you have mastered it, your opponent will have a difficult time striking you, at least hard enough to stop you from moving to close quarters.

When you do enter, there are two positions that will protect you from the number 1 strike: the arrow and the wall.

LEVEL 9: EMPTY-HAND DEFENSE AGAINST THE STICK   231

The Arrow   The Wall

The arrow and the wall as seen from the attacker's point of view.

The Arrow: The arrow is a technique in which you shoot yourself quickly across the gap. Stand just out of range, baiting the opponent with your head.

The opponent takes the bait and steps through to close the gap and strike you. At the same time, extend your arms in front of you as you duck your head and rush forward.

Angle slightly into his weapon arm, usually to your eleven o'clock position, ahead and slightly to your left. Your left forearm strikes his arm and checks the weapon as you drive your right forearm into the side of his neck.

Maintain pressure on the neck as you snake your rear hand around the opponent's weapon arm.

Maintain pressure on the neck as you complete the snake and dislodge the weapon from his grasp.

You now have the opponent's weapon.

The Wall: Stand just out of range, baiting the opponent with your head.

The opponent takes the bait and steps through to close the gap and strike you. At the same time, raise your right hand over your left shoulder, palm away, to protect the left side of your head. Raise your left shoulder and tuck your head into it to protect your chin.

LEVEL 9: EMPTY-HAND DEFENSE AGAINST THE STICK   233

Turn your body slightly to the right to protect your centerline as you drive forward and shoulder-check the opponent's right upper arm and shoulder area.

Deliver a right chop to the opponent's neck.

Hook behind his head and pull him down into a knee strike.

Pivot to your right, delivering a right downward elbow strike to the opponent's back. If the opponent still has his stick, grasp it with your left hand and lever it out of his grip.

Evasion

If you have no weapon, it is not advised that you use your arm to block the weapon. Instead, you should evade whenever possible. In both of the evasion techniques presented here, the rope-a-dope and the duck, you must avoid moving on a 1–2 count in which the opponent attacks, then you enter after he has finished his swing. Rather, strive to move on a much quicker, 1–1.2 count, entering the instant the opponent's stick passes by and before he can rechamber to attack again. The distinction is subtle, but understanding it can make the difference between success and failure.

Rope-a-Dope: The rope-a-dope is a boxing style made famous by Muhammad Ali in his 1974 match slated "The Rumble in the Jungle," in which he made George Foreman miss him repeatedly by leaning just out of range of his attacks. Begin by exposing your head to draw a strike.

When the opponent swings, lean your body backward just out of range of his strike.

As soon as the weapon goes by, straighten back up.

The opponent returns with a horizontal backhand strike.

Stop the opponent's weapon arm, jamming him at the wrist and elbow.

Grasp his stick and deliver a hard palm strike to the back of his arm to dislodge the weapon from his grasp.

LEVEL 9: EMPTY-HAND DEFENSE AGAINST THE STICK 235

Ducking: Hopefully you have been practicing with your evasion bopper, because you will need good timing and quick footwork for this technique. Draw a strike by exposing your head.

Hold your position until he is fully committed to the angle of his attack.

Step to your left and duck under his strike.

As his strike goes by, pop up behind his right shoulder into a dead spot where it is difficult for him to hit you.

Turn his head with your right hand and check his weapon arm with your left.

Pull him backward and grasp his stick in preparation to lever it out of his grip.

Improvised Armament

Learn to quickly scan your environment for improvised weapons and things you can use to arm yourself. On the street, this may be a jacket, purse, shopping bag, or backpack. In a residence, you might find a cushion, pillow, or other object. In a bar or restaurant, it could be a chair or bottle. Look for anything you might be able to use as a projectile or shield.

Throwing: Draw a strike and read the opponent's movements.

As he begins his swing, throw your jacket or other object at his face.

Immediately move in behind the projectile, taking advantage of his temporary blindness.

Step in and check his weapon hand as you deliver a right forearm strike to his neck.

Slide your hand down and grasp the stick, then strike his arm to dislodge the stick from his grasp.

Back out to establish distance, then switch to stick-versus-empty-hand tactics.

LEVEL 9: EMPTY-HAND DEFENSE AGAINST THE STICK 237

Shield: You can also use a coat, backpack, or other object as a shield to block the opponent's weapon. Wrap a jacket around your arm and use it to block the stick.

Then, step in and strike at his eyes; he will have a hard time hitting you if he can't see you.

Level 9 Workout

Objective: This sixty-to-ninety-minute workout will help you learn to disarm an opponent with a stick.

1. Warm-Up: 5–10 Minutes. Start with some light stretching. See the guide at the beginning of this book for a sample stretching routine. Follow this with five to ten minutes of jumping rope. Do some light stretching until your heart rate returns to normal.

2. Distancing and Control: 10–15 Minutes. Do a few rounds of armed and unarmed no-contact sparring with a partner. Even though this is a control drill, it is recommended that you wear protective gear on your head and hands. Use light rattan or padded sticks. Begin by facing your opponent, who is armed while you are not, and *slowly* work through the various techniques presented in this level. Stop the action after each exchange, reset, and repeat. This drill should be performed at half speed, gradually increasing in tempo only after both practitioners have become proficient at controlling their strikes.

3. Accuracy and Timing: 15–20 Minutes. As just mentioned, after a while, both partners will begin speeding up, making it harder and harder to control your strikes. This is the natural evolution of the drill, but it should be postponed as long as possible. When you do start inadvertently hitting each other, it is time to switch to the next phase. Armor up fully and begin fighting at 75 percent speed. Maintain a sense of control and do not strike with full force. Let each exchange run its course, then break and reset. Concentrate on closing in on the opponent, controlling the weapon, and disarming him. Be mindful and move with purpose. Your mission now is to methodically test each technique in your arsenal at speed to figure out what works when, and why.

4. Speed and Power: 10–15 Minutes. It is important that you end your workout with a few rounds of full-speed and full-power sparring. The time for drills is over. The idea is to push yourself and your partner slightly out of your comfort zones. Push yourself to be courageous and confident. Swing hard, but do not intentionally injure your partner. Remember that any hit could be dangerous, so fight smart.

5. Cooldown: 5–10 Minutes. Finish up with some light stretching to help your muscles stay loose and recover more quickly. Faster recovery time means you will feel better and can get back to training again that much sooner.

Follow-Up: Don't forget to continue recording each of your workouts in your training log. Keep pushing yourself by setting new goals. Use these goals to stay motivated and to keep your training fresh and exciting.

Appendix

Training Equipment

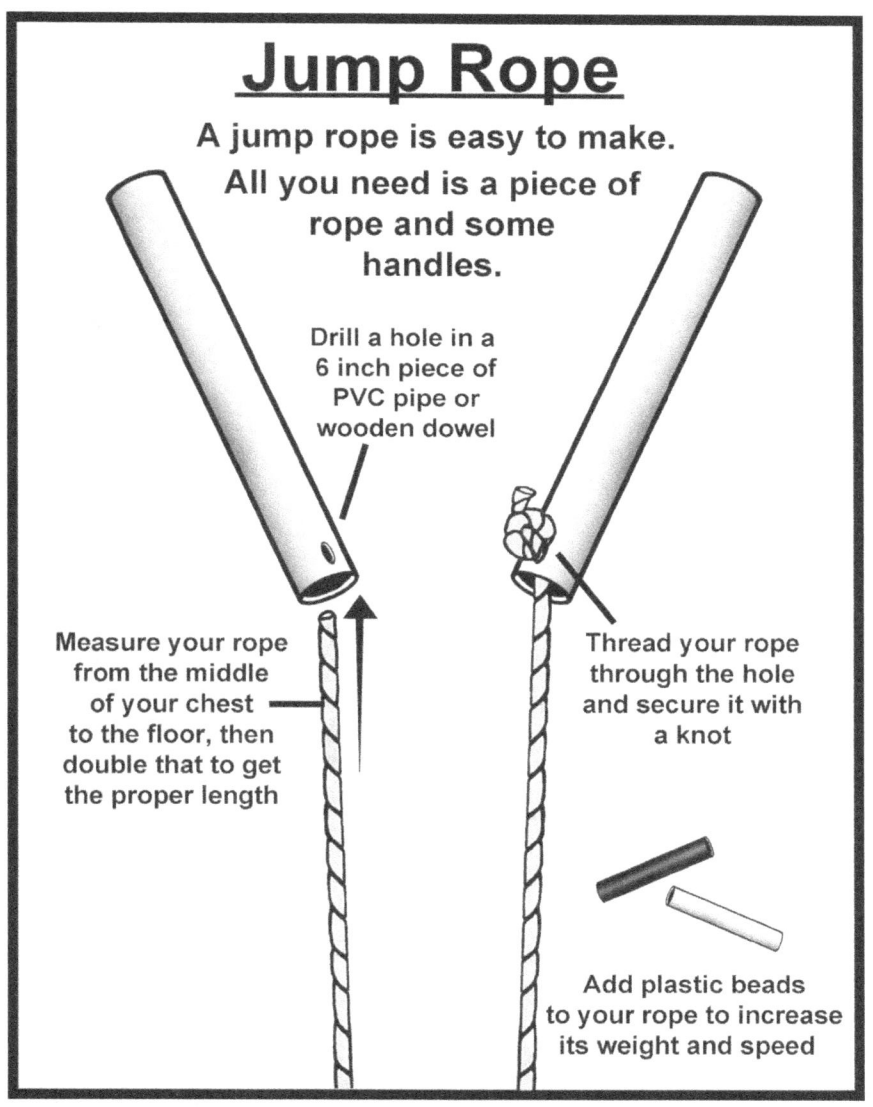

Floor Patterns

Floor patterns are used to help develop good footwork.
There are many different patterns to chose from.
Each teaches you something different.

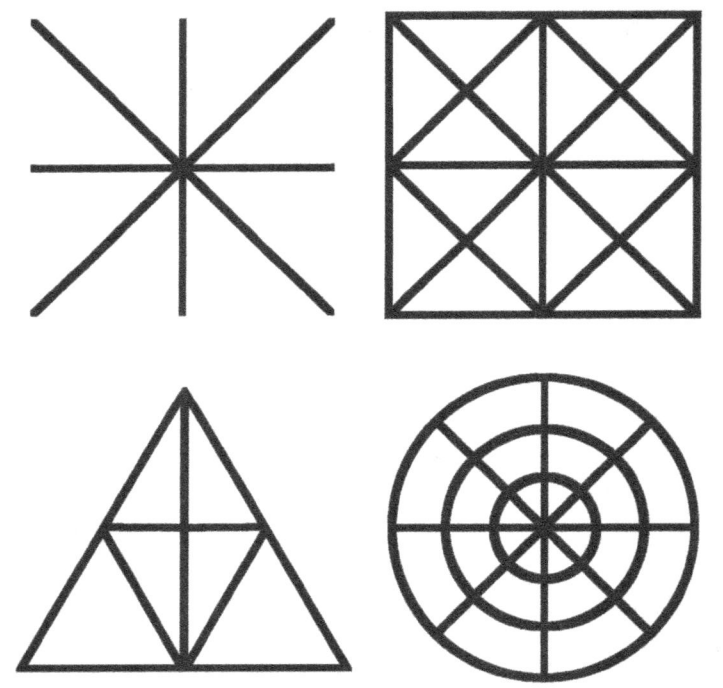

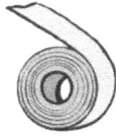 Mark out your floor pattern in masking tape, duct tape, or paint.

**Warning: sometimes tape can leave marks
on your floor that cannot be removed!**

Tire Bag

Drill holes in old tires using a paddle bit.

Thread strong rope through the holes and knot them at the top.

The number of tires can vary to suit your needs.

Hang it from a sturdy frame.

Knot the ends so they can't pull through the holes.

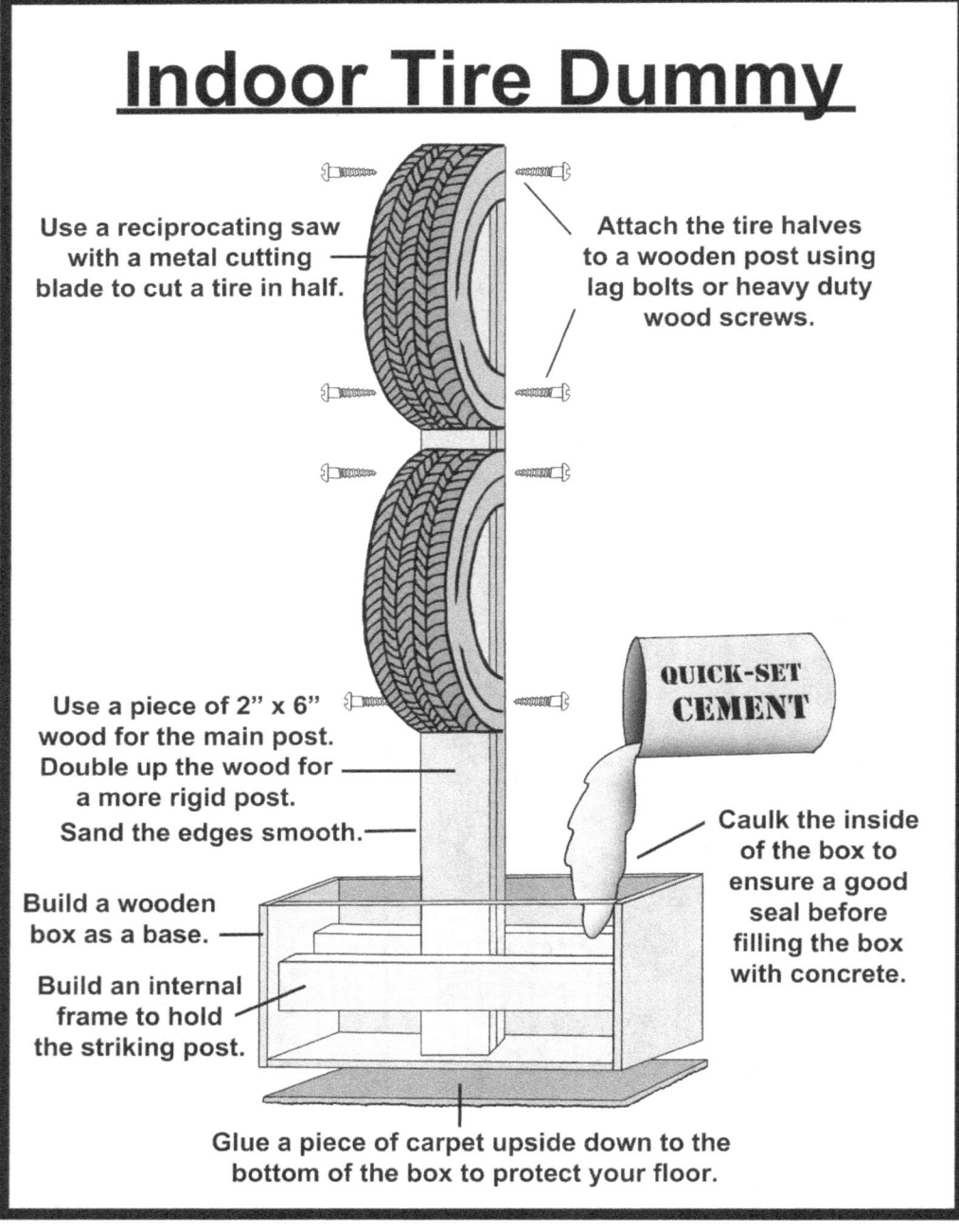

Evasion Bopper

18-20" stick

About 3 feet of pool noodle

Insert the stick only halfway into the pool noodle, leaving about 2 feet at the striking end.

Use some tape to hold them together.

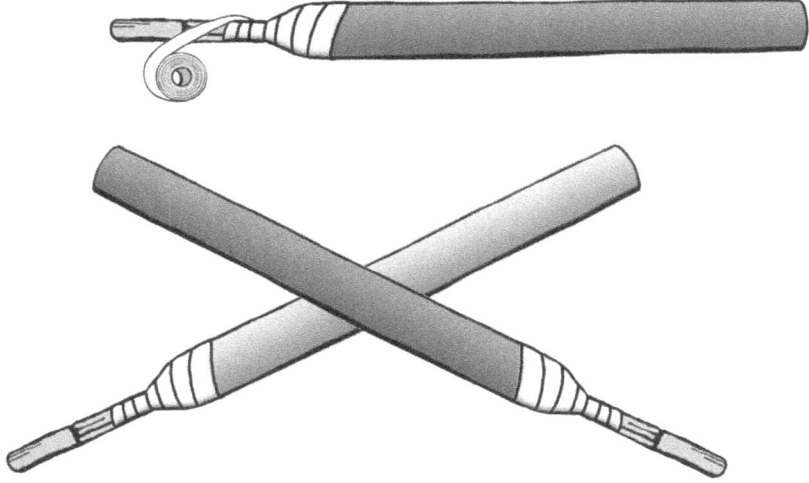

Remember, evasion boppers are <u>NOT</u> for sparring! Use them to learn how to stay on the <u>outside.</u>

Target Stick

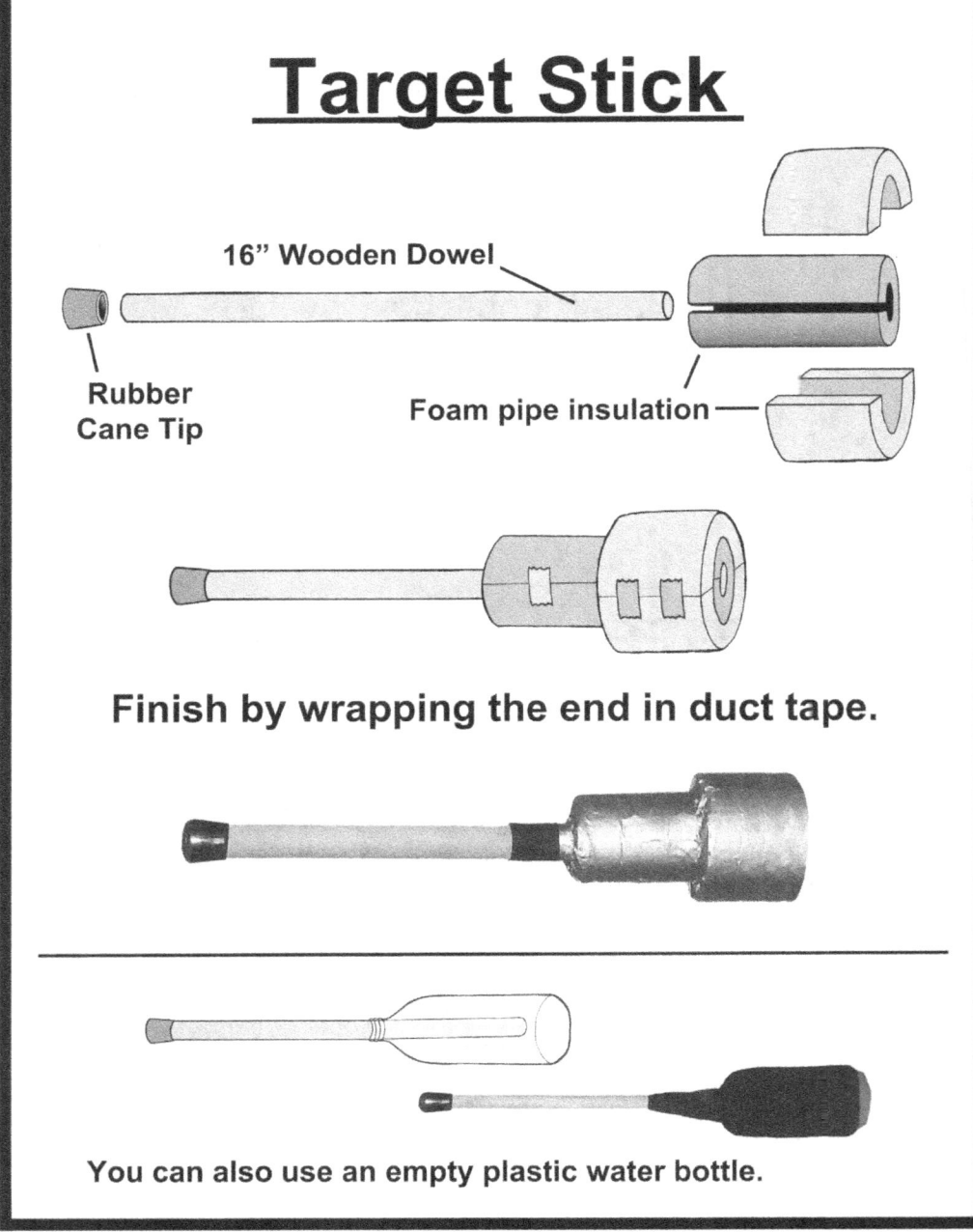

16" Wooden Dowel

Rubber Cane Tip

Foam pipe insulation

Finish by wrapping the end in duct tape.

You can also use an empty plastic water bottle.

Striking Point

The striking point is used to develop accuracy, distancing, and control. It is not intended to be hit with full power.

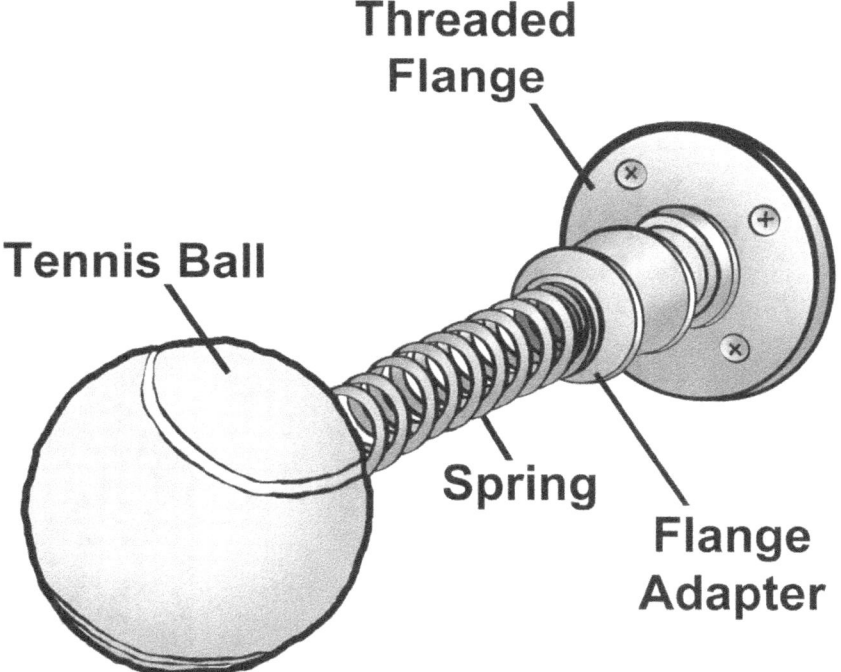

Slit the ball and insert the spring. Screw the apparatus to a firm support.

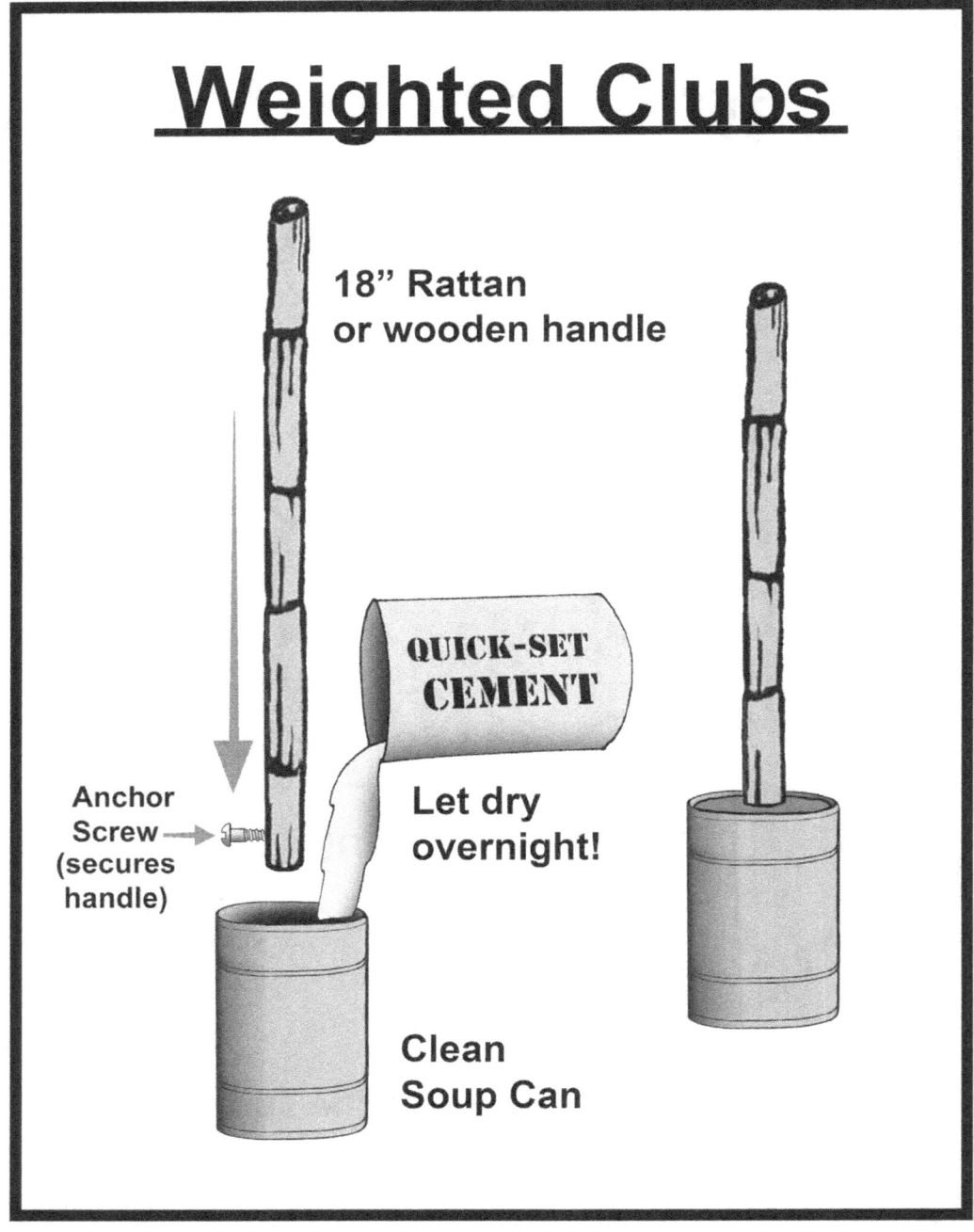

APPENDIX: TRAINING EQUIPMENT 247

Arm Compression Dummy

The arm compression dummy mimics the dual bones of the forearm.

Start with a length of 1/2" to 3/4" PVC.

Wrap the ends in tape, then cover one end with foam pipe insulation.

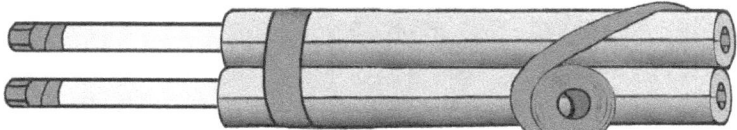

Make two sticks and tape them together.

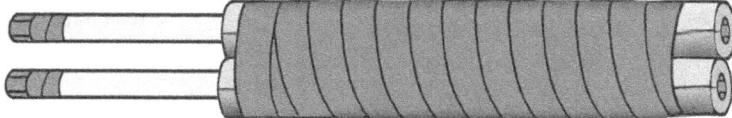

The completed arm compression dummy.

Neck Compression Dummy

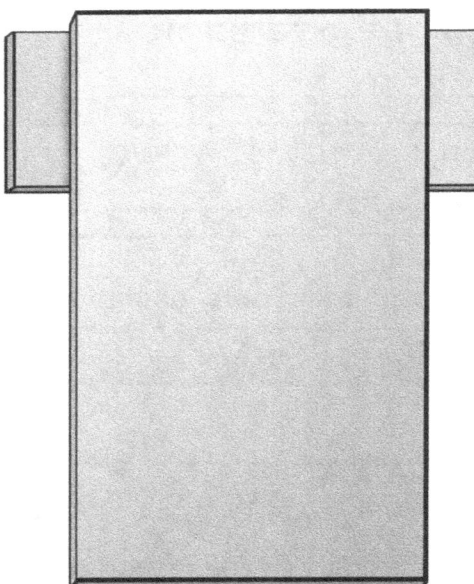

Roll the a piece of foam rubber, carpeting, or even thick cardboard to a circumference of 14-15 inches. Wrap an additional piece around one end to represent the head.

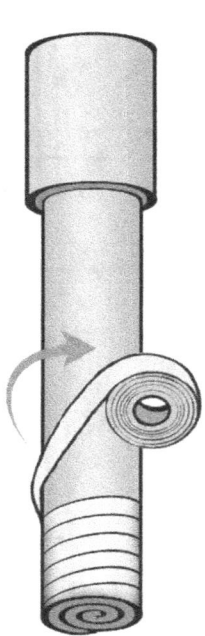

Wrap the entire apparatus in duct tape for durability.

APPENDIX: TRAINING EQUIPMENT 249

Padded Sticks

1. Start with a length of 3/4" PVC pipe.

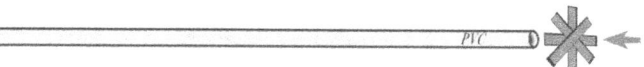

2. Cover the ends with electrical tape.

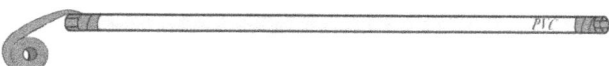

3. Cover the entire stick with 3/4" foam pipe insulation.

4. Cut and attach three foam disks to each end.

5. Wrap the entire stick in a smooth layer of duct tape.

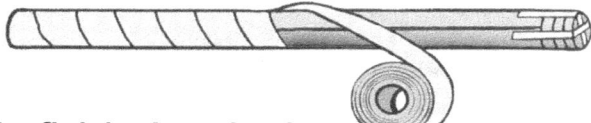

6. The finished product!

You can used colored tape for a more professional result.

Always inspect your sticks carefully before each use.

Padded Knife

Begin with a quality, name brand foam sword.

Use a hacksaw to cut the blade into knife-sized pieces.

Tape the handle and you are ready to go!

You can also use the handle piece.

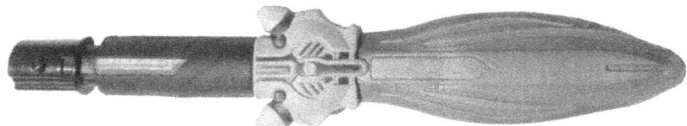

Use a hot glue gun to fashion a new tip.

APPENDIX: TRAINING EQUIPMENT 251

Padded Staff

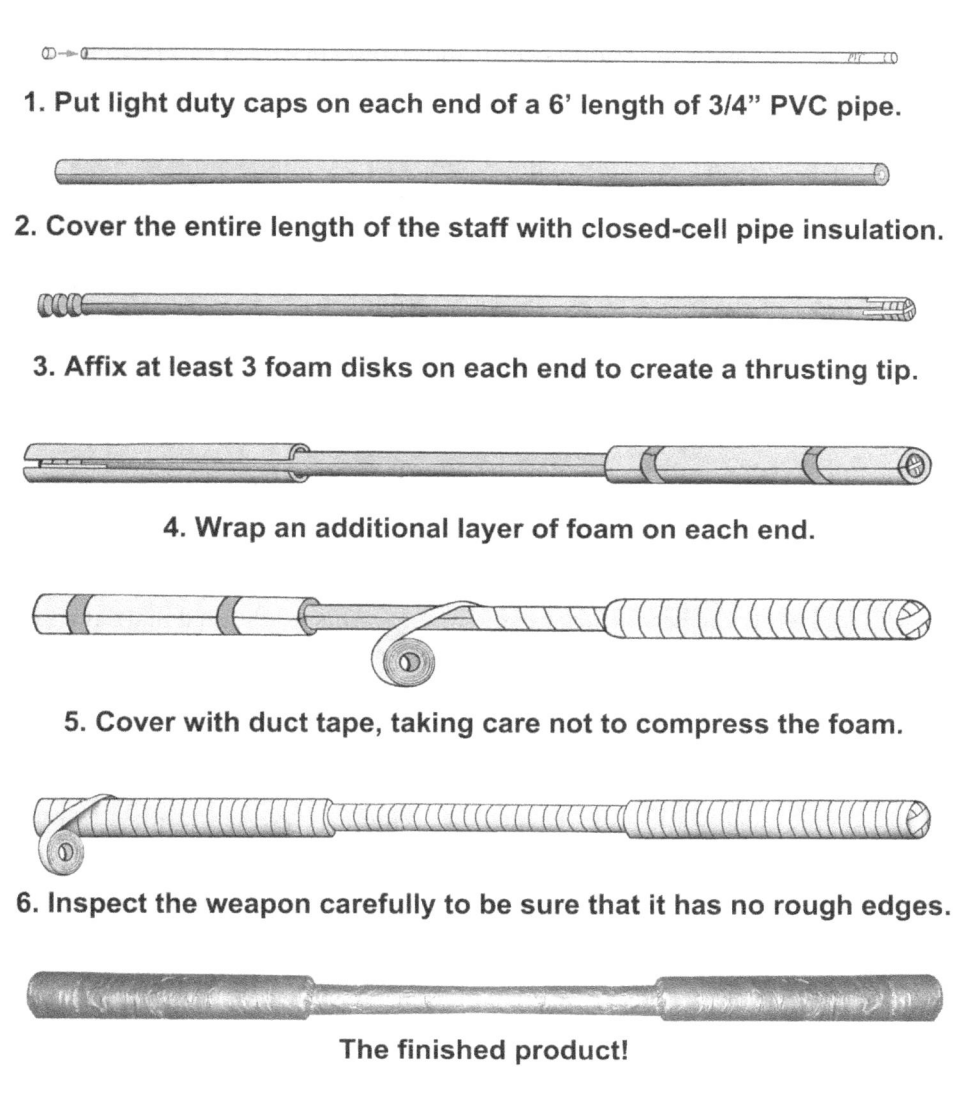

1. Put light duty caps on each end of a 6' length of 3/4" PVC pipe.

2. Cover the entire length of the staff with closed-cell pipe insulation.

3. Affix at least 3 foam disks on each end to create a thrusting tip.

4. Wrap an additional layer of foam on each end.

5. Cover with duct tape, taking care not to compress the foam.

6. Inspect the weapon carefully to be sure that it has no rough edges.

The finished product!

About the Author

Master Joe Varady has over thirty years' experience in the martial arts. He began Cuong Nhu Martial Arts in 1987 and currently holds a sixth-degree black belt. Over the past three decades, he has cross-trained in Eastern martial arts, including karate, tae kwon do, judo, wing chun, and eskrima (to name a few), and various Western martial arts, such as boxing, fencing, long sword, and sword and shield.

Joe is currently the head instructor of two programs: traditional martial arts through Satori Dojo and eclectic weapons systems through Modern Gladiatorial Arts, both located in Phoenixville, Pennsylvania. He has served as president and is currently an active member of the Universal Systems of Martial Arts Organization, a fellowship of instructors from different styles of martial arts who share techniques and principles. Joe was inducted into the Philadelphia Historic Martial Arts Hall of Fame in 2016.

Joe holds a master's degree in elementary education and has written and illustrated four Cuong Nhu training manuals for adults, as well as two full-color volumes for kids. YMAA Publication Center released the precursor to this book, *The Art and Science of Staff Fighting*, in October 2016.

BOOKS FROM YMAA

101 REFLECTIONS ON TAI CHI CHUAN
108 INSIGHTS INTO TAI CHI CHUAN
A SUDDEN DAWN: THE EPIC JOURNEY OF BODHIDHARMA
A WOMAN'S QIGONG GUIDE
ADVANCING IN TAE KWON DO
ANALYSIS OF SHAOLIN CHIN NA 2ND ED
ANCIENT CHINESE WEAPONS
THE ART AND SCIENCE OF STAFF FIGHTING
THE ART AND SCIENCE OF STICK FIGHTING
ART OF HOJO UNDO
ARTHRITIS RELIEF, 3D ED.
BACK PAIN RELIEF, 2ND ED.
BAGUAZHANG, 2ND ED.
BRAIN FITNESS
CARDIO KICKBOXING ELITE
CHIN NA IN GROUND FIGHTING
CHINESE FAST WRESTLING
CHINESE FITNESS
CHINESE TUI NA MASSAGE
CHOJUN
COMPLETE MARTIAL ARTIST
COMPREHENSIVE APPLICATIONS OF SHAOLIN CHIN NA
CONFLICT COMMUNICATION
CROCODILE AND THE CRANE: A NOVEL
CUTTING SEASON: A XENON PEARL MARTIAL ARTS THRILLER
DAO DE JING
DAO IN ACTION
DEFENSIVE TACTICS
DESHI: A CONNOR BURKE MARTIAL ARTS THRILLER
DIRTY GROUND
DR. WU'S HEAD MASSAGE
DUKKHA HUNGRY GHOSTS
DUKKHA REVERB
DUKKHA, THE SUFFERING: AN EYE FOR AN EYE
DUKKHA UNLOADED
ENZAN: THE FAR MOUNTAIN, A CONNOR BURKE MARTIAL ARTS THRILLER
ESSENCE OF SHAOLIN WHITE CRANE
EVEN IF IT KILLS ME
EXPLORING TAI CHI
FACING VIOLENCE
FIGHT BACK
FIGHT LIKE A PHYSICIST
THE FIGHTER'S BODY
FIGHTER'S FACT BOOK
FIGHTER'S FACT BOOK 2
THE FIGHTING ARTS
FIGHTING THE PAIN RESISTANT ATTACKER
FIRST DEFENSE
FORCE DECISIONS: A CITIZENS GUIDE
FOX BORROWS THE TIGER'S AWE
INSIDE TAI CHI
THE JUDO ADVANTAGE
THE JUJI GATAME ENCYCLOPEDIA
KAGE: THE SHADOW, A CONNOR BURKE MARTIAL ARTS THRILLER
KARATE SCIENCE
KATA AND THE TRANSMISSION OF KNOWLEDGE
KRAV MAGA COMBATIVES
KRAV MAGA PROFESSIONAL TACTICS
KRAV MAGA WEAPON DEFENSES
LITTLE BLACK BOOK OF VIOLENCE
LIUHEBAFA FIVE CHARACTER SECRETS
MARTIAL ARTS ATHLETE
MARTIAL ARTS INSTRUCTION
MARTIAL WAY AND ITS VIRTUES
MASK OF THE KING
MEDITATIONS ON VIOLENCE
MERIDIAN QIGONG EXERCISES
MIND/BODY FITNESS
MINDFUL EXERCISE
THE MIND INSIDE TAI CHI
THE MIND INSIDE YANG STYLE TAI CHI CHUAN
MUGAI RYU
NATURAL HEALING WITH QIGONG
NORTHERN SHAOLIN SWORD, 2ND ED.
OKINAWA'S COMPLETE KARATE SYSTEM: ISSHIN RYU
THE PAIN-FREE BACK

PAIN-FREE JOINTS
POWER BODY
PRINCIPLES OF TRADITIONAL CHINESE MEDICINE
THE PROTECTOR ETHIC
QIGONG FOR HEALTH & MARTIAL ARTS 2ND ED.
QIGONG FOR LIVING
QIGONG FOR TREATING COMMON AILMENTS
QIGONG MASSAGE
QIGONG MEDITATION: EMBRYONIC BREATHING
QIGONG MEDITATION: SMALL CIRCULATION
QIGONG, THE SECRET OF YOUTH: DA MO'S CLASSICS
QUIET TEACHER: A XENON PEARL MARTIAL ARTS THRILLER
RAVEN'S WARRIOR
REDEMPTION
ROOT OF CHINESE QIGONG, 2ND ED.
SAMBO ENCYCLOPEDIA
SCALING FORCE
SELF-DEFENSE FOR WOMEN
SENSEI: A CONNOR BURKE MARTIAL ARTS THRILLER
SHIHAN TE: THE BUNKAI OF KATA
SHIN GI TAI: KARATE TRAINING FOR BODY, MIND, AND SPIRIT
SIMPLE CHINESE MEDICINE
SIMPLE QIGONG EXERCISES FOR HEALTH, 3RD ED.
SIMPLIFIED TAI CHI CHUAN, 2ND ED.
SOLO TRAINING
SOLO TRAINING 2
SPOTTING DANGER BEFORE DANGER SPOTS YOU
SUMO FOR MIXED MARTIAL ARTS
SUNRISE TAI CHI
SUNSET TAI CHI
SURVIVING ARMED ASSAULTS
TAE KWON DO: THE KOREAN MARTIAL ART
TAEKWONDO BLACK BELT POOMSAE
TAEKWONDO: A PATH TO EXCELLENCE
TAEKWONDO: ANCIENT WISDOM FOR THE MODERN WARRIOR
TAEKWONDO: DEFENSE AGAINST WEAPONS
TAEKWONDO: SPIRIT AND PRACTICE
TAO OF BIOENERGETICS
TAI CHI BALL QIGONG: FOR HEALTH AND MARTIAL ARTS
TAI CHI BALL WORKOUT FOR BEGINNERS
THE TAI CHI BOOK
TAI CHI CHIN NA: THE SEIZING ART OF TAI CHI CHUAN, 2ND ED.
TAI CHI CHUAN CLASSICAL YANG STYLE, 2ND ED.
TAI CHI CHUAN MARTIAL POWER, 3RD ED.
TAI CHI CONNECTIONS
TAI CHI DYNAMICS
TAI CHI FOR DEPRESSION
TAI CHI IN 10 WEEKS
TAI CHI QIGONG, 3RD ED.
TAI CHI SECRETS OF THE ANCIENT MASTERS
TAI CHI SECRETS OF THE WU & LI STYLES
TAI CHI SECRETS OF THE WU STYLE
TAI CHI SECRETS OF THE YANG STYLE
TAI CHI SWORD: CLASSICAL YANG STYLE, 2ND ED.
TAI CHI SWORD FOR BEGINNERS
TAI CHI WALKING
TAIJIQUAN THEORY OF DR. YANG, JWING-MING
TAO OF BIOENERGETICS
TENGU: THE MOUNTAIN GOBLIN, A CONNOR BURKE MARTIAL ARTS THRILLER
TIMING IN THE FIGHTING ARTS
TRADITIONAL CHINESE HEALTH SECRETS
TRADITIONAL TAEKWONDO
TRAINING FOR SUDDEN VIOLENCE
TRUE WELLNESS
TRUE WELLNESS: THE MIND
TRUE WELLNESS: THE HEART
THE WARRIOR'S MANIFESTO
WAY OF KATA
WAY OF KENDO AND KENJITSU
WAY OF SANCHIN KATA
WAY TO BLACK BELT
WESTERN HERBS FOR MARTIAL ARTISTS
WILD GOOSE QIGONG
WINNING FIGHTS
WISDOM'S WAY
XINGYIQUAN

DVDS FROM YMAA

ADVANCED PRACTICAL CHIN NA IN-DEPTH
ANALYSIS OF SHAOLIN CHIN NA
ATTACK THE ATTACK
BAGUA FOR BEGINNERS 1
BAGUA FOR BEGINNERS 2
BAGUAZHANG: EMEI BAGUAZHANG
BEGINNER QIGONG FOR WOMEN 1
BEGINNER QIGONG FOR WOMEN 2
BEGINNER TAI CHI FOR HEALTH
CHEN STYLE TAIJIQUAN
CHEN TAI CHI FOR BEGINNERS
CHIN NA IN-DEPTH COURSES 1—4
CHIN NA IN-DEPTH COURSES 5—8
CHIN NA IN-DEPTH COURSES 9—12
FACING VIOLENCE: 7 THINGS A MARTIAL ARTIST MUST KNOW
FIVE ANIMAL SPORTS
FIVE ELEMENTS ENERGY BALANCE
INFIGHTING
INTRODUCTION TO QI GONG FOR BEGINNERS
JOINT LOCKS
KNIFE DEFENSE: TRADITIONAL TECHNIQUES AGAINST A DAGGER
KUNG FU BODY CONDITIONING 1
KUNG FU BODY CONDITIONING 2
KUNG FU FOR KIDS
KUNG FU FOR TEENS
LOGIC OF VIOLENCE
MERIDIAN QIGONG
NEIGONG FOR MARTIAL ARTS
NORTHERN SHAOLIN SWORD : SAN CAI JIAN, KUN WU JIAN, QI MEN JIAN
QI GONG 30-DAY CHALLENGE
QI GONG FOR ANXIETY
QI GONG FOR ARMS, WRISTS, AND HANDS
QIGONG FOR BEGINNERS: FRAGRANCE
QI GONG FOR BETTER BREATHING
QI GONG FOR CANCER
QI GONG FOR ENERGY AND VITALITY
QI GONG FOR HEADACHES
QI GONG FOR HEALING
QI GONG FOR HEALTHY JOINTS
QI GONG FOR HIGH BLOOD PRESSURE
QIGONG FOR LONGEVITY
QI GONG FOR STRONG BONES
QI GONG FOR THE UPPER BACK AND NECK
QIGONG FOR WOMEN
QIGONG FOR WOMEN WITH DAISY LEE
QIGONG MASSAGE
QIGONG MINDFULNESS IN MOTION
QIGONG: 15 MINUTES TO HEALTH
SABER FUNDAMENTAL TRAINING
SAI TRAINING AND SEQUENCES
SANCHIN KATA: TRADITIONAL TRAINING FOR KARATE POWER
SCALING FORCE
SHAOLIN KUNG FU FUNDAMENTAL TRAINING: COURSES 1 & 2
SHAOLIN LONG FIST KUNG FU: ADVANCED SEQUENCES 1
SHAOLIN LONG FIST KUNG FU: ADVANCED SEQUENCES 2
SHAOLIN LONG FIST KUNG FU: BASIC SEQUENCES
SHAOLIN LONG FIST KUNG FU: INTERMEDIATE SEQUENCES
SHAOLIN SABER: BASIC SEQUENCES
SHAOLIN STAFF: BASIC SEQUENCES
SHAOLIN WHITE CRANE GONG FU BASIC TRAINING: COURSES 1 & 2
SHAOLIN WHITE CRANE GONG FU BASIC TRAINING: COURSES 3 & 4
SHUAI JIAO: KUNG FU WRESTLING
SIMPLE QIGONG EXERCISES FOR HEALTH
SIMPLE QIGONG EXERCISES FOR ARTHRITIS RELIEF
SIMPLE QIGONG EXERCISES FOR BACK PAIN RELIEF
SIMPLIFIED TAI CHI CHUAN: 24 & 48 POSTURES
SIMPLIFIED TAI CHI FOR BEGINNERS 48
SUNRISE TAI CHI
SUNSET TAI CHI
SWORD: FUNDAMENTAL TRAINING
TAEKWONDO KORYO POOMSAE
TAI CHI BALL QIGONG: COURSES 1 & 2
TAI CHI BALL QIGONG: COURSES 3 & 4
TAI CHI BALL WORKOUT FOR BEGINNERS
TAI CHI CHUAN CLASSICAL YANG STYLE
TAI CHI CONNECTIONS
TAI CHI ENERGY PATTERNS
TAI CHI FIGHTING SET
TAI CHI FIT: 24 FORM
TAI CHI FIT: FLOW
TAI CHI FIT: FUSION BAMBOO
TAI CHI FIT: FUSION FIRE
TAI CHI FIT: FUSION IRON
TAI CHI FIT IN PARADISE
TAI CHI FIT: OVER 50
TAI CHI FIT OVER 50: SEATED WORKOUT FOR HEALTH
TAI CHI FIT OVER 50: BALANCE EXERCISES
TAI CHI FIT OVER 60: HEALTHY JOINTS
TAI CHI FIT OVER 60: LIVE LONGER, FEEL YOUNGER
TAI CHI FIT: STRENGTH
TAI CHI FIT: TO GO
TAI CHI FOR WOMEN
TAI CHI FUSION: FIRE
TAI CHI QIGONG
TAI CHI PUSHING HANDS: COURSES 1 & 2
TAI CHI PUSHING HANDS: COURSES 3 & 4
TAI CHI SWORD: CLASSICAL YANG STYLE
TAI CHI SWORD FOR BEGINNERS
TAI CHI SYMBOL: YIN YANG STICKING HANDS
TAIJI & SHAOLIN STAFF: FUNDAMENTAL TRAINING
TAIJI CHIN NA IN-DEPTH
TAIJI 37 POSTURES MARTIAL APPLICATIONS
TAIJI SABER CLASSICAL YANG STYLE
TAIJI WRESTLING
TRAINING FOR SUDDEN VIOLENCE
UNDERSTANDING QIGONG 1: WHAT IS QI? • HUMAN QI CIRCULATORY SYSTEM
UNDERSTANDING QIGONG 2: KEY POINTS • QIGONG BREATHING
UNDERSTANDING QIGONG 3: EMBRYONIC BREATHING
UNDERSTANDING QIGONG 4: FOUR SEASONS QIGONG
UNDERSTANDING QIGONG 5: SMALL CIRCULATION
UNDERSTANDING QIGONG 6: MARTIAL QIGONG BREATHING
WATER STYLE FOR BEGINNERS
WHITE CRANE HARD & SOFT QIGONG
YANG TAI CHI FOR BEGINNERSS
WUDANG KUNG FU: FUNDAMENTAL TRAINING
WUDANG SWORD
WUDANG TAIJIQUAN
XINGYIQUAN
YANG TAI CHI FOR BEGINNERS

more products available from . . .
YMAA Publication Center, Inc. 楊氏東方文化出版中心
1-800-669-8892 • info@ymaa.com • www.ymaa.com

www.ingramcontent.com/pod-product-compliance
Lightning Source LLC
Chambersburg PA
CBHW081428070526
44586CB00020B/2518